CARRY ON REVISITED

Ryan Valmont

© Copyright 2024 Ryan Valmont

All Rights Reserved.

CONTENTS

DISCLAIMER	1
INTRODUCTION	3
PRODUCTION PROFILES	5
Peter Rogers	5
Gerald Thomas	6
Talbot Nelson Conn Rothwell	7
Norman Hudis	8
STARS ON SCREEN: A FILM AND ACTOR OVERVIEW	11
CARRY ON CHRONICLES: TRIVIA, ACTOR PROFILES, AND FILM INSIGHTS	13
Carry On 50's	13
Carry On 60's	34
Carry on 70's	127
Carry on 90's	170
A FESTIVE FARCE: THE HILARIOUS ANTICS OF CARRY ON CHRISTMAS (1969-1973)	174
Carry On Christmas (1969)	174
Carry On Again Christmas (1970)	175
Carry On Christmas (or Carry On Stuffing) (1972)	176
Carry On Christmas (1973)	177
CARRY ON LAUGHING (1975)	179
Carry On Laughing – Series One	180
Carry On Laughing – Series Two	183
CARRY ON STAGE: THEATRE AND PLAYHOUSE ANTICS	188
Carry On London! (4 October 1973 – March 1975)	188

Carry On Laughing: The Slimming Factory (16 June – September 1976)	189
Wot a Carry On in Blackpool (22 May – 25 October 1992)	190
CARRY ON LEGENDS: FILMS BEYOND THE CLASSICS	**192**
Cor, Blimey! (2000)	192
Kenneth Williams: Fantabulosa! (2006)	195
Hattie (2011)	197
Babs (2017)	198
THE LOST STORIES: UNFILMED CARRY ON SCRIPTS	**201**
FILMOGRAPHY: A SCREEN LEGACY	**205**
CARRY ON QUOTING	**218**
CARRY ON GUESSING: THE ULTIMATE CARRY ON QUIZ	**221**
QUIZ ANSWERS	**231**

DISCLAIMER

The author is not responsible for any errors or omissions, or for any actions taken based on the information contained in this book. This book is provided for informational purposes only, and the author and publisher shall not be liable for any errors or omissions, or for any actions taken based on the information contained in this book.

INTRODUCTION

Step into the hysterical realm of the Carry On Films, where laughter knows no boundaries and wit reigns supreme. Within the pages of this delightful exploration, we immerse ourselves in the iconic and timeless collection of The Carry On Collection that has been tickling funny bones and leaving audiences in stitches for decades.

"Carry On" is a British comedy franchise comprising 31 films produced between 1958 and 1992. Under the helm of Peter Rogers, the films were directed by Gerald Thomas and boasted a recurring ensemble cast.

The humour of "Carry On" finds its roots in the British comic tradition of music hall and cheeky seaside postcards. The success of these films spawned spin-offs, including four Christmas television specials (1969–1973), a 1975 television series with 13 episodes, and three West End stage shows that toured the United Kingdom.

The "Carry On" series holds the record for the largest number of films in any British film franchise and is the second longest-running, with a 14-year hiatus (1978–1992) between the 30th and 31st entries. (The James Bond film series is the longest-running, having started in 1962, four years after the first "Carry On," though with fewer films.)

Rogers and Thomas were the driving forces behind all 31 films, consistently delivering within the allotted time and budget. Between 1958 and 1992, the series had seven writers, with Norman Hudis (1958–1962) and Talbot Rothwell (1963–1974) being the most frequent contributors. Anglo Amalgamated Film

Distributors Ltd produced 12 films (1958–1966), the Rank Organisation made 18 (1966–1978), and United International Pictures produced one (1992).

All the films were created at Pinewood Studios near Iver Heath, Buckinghamshire. Due to budgetary constraints, a significant portion of the location filming occurred in the vicinity of the studios, primarily in and around south Buckinghamshire, including areas of Berkshire and Middlesex. However, during the late 1960s, at the peak of the series' success, more elaborate plots occasionally required filming in locations further afield. Notable examples include Snowdonia National Park, Wales, where the foot of Snowdon stood in for the Khyber Pass in "Carry On Up the Khyber," and the beaches of the Sussex coast doubling as Saharan sand dunes in "Follow That Camel."

Join us as we embark on a laughter-filled adventure through the golden age of British comedy, where every "Carry On" film is a timeless testament to the power of laughter and the enduring charm of classic cinema.

PRODUCTION PROFILES

PETER ROGERS

Peter Rogers, born on 20th February 1914, led a distinguished life as an English film producer, with his notable contributions immortalised in the creation of the beloved Carry On series of films.

In his personal sphere, Rogers was married to film producer Betty Box, credited with the Doctor series of films. Together, the couple resided for an extended period at "Drummers Yard" in Beaconsfield, a substantial property previously owned by actor Dirk Bogarde.

Rogers commenced his professional journey as a journalist for the local newspaper before transitioning into scripting religious informational films. Collaborating with director Gerald Thomas, he ventured into film production, starting with a project for the Children's Film Foundation. However, Rogers truly made his mark as the producer of the Carry On series, a celebrated collection of British comedy films that kicked off with Carry On Sergeant in 1958.

The majority of Rogers' prolific work, including all the Carry On films, found its creative space at Pinewood Studios in Iver Heath, Buckinghamshire, England. Beyond the Carry On series, his diverse credits included notable projects such as Appointment with Venus, featuring David Niven, and Time Lock, showcasing one of Sean Connery's earliest film appearances.

Rogers' contributions extended beyond film, with involvement in the television series Ivanhoe alongside Roger Moore and the film adaptation of the long-running sitcom Bless This House, starring Carry On regular Sid James.

Rogers' legacy was explored in the authorised biography, "Mr Carry On: The Life and Work of Peter Rogers" (BBC), co-authored by Morris Bright and Robert Ross. Published in 2000, the biography, enriched by Rogers' insights, aimed to address accusations of exploiting the Carry On cast by highlighting the consistent £5,000 payment to lead actors from the series' inception in 1958 until the penultimate film.

Despite facing health challenges, Rogers actively participated in the 50th-anniversary celebration of the Carry On films held at Pinewood Studios in March 2008. His passing on 14th April 2009 marked the end of a remarkable career, leaving an indelible imprint on the British film industry.

GERALD THOMAS

Gerald Thomas (10th December 1920 – 9th November 1993), an esteemed English film director renowned for the enduring Carry On series of British film comedies, led a life intertwined with both family and cinematic achievements.

Born in Hull, East Riding of Yorkshire, England, Thomas received his education in Bristol and London. Initially on a path towards medicine, his plans were interrupted by the outbreak of World War II. After serving four years in the British Army during the conflict, Thomas returned to civilian life with the belief that it was too late to resume his medical studies.

Embarking on his movie career at Denham Studios, Thomas ascended to the role of an assistant film editor, starting with Laurence Olivier's Hamlet (1948). Notably, his editing skills were employed in various films directed by his older brother, Ralph Thomas. Thomas made his directorial debut with the short film

Circus Friends (1956), a production by the Children's Film Foundation. The following year saw his first feature, the thriller Time Lock.

Gerald Thomas achieved significant acclaim as the director of the Carry On series, commencing with the uproarious Carry On Sergeant (1958) and overseeing all 30 films in the series of British comedies. Produced by Peter Rogers, this collaboration spanned until Carry On Emmannuelle (1978) and the later Carry On Columbus (1992). Additionally, he directed the framing sequences for the compilation film That's Carry On! (1977). His directorial repertoire also included the comedy Please Turn Over (1959) and the post-war Austrian drama The Second Victory (1986).

Personal life brought joy to Thomas through marriage, and the couple was blessed with three daughters. Tragically, he succumbed to a heart attack at home.

Thomas's nephew, Jeremy Thomas, continued the family's cinematic legacy as a film producer. In honour of his contributions, a green plaque adorns The Avenues in Kingston upon Hull, commemorating the life and impact of Gerald Thomas.

TALBOT NELSON CONN ROTHWELL

Talbot Nelson Conn Rothwell, commonly known as "Tolly" Rothwell, OBE, was an esteemed English screenwriter born on 12th November 1916 in Bromley, Kent, England. His diverse early career encompassed roles such as town clerk, police officer, and Royal Air Force pilot.

During World War II, Rothwell faced adversity as a prisoner of war in Stalag Luft III after being shot down over Norway. It was within the confines of captivity that he discovered his passion for writing. Bonding with fellow inmate Peter Butterworth, Rothwell penned scripts for camp concerts, providing entertainment and cover for escape efforts.

Post-war, Rothwell transitioned to a career in writing, contributing scripts for renowned figures like The Crazy Gang, Arthur Askey, Ted Ray, and Terry-Thomas. His hit play, "Queen Elizabeth Slept Here," enjoyed a successful run in London's West End.

Rothwell's association with the iconic Carry On film series began with the submission of "Carry On Jack," leading to his role as the series' staff writer. He brought a more risqué and lively tone to the films while preserving the essence of music hall entertainment inspired by his hero, Max Miller.

His contributions extended beyond films; Rothwell wrote numerous Carry On TV specials for Christmas and co-wrote "Up Pompeii!" starring Frankie Howerd. Recognising his significant impact on the cinema industry, Rothwell was honoured with an OBE in 1977.

In the mid-1970s, facing a prolonged illness, Rothwell retired from his prolific career. He spent his final years in Worthing, passing away at the age of 64. In April 2007, Rothwell's memorable line "Infamy! Infamy! They've all got it in for me!" from Carry On Cleo was voted the greatest one-liner in movie history, showcasing the enduring legacy of his wit. Notably, Rothwell "borrowed" the line with permission from Frank Muir and Denis Norden, who had used it on their radio show Take It From Here.

NORMAN HUDIS

Norman Hudis was born on 27th July 1922 in Stepney, London; Hudis started his writing journey at the local newspaper, the

Hampstead & Highgate Express. With the outbreak of World War II, he joined the RAF and was stationed in the Middle East, where he contributed to Air Force News. After the war, Hudis began writing for camp concerts before transitioning to playwriting. Although only one of his plays, "Here Is The News", received critical acclaim, it caught the attention of Pinewood Studios, leading to a trainee screenwriter position. However, none of his screenplays were produced during his two-year stint at Pinewood.

Subsequently, Hudis became a freelance writer and gained prominence as a screenwriter for B movies in the 1950s. He wrote the screenplay for the biopic "The Tommy Steele Story" (1957). Following its release, film producer Peter Rogers offered him another screenplay opportunity for Tommy Steele's "The Duke Wore Jeans" (1958), directed by Gerald Thomas. Rogers and Thomas then chose Hudis to rewrite R. F. Delderfield's "The Bull Boys".

After the success of his initial Carry On film (Sergeant), Hudis penned an additional five entries in the series: Carry On Nurse, Carry On Teacher, Carry On Constable, Carry On Regardless (being his least favourite), and Carry On Cruising. The pinnacle of these was his second effort, Carry On Nurse, which became the highest-grossing film in the UK in 1959.

In 1966, following the success of Carry On Nurse in the United States, Hudis permanently relocated to the US. His American television writing credits include popular shows like "The Wild Wild West", "The F.B.I.", "The Man From U.N.C.L.E.", "Hawaii Five-O", "Cannon", and "Baretta".

Hudis remained active in writing for film, TV, and theatre throughout his life. He co-wrote the long-running play "Seven Deadly Sins Four Deadly Sinners", which has been staged globally since 2003. He also penned the one-man play "Jeffrey Archer's

Prison Diaries by FF 8282", an authorised adaptation of Jeffrey Archer's diaries from his time in prison. Another notable work is the semi-autobiographical play "Dinner with Ribbentrop", reflecting his experiences with the actor Eric Portman, known for his anti-Semitic views.

Norman Hudis passed away at the age of 93 on 8th February 2016. His son, Stephen R. Hudis, is a Hollywood director, and his sister, Sylvia Holness, resides in England. In 2008, Hudis published his autobiography, "No Laughing Matter: How I Carried On", through Apex Publishing Ltd.

STARS ON SCREEN: A FILM AND ACTOR OVERVIEW

Films & Dates			
Sergeant	1958	Up the Khyber	1968
Nurse	1959	Camping	1969
Teacher	1959	Again Doctor	1969
Constable	1960	Up the Jungle	1970
Regardless	1961	Loving	1970
Cruising	1962	Henry	1971
Cabby	1963	At Your Convenience	1971
Jack	1963	Matron	1972
Spying	1964	Abroad	1972
Cleo	1964	Girls	1973
Cowboy	1965	Dick	1974
Screaming!	1966	Behind	1975
Don't Lose Your Head	1966	England	1976
Follow That Camel	1967	That's Carry On!	1977
Doctor	1967	Emmannuelle	1978
		Columbus	1992

Actor	# Films	Recurring Actors in Main Roles		Recurring Actors	
Kenneth Williams	25	Eric Barker	4	Peter Gilmore	11
Joan Sims	24	Bill Owen	4	Michael Nightingale	9
Charles Hawtrey	23	Terence Longdon	4	Marianne Stone	9
Sid James	19	Leslie Phillips	4	Julian Holloway	7
Kenneth Connor	17	June Whitfield	4	Cyril Chamberlain	7
Peter Butterworth	16	Esma Cannon	4	Anthony Sagar	6

Carry On Revisited | 11

Actor	# Films	Recurring Actors in Main Roles		Recurring Actors	
Hattie Jacques	14	Liz Fraser	4	Margaret Nolan	6
Bernard Bresslaw	14	Dilys Laye	4	Valerie Leon	5
Jim Dale	11	Angela Douglas	4	Joan Hickson	5
Barbara Windsor	9	Jacki Piper	4	Bill Maynard	5
Patsy Rowlands	9	Bernard Cribbins	3	Lucy Griffiths	4
Jack Douglas	8	Shirley Eaton	3		
Terry Scott	7	Kenneth Cope	2		

* Film count does not include deleted scenes, uncredited roles, or That's Carry On!

CARRY ON CHRONICLES: TRIVIA, ACTOR PROFILES, AND FILM INSIGHTS

CARRY ON 50'S

CARRY ON SERGEANT (1958)

The film follows the story of Mary Sage, newly married to Charlie, who receives a call-up during their wedding breakfast. Assigned to Sergeant Grimshaw, the recruits, including hypochondriac Horace Strong, strive to become the best platoon under Grimshaw's command. Mary, determined to spend her wedding night with Charlie, infiltrates the depot, leading to comedic situations.

Directed by Gerald Thomas and produced by Peter Rogers, Carry On Sergeant established a partnership that endured until 1978. Notably, this film introduced key actors, including Kenneth Williams, Charles Hawtrey, Hattie Jacques, Kenneth Connor, and Terry Scott, who would become integral to the Carry On series. Following its success, the film paved the way for the evolution of the Carry On film franchise.

CAST:

William Hartnell as **Sergeant Grimshaw**
Bob Monkhouse as **Private Charlie Sage**
Shirley Eaton as **Mary Sage**
Eric Barker as **Captain Potts**
Dora Bryan as **Norah**
Bill Owen as **Corporal Copping**
Charles Hawtrey as **Private Peter Golightly**

Kenneth Connor as **Private Horace Strong**
Kenneth Williams **as Private James Bailey**
Terence Longdon as **Private Miles Heywood**
Norman Rossington as **Herbert Brown**
Gerald Campion as **Private Andy Galloway**
Hattie Jacques as **Captain Clark, R.A.M.C.**
Cyril Chamberlain as **Bren Gun instructor**
Terry Scott as Sergeant **Paddy O'Brien**

FACTS AND TRIVIA:

The title "Carry On Sergeant" reflects a common military expression, equivalent to the American "As you were." It was inspired by the success of the 1957 film "Carry On Admiral." Composer Bruce Montgomery composed the score, performed by the Band of the Coldstream Guards.

Variety described Carry On Sergeant as a "Corny but mostly very funny Army farce," with talented character comedians elevating the humour beyond the script's provisions. The Monthly Film Bulletin highlighted the film's traditionally English blend of farcical situations, well-worn jokes, and comic characters, praising performances by Charles Hawtrey and Kenneth Williams.

- Filming Dates: 24th March - 2nd May 1958
- Exteriors: Stoughton Barracks, Surrey (Army camp), Harefield, Middlesex (Wedding scene), Beaconsfield, Buckinghamshire (Church scenes)
- The film was adapted from a play titled "The Bull Boys" by R. F. Delderfield.
- Norman Hudis crafted the screenplay with additional material by John Antrobus.
- The original novel's conscripted ballet dancers were transformed into a married couple for the film.

- Budget: £74,000
- Ranked third at the British box office in 1958.

After being shown to the trade and cinema-bookers on 1st August 1958, "Carry On Sergeant" had regional screenings from 31st August. The London cinema release at the Plaza occurred on 19th September with a nationwide general release following from 20th September onwards.

PROFILES:

Kenneth Charles Williams born on 22nd February 1926, was a renowned British actor and comedian who experienced a life marked by both professional success and personal struggles. Born in Bingfield Street, King's Cross, London, to Charles George Williams and Louisa Alexandra (née Morgan), he grew up in a working-class family in Central London. Williams' educational journey took him to The Lyulph Stanley Boys' Central Council School in Camden Town, North London. While apprenticing as a draughtsman to a mapmaker, he found his career trajectory momentarily disrupted by World War II, during which he served as a sapper in the Royal Engineers Survey Section.

Post-war, Williams transitioned into the entertainment world, joining the Combined Services Entertainment Unit, where he honed his skills in revue shows alongside notable figures like Stanley Baxter, Peter Vaughan, Peter Nichols, and John Schlesinger. His professional journey commenced in 1948 in repertory theatre, initially aspiring to be a serious dramatic actor. However, his comedic prowess shone through, leading to his breakthrough in Bernard Shaw's St Joan in the West End (1954). This caught the attention of radio producer Dennis Main Wilson, propelling Williams into the radio series Hancock's Half Hour, where he played funny voice roles.

Williams achieved continued success in the 1950s, '60s, and '70s, becoming a fixture in the Carry On film series from 1958 to 1978, contributing to the franchise's popularity. Despite his private criticism of the films, his collaboration with producer Peter Rogers proved financially beneficial. Williams's contribution to British film extended beyond Carry On, with appearances in various productions during the same period.

A regular on BBC Radio's Just a Minute from 1968 until his death, Williams displayed his wit and often engaged in spirited exchanges with host Nicholas Parsons. His television career included co-hosting Meanwhile, On BBC2, contributing to What's My Line?, hosting International Cabaret, and narrating the children's cartoon Willo the Wisp (1981).

In his private life, Williams battled loneliness and despondency, as reflected in his diaries and interviews. His asexuality and celibacy were prominent aspects of his personal narrative. On 15th April 1988, Williams passed away in his flat, leaving behind a legacy marked by both his comedic genius and personal challenges. The circumstances surrounding his death remain subject to debate, with an inquest recording an open verdict.

Williams left an indelible mark on the entertainment industry, and his life has been explored in various biographies. Radio 4's The Pain of Laughter and biographies like Kenneth Williams Unseen, and Born Brilliant shed light on different facets of his life, contributing to a deeper understanding of this multifaceted individual.

Various portrayals, such as David Benson's show Think No Evil of Us and Michael Sheen's portrayal in Kenneth Williams: Fantabulosa!, have kept Williams's memory alive. Blue plaques unveiled at locations significant to his life, including his father's barber shop and Farley Court, serve as enduring tributes to a true original in British comedy.

Title	Year	Kenneth Williams
Sergeant	1958	James Bailey
Nurse	1959	Oliver Reckitt
Teacher	1959	Edwin Milton
Constable	1960	Const. Stanley Benson
Regardless	1961	Francis Courtenay
Cruising	1962	Leonard Marjoribanks
Jack	1963	Captain Fearless
Spying	1964	Desmond Simpkins
Cleo	1964	Julius Caesar
Cowboy	1965	Judge Burke
Screaming!	1966	Dr. Watt
Don't Lose Your Head	1966	Citizen Camembert
Follow That Camel	1967	Cmdnt. Burger
Doctor	1967	Dr. Kenneth Tinkle
Up the Khyber	1968	Randy Lal, The Khasi of Kalabar
Camping	1969	Dr. Kenneth Soaper
Again Doctor	1969	Frederick Carver
Loving	1970	Percival Snooper
Henry	1971	Thomas Cromwell
At Your Convenience	1971	W C Boggs
Matron	1972	Sir Bernard Cutting
Abroad	1972	Stuart Farquhar
Dick	1974	Desmond Fancey
Behind	1975	Prof. Roland Crump
That's Carry On!	1977	Presenter
Emmannuelle	1978	Emile Prevert

William Henry Hartnell was born on 8th January 1908 in St Pancras, London, and his early life was marked by uncertainty about his father's identity. Raised partially by a foster mother, he spent holidays in Devon, learning to ride horses. Despite a fall and a mishandled wound, leaving a scar on his temple, Hartnell pursued acting.

In 1925, Hartnell began his theatrical journey under Frank Benson as a general stagehand. His repertoire included numerous Shakespearean plays such as The Merchant of Venice, Julius Caesar, As You Like It, Hamlet, The Tempest, and Macbeth in 1926. Additional appearances in She Stoops to Conquer, The School for Scandal (both 1926), Good Morning, Bill (1927), and Miss Elizabeth's Prisoner (1928) followed. Hartnell married actress Heather McIntyre, featured in the latter play, in the subsequent year. His film career took off with Say It With Music in 1932.

Radio work became a notable part of his career, with his earliest known performance in the Chinese Moon Party broadcast by the BBC on 11th May 1931.

During World War II, Hartnell attempted to volunteer for the RAF but ended up serving in the British Army's Tank Corps. After 18 months, a nervous breakdown led to his invalidation, and he returned to acting. In 1942, he was cast in Noël Coward's film In Which We Serve, but an incident on set resulted in his dismissal. He rebounded with a robust role as Sergeant Ned Fletcher in The Way Ahead (1944).

Hartnell's career after that became defined by roles as policemen, soldiers, and thugs, a typecasting that bothered him. Notable films during this period include Brighton Rock (1947), where he played tough gang underboss Dallow, and Carry On Sergeant (1958), his role in the first Carry On comedy film. He continued with military characters in The Mouse That Roared (1959) and a town councillor in Heavens Above! (1963).

On television, his first regular role was as Sergeant Major Percy Bullimore in The Army Game (1957). Despite being a comedy series, Hartnell often found himself cast in "tough guy" roles. He also played a supporting role in the film version of This Sporting Life (1963), portraying an ageing rugby league talent scout known as "Dad."

Impressed by Hartnell's performance in This Sporting Life, Verity Lambert offered him the role of the first Doctor in Doctor Who. Despite initial hesitation, he accepted, enjoying the character's departure from his usual military roles. Hartnell's Doctor debuted in 1963 and earned him £315 per episode by 1966.

Describing the character as a wizard, he occasionally portrayed the Doctor as tongue-tied. Colleagues accused him of being challenging to work with, citing racism or antisemitism. His declining health due to arteriosclerosis affected his ability to learn lines, leading to his departure from Doctor Who in 1966. The show introduced regeneration, and Hartnell suggested Patrick Troughton as his successor.

Returning briefly in The Three Doctors in 1972–1973, Hartnell's declining health required him to read lines from cue cards. This marked his final acting role. Many of his Doctor Who episodes are missing due to the standard practice of discarding old shows.

Hartnell's health deteriorated, resulting in his extended hospitalisation in December 1974. Afflicted by strokes linked to cerebrovascular disease, he peacefully passed away in his sleep due to heart failure on 23rd April 1975, at the age of 67.

Bob Monkhouse born Robert Alan Monkhouse OBE, on 1st June 1928, was an English comedian and TV host. He presented shows like The Golden Shot and Family Fortunes. Monkhouse's early life included writing for comics and completing National Service with the Royal Air Force.

His career began on stage in London and expanded to quiz shows like Do You Trust Your Wife? (1956). Monkhouse gained fame as a writer and comedian, forming a successful partnership with Denis Goodwin. He hosted over 30 quiz shows, with notable success on The Golden Shot.

Monkhouse was known for stand-up comedy, ad-libbing skills, and hosting chat shows. In later years, he presented The National Lottery Live and hosted Wipeout until shortly before he died in 2003. A film collector and expert on silent cinema, Monkhouse's archive was acquired by the British Film Institute in 2008. His legacy includes influencing British comedy, receiving awards, and a posthumous prostate cancer awareness advertisement.

Monkhouse passed away from prostate cancer on 29th December 2003.

CARRY ON NURSE (1959)

Journalist Ted York is hurried to Haven Hospital with appendicitis, experiencing a whirlwind of events. Amidst Nurse Denton's charm, the hospital is a hub of chaos. The arrival of boxer Bernie Bishop and a cast of quirky characters adds to the comedic atmosphere. Matron's inspections, often thwarted by clumsy Nurse Dawson, create hilarious moments. Personal relationships develop, including Ted's realisation of Nurse Denton's unrequited love and Oliver's budding romance with Jill. The narrative unfolds through amusing incidents, medical blunders, and pranks, showcasing the lively dynamics within the hospital.

Filmed at Pinewood Studios in Buckinghamshire, Carry On Nurse was produced from 3rd November to 12th December 1958. The film features a memorable score played by the Band of the Coldstream Guards.

CAST:

Kenneth Connor as **Bernie Bishop**
Shirley Eaton as **Staff Nurse Dorothy Denton**
Charles Hawtrey as **Humphrey Hinton**

Hattie Jacques as **Matron**
Terence Longdon as **Ted York**
Bill Owen as **Percy Hickson**
Leslie Phillips as **Jack Bell**
Joan Sims as **Student Nurse Stella Dawson**
Susan Stephen as **Nurse Georgie Axwell**
Kenneth Williams as **Oliver Reckitt**
Wilfrid Hyde White as **the Colonel**
Susan Beaumont as **Nurse Frances James**
Ann Firbank as **Staff Nurse Helen Lloyd**
Joan Hickson as **Sister**
Cyril Chamberlain as **Bert Able**
Harry Locke as **Mick the Orderly**
Norman Rossington as **Norm**
Brian Oulton as Henry Bray
Susan Shaw as **Mrs Jane Bishop**
Jill Ireland as **Jill Thompson**
Irene Handl as **Mrs Marge Hickson**
Michael Medwin as **Ginger**
Leigh Madison as **Doctor Winn**
John Van Eyssen as **Mr Stephens, the surgeon**
Marianne Stone as **Mrs Alice Able**
Rosalind Knight as **Student Nurse Nightingale**
June Whitfield as **Meg**
Ed. Devereaux as **Alec Lawrence**

Bernard Bresslaw (uncredited): *his feet were used as stand-ins for Terence Longdon's, when the latter's character was supposedly standing in a bath.*

FACTS AND TRIVIA:

- Budget: £71,000
- The film topped the British box office in 1959, grossing $843,000 and garnering an estimated ten million admissions.

- It was the most successful Carry On film and enjoyed significant success in the United States, playing at some cinemas for three years.
- Premiering at the Carlton Cinema in London on 5th March 1959, the film went on nationwide release from 23rd March 1959.
- Variety praised "Carry On Nurse" as the second entry in a potentially golden series, describing it as an unabashed assault on the patrons' funny bones. However, The Monthly Film Bulletin offered a negative perspective, labelling it a somewhat stale farce with cheerlessly rollicking elements. Despite mixed reviews, the film achieved significant success in Britain, leaving critics intrigued by its popularity.

PROFILES:

Irene Joan Marion Sims was born on 9th May 1930, the only child of John Henry Sims, the Station Master of Laindon railway station in Essex, and Gladys Marie Sims (née Ladbrook). Growing up at the railway station, Sims's early interest in acting was nurtured by the performances she would stage for waiting passengers. Her desire to pursue a career in show business solidified during her teenage years, as she became a familiar face in numerous local amateur productions.

In 1946, Sims made one of her initial stage appearances as Miranda Bute in Esther McCracken's comedy "Quiet Wedding." Although her first attempt to gain admission to the Royal Academy of Dramatic Art (RADA) was unsuccessful, she persevered and eventually joined RADA's preparatory school, PARADA. After four attempts, Sims succeeded in gaining admission to RADA, graduating in 1950 at the age of 19. Her early-stage performances included roles in the pantomime "The Happy Ha'penny" at Glasgow's Citizens Theatre in 1951.

Sims embarked on her film career in 1953 with "Will Any Gentleman?" and "Trouble in Store." Notably, in 1958, she received the script for "Carry On Nurse," marking the beginning of her enduring association with the Carry On series. Her performances in subsequent films like "Carry On Teacher" and "Carry On Constable" solidified her status as a regular Carry On performer.

Beyond the Carry On series, Sims made significant contributions to television, portraying characters like Gran in "Till Death Us Do Part," Mrs Wembley in "On the Up," and Madge Hardcastle in "As Time Goes By." Her versatility extended to film, where she played roles in productions like "Love Among the Ruins" (1975) alongside Katharine Hepburn and Laurence Olivier, as well as appearances in "Doctor Who" and "A Murder is Announced."

In 1963, Sims ventured into the music industry, releasing several recordings. Although her singles failed to make an impact on the UK Singles Chart, her contributions to comedy compilation albums and original cast recordings showcase her diverse talents.

Sims, akin to her fellow Carry On star Kenneth Williams, chose not to marry. Despite a proposal of a marriage of convenience from Williams, she declined. Her romantic life included a three-year cohabitation with actor Tony Baird and a subsequent relationship with John Walters. Sims attributed the strain on her relationship with Baird to his lack of success as an actor, and her relationship with Walters eventually ended after approximately two years.

Sims faced health challenges, including depression, in her later years. The deaths of her agent, Peter Eade, close friend Hattie Jacques, and her mother within a two-year period exacerbated her struggles. She also experienced Bell's palsy in 1999 and a fractured hip in 2000, recovering well from both incidents.

However, her battles with alcoholism began to dominate her life in her later years.

Sims's 2000 autobiography, "High Spirits," provided candid insights into her life, revealing moments of disappointment, resilience, and self-reflection. The autobiography concluded on a poignant note, encapsulating Sims's enduring philosophy to "carry on" regardless of life's challenges.

Admitted to the hospital in November 2000, Sims faced complications during a routine operation, slipping into a coma. She passed away on 27th June 2001, ten minutes after her friend Norah Holland spoke to her about their shared memories with Kenneth Williams and their time on the Carry On films. Sims succumbed to liver failure and diverticulitis, with diabetes and COPD cited as contributory factors. She was cremated at Putney Vale Crematorium, and her ashes were scattered on the grounds. In 2014, Andrew Ross authored her authorised biography, "Too Happy A Face," offering a comprehensive exploration of Sims's remarkable life and contributions to British entertainment.

Title	Year	Joan Sims
Nurse	1959	Nurse Stella Dawson
Teacher	1959	Sarah Allcock
Constable	1960	Policewoman Gloria Passworthy
Regardless	1961	Lily Duveen
Cleo	1964	Calpurnia
Cowboy	1965	Belle Armitage
Screaming!	1966	Emily Bung
Don't Lose Your Head	1966	Desiree Dubarry
Follow That Camel	1967	Zig-Zig
Doctor	1967	Chloe Gibson
Up the Khyber	1968	Lady Joan Ruff-Diamond
Camping	1969	Joan Fussey
Again Doctor	1969	Ellen Moore

Up the Jungle	1970	Lady Evelyn Bagley
Loving	1970	Esme Crowfoot
Henry	1971	Queen Marie of Normandy
At Your Convenience	1971	Chloe Moore
Matron	1972	Mrs. Tidey
Abroad	1972	Cora Flange
Girls	1973	Connie Philpotts
Dick	1974	Madame Desiree
Behind	1975	Daphne Barnes
England	1976	Pvt. Ffoukes Sharpe
That's Carry On!	1977	Archive
Emmannuelle	1978	Mrs. Dangle

Leslie Samuel Phillips CBE, the renowned English actor, was born on 20th April 1924 in Tottenham, the third child of Cecelia Margaret (née Newlove) and Frederick Samuel Phillips. His father worked at Glover and Main, manufacturers of cookers in Edmonton. In 1931, the family moved to Chingford, where Phillips attended Larkswood Primary School. Tragically, in 1935, his father passed away at the age of 44 due to health issues exacerbated by the factory's polluted air.

After his father's death, Phillips was sent to the Italia Conti Academy at his mother's insistence. There, he engaged in drama, dance, and elocution to shed his cockney accent, considered a hindrance for aspiring actors at the time. His education at Italia Conti played a crucial role in refining his Received Pronunciation accent. He left school at the age of 14 in 1938.

Phillips made his stage debut in 1937 as a wolf in Peter Pan at the London Palladium. In the following years, he took on various roles to support his family financially. His first film appearance was in the 1938 musical comedy Lassie from Lancashire, followed by uncredited roles in Climbing High (1938) and The Mikado (1939) at Pinewood Studios. During the early years of World War

II, Phillips worked in the West End while being intermittently called up to the British Army.

He rose to the rank of lance-bombardier in the Royal Artillery but was later declared unfit for service just before D-Day due to a neurological condition causing partial paralysis. Demobbed as a lieutenant in December 1944, Phillips resumed his acting career, initially performing in the north of England's playhouses and music halls. He gained momentum in films featuring Anna Karenina and Powell and Pressburger's The Red Shoes (both 1948).

Phillips breakthrough in films came with the Gene Kelly musical Les Girls (1957), leading to more character roles in British comedies.

Phillips secured a minor role as Jack Bell in **Carry On Nurse** (1959). His character's exclamation of "Ding dong" in the film resonated with audiences, transforming it into a widely popular catchphrase. Renowned for his suave and amorous portrayals, he became closely identified with additional catchphrases such as "I say" and "Hello,". He further solidified his on-screen persona in two additional early Carry On films - **Carry On Teacher** (1959) and **Carry On Constable** (1960); later, he returned to the film franchise in **Carry On Columbus** (1992). He also made significant contributions to radio, notably as Sub-Lieutenant Phillips in The Navy Lark between 1959 and 1977.

In the early 1980s, Phillips transitioned to dramatic roles, securing parts in Out of Africa (1985) and Steven Spielberg's Empire of the Sun (1987). He continued as a character actor in stage and television productions, featuring in Scandal (1989) and Lara Croft: Tomb Raider (2001). He also lent his voice to the Sorting Hat in the Harry Potter films. His career extended into television sitcoms, with appearances in shows like Honey for Tea. He received the OBE in 1998 and was later promoted to CBE in

2008. In collaboration with Jules Williams and Back Door Productions, he co-produced the Sky Arts series Living The Life, which ran until 2013.

Encountering health difficulties, he experienced two strokes at the age of 90 and peacefully departed in his sleep on 7th November 2022, reaching the age of 98.

Shirley Jean Eaton was born on 12th January 1937 at Edgware General Hospital, Middlesex, and grew up in the Kingsbury suburb. Despite residing near Kingsbury County Grammar School and Tylers Croft Secondary Modern School, she secured a place at the Aida Foster Theatre School, a specialised drama school, until the age of sixteen. Her stage debut was in Benjamin Britten's Let's Make an Opera!, and in 1954, she made her West End debut in Going to Town.

Throughout the 1950s, Eaton was a singing star, performing on stage and television. She appeared in variety shows nationwide, headlining at the Prince of Wales Theatre in London with her solo singing act. Eaton also participated in the British heat of the 1957 Eurovision Song Contest. Collaborating with renowned British male comedy stars like Jimmy Edwards, Max Bygraves, Bob Monkhouse, and Arthur Askey, she featured in several films and television productions. Notable early roles include Three Men in a Boat (1956), Date with Disaster (1957), and The Belles of St Trinian's (1954).

Eaton's Carry On appearances include: **Carry On Sergeant** (1958), **Carry On Nurse** (1959) and **Carry On Constable** (1960).

Eaton transitioned from comedy roles with The Girl Hunters (1963), opposite Mickey Spillane. Her significant recognition came with the role of Jill Masterson in Goldfinger (1964). Despite her character's memorable death in gold paint, Eaton dispelled the rumour of her demise and appeared on MythBusters in 2003.

Following Goldfinger, Eaton made a few more films, including Rhino! (1964), Around the World Under the Sea (1966), Ten Little Indians (1965), Eight on the Lam (1967), and The Million Eyes of Sumuru (1967). She decided to retire after The Girl from Rio (1969) to focus on family life, stating in a 2014 interview that being away from her children influenced her decision. Eaton published her autobiography, Golden Girl, in 1999, followed by two more books showcasing her film photos, art, and sculptures.

CARRY ON TEACHER (1959)

At Maudlin Street Secondary Modern School, William Wakefield, the acting headmaster, considers applying for a new position near his birthplace after spotting an advertisement. During a visit by Ministry of Education Inspector Miss Wheeler and child psychiatrist Alistair Grigg, Wakefield seeks staff assistance to ensure a smooth inspection. Senior pupil Robin Stevens overhears Wakefield's plan to leave, prompting students to sabotage efforts to deter him.

Carry On Teacher was released on 3rd September 1959 at the Plaza Cinema in London. Ted Ray makes his sole appearance in the Carry On series, joining regulars Kenneth Connor, Charles Hawtrey, Kenneth Williams, and Hattie Jacques. Leslie Phillips and Joan Sims, who debuted in the previous film, Carry On Nurse also return. Emerging talents Richard O'Sullivan and Larry Dann, make their initial appearance, taking on roles as pupils. Dann commemorated his experience in the film by devoting a chapter of his autobiography, titled "Oh, What A Lovely Memoir," to share recollections in 2023.

CAST:

Ted Ray as **Mr William Wakefield**
Kenneth Connor as **Mr Gregory Adams**
Charles Hawtrey as **Mr Michael Bean**

Leslie Phillips as **Mr Alistair Grigg**
Kenneth Williams as **Mr Edwin Milton**
Hattie Jacques as **Miss Grace Short**
Joan Sims as **Miss Sarah Allcock**
Rosalind Knight as **Miss Felicity Wheeler**
Cyril Chamberlain as **Mr Alf Hodgson**
Richard O'Sullivan as **Robin Stevens**
George Howell as **Billy Haig**
Roy Hines as **Harry Bird**
Diana Beevers as **Penny Lee**
Jacqueline Lewis as **Pat Gordon**
Carol White as **Sheila Dale**
Jane White as **Irene Ambrose**
Paul Cole as **John Atkins**
Larry Dann as **Pupil**

FACTS AND TRIVIA:

- Budget: £78,000
- Filming Dates: March - April 1959
- Exterior Filming: Drayton Green Primary School, Ealing
- During filming, an amusing incident involving Charles Hawtrey's mother occurred. While she was enjoying a cigarette on set, lit ash accidentally fell into her handbag. Joan Sims, the first to notice, urgently exclaimed, "Charlie, Charlie, your mother's bag is on fire!" Charles Hawtrey nonchalantly poured his tea into the bag, closed it and continued chatting as if nothing had happened.
- Variety praised the film as "an unabashed collection of uninhibited gag situations and dialogues." Screenplay writer Norman Hudis introduced a slightly stronger storyline, making the characters more credible. Despite some telegraphed gags, the cheerful impudence with which they are delivered is disarming.

- Margaret Harford of the Los Angeles Times commended Carry On Teacher for its "high mark for low comedy" in the slapstick tradition of previous films, labelling it as silly nonsense but fun.
- The Monthly Film Bulletin noted it as another slapstick farce in the 'Carry On' series, acknowledging some predictability but appreciating skilfully timed humour.
- According to Kinematograph Weekly, the film performed "better than average" at the British box office in 1959.

PROFILES:

Charles Hawtrey, born George Frederick Joffre Hartree on 30th November 1914, embraced a multifaceted career as an English actor, comedian, singer, pianist, and theatre director. Despite his public persona, little is known about his private life, which he guarded carefully, especially during a time when male homosexual relationships were illegal in England until 1967.

Hawtrey's early years involved study at the Italia Conti Academy of Theatre Arts in London, where he embarked on a theatre career as both an actor and director. Born in Hounslow, Middlesex, in 1914 to William John Hartree and Alice Crow, he adopted the stage name Charles Hawtrey, inspired by the theatrical knight Sir Charles Hawtrey. It's worth noting that while he encouraged the notion of being Hawtrey's son, his father was, in reality, a London car mechanic.

The actor's personal eccentricities extended beyond the stage. In 1968, Hawtrey relocated to Deal, Kent, where he became known for his unique attire, frequenting local establishments, and promenading along the seafront. Despite his public visibility, he maintained an air of mystery about his private affairs.

Hawtrey's personal life was marked by his close relationship with his mother, who suffered from Alzheimer's disease in her later years. During film shoots, he would bring her onto the set, occasionally locking her in his dressing room when he needed to film a scene.

However, his relationships with fans were less welcoming. When approached for autographs, Hawtrey would often swear at them and rip their paper in half, displaying a peevish demeanour that did not earn him many close friends.

In the later years of his life, Hawtrey faced health challenges, including a heart attack in 1981. In 1984, his house caught fire, a dramatic incident that further highlighted his eccentric lifestyle. On 24th October 1988, he collapsed, suffering a shattered femur, and was subsequently diagnosed with peripheral vascular disease, likely a result of heavy smoking throughout his life. Refusing a life-saving amputation, Hawtrey passed away on 27th October 1988 at Windthorpe Lodge Nursing Home in Walmer, near Deal.

Title	Year	Charles Hawtrey
Sergeant	1958	Peter Golightly
Nurse	1959	Humphrey Hinton
Teacher	1959	Michael Bean
Constable	1960	Special Const. Timothy Gorse
Regardless	1961	Gabriel Dimple
Cabby	1963	Pint-Pot (Terry Tankard)
Jack	1963	Walter
Spying	1964	Charlie Bind
Cleo	1964	Seneca
Cowboy	1965	Big Heap
Screaming!	1966	Dan Dann
Don't Lose Your Head	1966	Duc De Pommfrit
Follow That Camel	1967	Capt. Le Pice
Doctor	1967	Mr. Barron
Up the Khyber	1968	Pvt. James Widdle

Camping	1969	Charlie Muggins
Again Doctor	1969	Dr. Ernest Stoppidge
Up the Jungle	1970	King Tonka / Walter Bagley
Loving	1970	James Bedsop
Henry	1971	Sir Roger de Lodgerley
At Your Convenience	1971	Charles Coote
Matron	1972	Dr. F A Goode
Abroad	1972	Eustace Tuttle
That's Carry On!	**1977**	*Archive*

Ted Ray, originally named Charles Olden, was born on 21st November 1905 in Wigan, Lancashire, England. Born to comic singer and mimic Charles Olden, stage-named Charlie Alden, and Margaret Ellen (née Kenyon). Despite his birth in Wigan, his family relocated to Liverpool shortly after his birth, and he became embraced as a local by Liverpudlians. Ray received his education at Anfield council school and Liverpool Collegiate School. In his youth, he aspired to be a footballer.

As a comedian of the 1940s and 1950s, Ray showcased his improvisational skills in the weekly radio show "Ray's A Laugh," which ran from 1949 to 1961. Renowned for his music hall performances, Ray often incorporated a poorly played violin into his act, initially as Hugh Neek and later as "Nedlo the Gypsy Violinist." Additionally, he played comedic roles in various British films.

His most notable contribution remains the BBC Radio show "Ray's a Laugh," a domestic comedy where Kitty Bluett portrayed his wife. The cast featured notable actors such as Peter Sellers, Fred Yule, Patricia Hayes, Kenneth Connor, Pat Coombs, and Graham Stark. Ray's involvement with the Grand Order of Water Rats and appearances on television and radio panel games further solidified his comedic legacy.

Ray married showgirl Dorothy Sybil, and the couple had two sons, Robin Ray and Andrew Ray, both of whom pursued successful careers in the entertainment industry. On 8th November 1977, Ted Ray suffered a fatal heart attack, marking the end of a comedic era. The legacy of "The Ted Ray Show," a BBC TV production that evolved over different series, remains a testament to his enduring impact on British comedy.

Rosalind Marie Knight born 3rd December 1933 in Marylebone, London, Knight was the daughter of actor Esmond Knight and his first wife, Frances Clare, and the stepdaughter of actress Nora Swinburne. Coming from a theatrical family, she was immersed in theatre from a young age. A visit to the bombed-out Old Vic Theatre in 1949 with her father sparked her interest, leading to two years of study under Glen Byam Shaw and George Devine. She started her career as an Assistant Stage Manager at the Midland Theatre Company in Coventry before moving to the Ipswich Repertory Company, where she worked alongside Joe Orton.

Her acting talent was noticed during her stint with the West of England Theatre Company, resulting in her cast as a schoolgirl in "Blue Murder at St Trinian's" (1957). Knight appeared in the BBC Radio comedy series "Ray's a Laugh" in the late 1950s and featured in two Carry On Films - **Carry On Nurse** (1959), she played Nurse Nightingale and in **Carry On Teacher** (1959), she played Felicity Wheeler, a prim school inspector whose romantic hopes toward Kenneth Connor's wimpy science master are continually thwarted.

Knight's film credits also include "Prick Up Your Ears" (1987) and "About a Boy" (2002). Throughout her career, she remained active in theatre, collaborating with prestigious institutions like the Royal Shakespeare Company, the Royal Court Theatre, and the Old Vic. She also contributed to the Manchester Royal Exchange and the Crucible Theatre in Sheffield. On television, she portrayed Beryl in the BBC sitcom "Gimme Gimme Gimme" (1999–2001) and Cynthia Goodman ("Horrible Grandma") in "Friday Night Dinner" (2012, 2016–2020). Additionally, she made numerous television appearances in popular shows such as "Coronation Street," "Sherlock Holmes," "Mapp & Lucia" and "Only Fools and Horses."

Rosalind Marie Knight passed away on 19th December 2020 at the age of 87. Her legacy endures through her extensive and diverse contributions to the world of entertainment.

CARRY ON 60'S

CARRY ON CONSTABLE (1960)

In a flu-hit suburban police station, Sergeant Wilkins welcomes three new recruits fresh from training school. The trio comprises intellectual PC Stanley Benson, playboy PC Tom Potter, and superstitious PC Charles Constable, joined by WPC Gloria Passworthy and Special Constable Timothy Gorse.

Despite earnest efforts, the new constables encounter mishaps, from nearly arresting an undercover detective to mistaking a radio play for a real murder. Their struggles culminate in a successful apprehension of thieves during a wage robbery, earning them a commendation. Inspector Mills is promoted to a training position, with Wilkins taking his place. Constable overcomes superstitions to win WPC Gloria Passworthy's heart, resulting in a mix of humour, mishaps, and eventual triumph for the newly-formed team.

CAST:

Charles Hawtrey as **Special Constable Timothy Gorse**
Sid James as **Sergeant Frank Wilkins**

Eric Barker as **Inspector Mills**
Kenneth Connor as **Constable Charlie Constable**
Kenneth Williams as **PC Stanley Benson**
Leslie Phillips as **PC Tom Potter**
Joan Sims as **WPC Gloria Passworthy**
Hattie Jacques as **Sergeant Laura Moon**
Shirley Eaton as **Sally Barry**
Joan Hickson as **Mrs May**
Irene Handl as **Distraught Mother**
Terence Longdon as **Herbert Hall**
Jill Adams as **WPC Harrison**
Freddie Mills as **Jewel thief**
Brian Oulton as **Store manager**
Victor Maddern as **Detective Sergeant Liddell**
Esma Cannon as **Deaf old lady**

FACTS AND TRIVIA:

ROLE OF SERGEANT WILKINS

- Originally intended for Ted Ray after his work on Carry On Teacher.
- Replaced by Sid James due to contractual issues with ABC, the distributor of Carry On films.
- Sid James then became a long-standing member of the Carry On team, featuring in 19 films.

FILMING SCHEDULE

- Filming dates: 9th November – 18th December 1959.
- Exteriors: The streets of Ealing, London.
- Budget: £82,500
- The police station exterior is Hanwell Library, Cherrington Road, W7.
- Other scenes were filmed along The Avenue in West Ealing, W13, with the Drayton Court Hotel visible.

- Royal Mail Sorting Office in Manor Road and the railway footbridge over the GWR out of West Ealing featured.
- Additional scenes on and around St Mary's Road (including St Mary's Church) and nearby streets, Ealing W5.
- F.H. Rowse department store, situated at the junction of Green Man Lane and Uxbridge Road in Ealing, is used in the film. Demolished in the early 1980s.

MISC

- Carry On Constable premiered at London's Plaza cinema on 25 February 1960.
- Third most popular film at the British box office in 1960 (Ranked after Doctor in Love and Sink the Bismarck!)

Variety mentioned the team's effort to maintain laughter pressure and deemed it successful in providing harmless merriment. Geoffrey M. Warren praised director Gerald Thomas for achieving good cinema, noting visual gags reminiscent of Laurel and Hardy and the Marx Bros.

PROFILES:

Sid James was born Solomon Joel Cohen on 8th May 1913 to a middle-class Jewish family in South Africa; later changing his name to Sidney Joel Cohen and eventually adopting the stage name Sidney James. His family resided on Hancock Street in Hillbrow, Johannesburg. While he claimed various previous occupations, including diamond cutter, dance tutor, and boxer, his actual profession was that of a trained hairdresser.

James's first marriage was to Berthe Sadie Delmont, known as Toots, in 1936. They had a daughter, Elizabeth, born in 1937, but the marriage ended in divorce in 1940. During the Second World War, James served as a lieutenant in the Union Defence Force Entertainment Unit in South Africa. His career shift towards acting occurred when he joined the Johannesburg Repertory

Players, leading to work with the South African Broadcasting Corporation.

In 1943, James married dancer Meg Sergei, with whom he had a daughter named Reina in 1947. However, this marriage also ended in divorce in 1952. On 21st August 1952, James married Valerie Elizabeth Patsy Assan, an actress using Ashton as her stage name. They had a son, Steve James, born in 1954, and a daughter, Sue. Despite his personal life being marked by multiple marriages and relationships, James's union with Valerie endured for a significant period.

James made his first credited film appearances in Night Beat and Black Memory in 1947, transitioning from bit parts to supporting roles in films like The Small Back Room (1949) and The Lavender Hill Mob (1951) alongside Alec Guinness. His move to the United Kingdom in December 1946 marked a pivotal moment in his career, supported by his service gratuity from the Union Defence Force.

In 1954, James began working with Tony Hancock in the BBC Radio series "Hancock's Half Hour," eventually transitioning to television. His portrayal of a character with his own name in the series established him as a regular performer. This partnership extended until 1960, after which James took on leading roles in television sitcoms like "Citizen James" (1960–1962) and "Taxi!" (1963–64). His ability to navigate both comedy and drama showcased his versatility.

Sidney James became an integral part of the Carry On films team, featuring in 19 films, often with top billing. His characters, typically named Sid or Sidney, were known for his trademark "dirty laugh" and a world-weary "Cor, blimey!" He continued to achieve success in TV situation comedies with shows like "Two in Clover" (1969–70) and "Bless This House" (1971–1976), the latter leading to a film adaptation in 1972.

James's life was marked by personal challenges, including his well-documented gambling addiction. Despite facing a severe heart attack in 1967, he made lifestyle changes, quitting heavy smoking and adopting a healthier routine. His marriage to Valerie also endured challenges, including a well-publicised affair with co-star Barbara Windsor.

Sidney James continued working until his untimely death on 26th April 1976, suffering a heart attack on stage during a performance of "The Mating Season" at the Sunderland Empire Theatre. Plans for future projects, including an additional series of "Bless This House" and a film, were abandoned due to his death. Sidney James was cremated, and his ashes were scattered at Golders Green Crematorium.

A Heritage Foundation commemorative blue plaque and a British Comedy Society plaque honour his contributions to British comedy at Teddington Studios and 35 Gunnersbury Avenue, respectively. Despite some theft incidents, these plaques serve as lasting reminders of Sidney James's significant impact on the world of entertainment.

Title	Year	Sid James
Constable	1960	Sgt. Frank Wilkins
Regardless	1961	Bert Handy
Cruising	1962	Captain Wellington Crowther
Cabby	1963	Charlie Hawkins
Cleo	1964	Mark Antony
Cowboy	1965	Johnny Finger / The Rumpo Kid
Don't Lose Your Head	1966	Sir Rodney Ffing / The Black Fingernail
Doctor	1967	Charlie Roper
Up the Khyber	1968	Sir Sidney Ruff-Diamond
Camping	1969	Sid Boggle
Again Doctor	1969	Gladstone Screwer
Up the Jungle	1970	Bill Boosey

Loving	1970	Sidney Bliss
Henry	1971	King Henry VIII
At Your Convenience	1971	Sid Plummer
Matron	1972	Sid Carter
Abroad	1972	Vic Flange
Girls	1973	Sidney Fiddler
Dick	1974	Reverend Flasher / Dick Turpin
That's Carry On!	1977	Archive

Joan Bogle Hickson, OBE, was born on 5th August 1906 in Kingsthorpe, Northampton, daughter of Edith Mary and Alfred Harold Hickson, a shoe manufacturer. After her education at Oldfield School in Swanage, Dorset, she pursued formal training at RADA in London, marking the beginning of a remarkable career.

Joan Hickson made her stage debut in 1927, showcasing a talent for comedic and eccentric roles in the West End of London. Her notable performances included the role of Ida in the original production of "See How They Run" at the Q Theatre in 1944. Agatha Christie herself expressed a desire for Hickson to portray Miss Marple after witnessing her in "Appointment with Death" in the 1940s.

In the realm of film, Hickson made her debut in 1934 and went on to play various supporting roles throughout her career. Notably, she featured in several Carry On films - **Carry On Nurse** (1959), **Carry On Constable** (1960), **Carry On Regardless** (1960), **Carry On Loving** (1970) and **Carry On Girls** (1973)

Joan's television and film career flourished, with roles in "Murder, She Said" (1961) and the TV series "Our Man at St Mark's" (1963–1966). She garnered acclaim, winning a Tony Award in 1979 for her performance in "Bedroom Farce" and portraying Mrs Trellis in "Clockwise" (1986).

However, it was her definitive portrayal of Miss Marple in the BBC adaptations from 1984 to 1992 that secured her legacy. Hickson received two BAFTA nominations for Best TV Actress and was awarded the OBE in June 1987.

Outside the limelight, Joan called Rose Lane, Wivenhoe, Essex, her home from 1958 until her passing in 1998. She married Dr Eric Norman Butler in 1932, and after he died in 1967, she continued to contribute to the world of acting until her retirement.

Hickson passed away at Colchester General Hospital from a stroke on 17th October 1998 at the age of 92. Her final resting place is at Sidbury Cemetery in Devon, under the name Joan Bogle Butler.

Terence Longdon was born as Hubert Tuelly Longdon in Newark-on-Trent, Nottinghamshire, England on 14th May 1922. Longdon initially served as a pilot with the Fleet Air Arm during World War II, safeguarding Atlantic convoys. It was during this time, stationed at a naval base near Blackpool, that he discovered his passion for acting. Encouraged by actor Douglas Hurn, he decided to pursue it further.

Post-war, Longdon honed his acting skills at RADA from 1946 to 1948. His debut on the stage occurred at the Lyceum, Sheffield, in 1948, followed by his West End debut the same year. Notably, he gained recognition for his lead role in the 1950s–1960s British TV series "Garry Halliday," portraying a pilot reminiscent of Biggles navigating various adventurous situations. Longdon even co-wrote an episode of the series in 1962.

In addition to his television success, Longdon made impactful contributions to British cinema. He played Drusus, Messala's personal aide, in the epic film "Ben-Hur" and had a significant supporting role in the 1958 film "Another Time, Another Place," sharing the screen with Sean Connery and Lana Turner. His versatility extended to comedy, appearing in four early Carry On films - **Carry On Sergeant** (1958), **Carry On Nurse** (1959), **Carry On Constable** (1960) and **Carry On Regardless** (1961)

Longdon's career also included character actor roles in British television productions like "The Sandbaggers," "Danger Man," and "The Avengers." Noteworthy among his leading roles was in the intense B-movie thriller "Clash by Night" (1963).

Residing on the border of Gloucestershire and Warwickshire, Terence Longdon battled cancer and passed away on 23rd April 2011, leaving behind a legacy of remarkable performances in both television and film. He was 88 years old.

CARRY ON REGARDLESS (1961)

In response to the complaints resonating within the local job market due to limited opportunities, Bert Handy and his secretary Miss Cooling, embarked on launching Helping Hand to address the job vacancies. Assembling a diverse team, their escapades unfold with humorous misadventures involving eccentric clients—a man speaking gobbledygook and a woman attempting to incite jealousy.

CAST:

Sid James as **Bert Handy**
Kenneth Connor as **Sam Twist**
Charles Hawtrey as **Gabriel Dimple**
Kenneth Williams as **Francis Courtenay**
Professor Stanley Unwin as **Landlord**
Joan Sims as **Lily Duveen**
Liz Fraser as **Delia King**
Esma Cannon as **Miss Cooling**
Bill Owen as **Mike Weston**

Freddie Mills as **'Lefty' Vincent**
Fenella Fielding as **Penny Panting**
Hattie Jacques as **Sister**
Joan Hickson as **Matron**
Sydney Tafler as **Strip Club Manager**
Judith Furse as **Headmistress**
Nicholas Parsons as **Wolf**
Cyril Chamberlain as **Policeman**
Terence Longdon as **Montgomery Infield-Hopping**

FACTS AND TRIVIA:

FILMING SCHEDULE

- 28th November 1960 – 17th January 1961
- Budget: £100,000
- Exteriors: The corner of Park Street and Sheet Street in Windsor, Berkshire, served as the setting for the Helping Hand Agency - This location was reused a decade later for the Wedded Bliss agency in Carry On Loving.
- Variety provided a mixed review, acknowledging scriptwriter Norman Hudis's ingenuity while noting occasional strains in the script. The dialogues, filled with double meanings and saucy vulgarity, were commended, and the extensive cast demonstrated their expertise in navigating the comedic challenges set by director Gerald Thomas.
- Margaret Harford from the Los Angeles Times found the film somewhat scrambled but suggested that devoted fans of the series would appreciate the inherent humour in an organisation labelled the Helping Hand Employment Agency.
- The Monthly Film Bulletin expressed a more critical view, stating that many gags seemed outdated, following the worn path of British music-hall and farce traditions. Despite this, the film's popularity allowed it to coast on its momentum for

some time, benefiting from the series' enduring appeal before potentially facing a reckoning from the audience.

PROFILES:

Kenneth Connor, MBE, was born on 6th June 1918, in Highbury, Islington, London, to a naval petty officer who organised concert parties. His early exposure to the stage began at the age of two, performing as an organ grinder's monkey in his father's shows in Portsmouth. Connor's own act emerged by the age of 11, and he later attended the Central School of Speech and Drama, winning a Gold Medal. In December 1936, he made his professional debut in J. M. Barrie's "The Boy David" at His Majesty's Theatre, London.

During World War II, Connor served as an infantry gunner with the Middlesex Regiment. Despite his military service, he continued acting by touring Italy and the Middle East with the Stars in Battledress concert party and ENSA. After being demobbed in Cairo, he received an invitation from William Devlin to join the newly formed Bristol Old Vic, where he gained a solid foundation in classical theatre.

Connor moved to the London Old Vic Company for a 1947–48 season at the New Theatre, where his notable performances included roles in "Saint Joan" and "The Government Inspector." Recognising his inclination towards comedy, he specialised in the genre. His early career included appearances in Talbot Rothwell's farce "Queen Elizabeth Slept Here" in the West End in 1949. His versatile talent was also evident in appearances on "The Goon Show" and TV series like "The Idiot Weekly, Price 2d" (1956) and "A Show Called Fred" (1956). Connor secured a small role in the film "The Ladykillers" (1955).

In 1958, Kenneth Connor was cast in the first Carry On film, "Carry On Sergeant," marking the beginning of his association with the renowned film series. Over the years, he appeared in seventeen of the original thirty Carry On films and associated television productions. His roles in the early Carry On films often portrayed him as the romantic lead or a sympathetic character. However, as the series progressed, he embraced less sympathetic roles, showcasing his comedic versatility.

Contrary to some of his Carry On co-stars, Connor found success on the London stage. He starred in the revue "One Over The Eight" (1962), the original London West End production of Stephen Sondheim's musical "A Funny Thing Happened on the Way to the Forum" (1963), and directed the show on tour. His stage credits also include "The Four Musketeers" (1967) and the revue "Carry On London" (1973).

Connor's television career continued with appearances in popular shows like "Dad's Army" radio comedy (1971–1973), "The Black and White Minstrel Show," "Rentaghost" (1983–84), "'Allo 'Allo!" (1984–1992), and "Hi-de-Hi!" (1986–88). He made guest appearances in sitcoms such as "That's My Boy," "You Rang, M'Lord?," and was featured in an episode of "Blackadder the Third" in 1987.

In 1991, Kenneth Connor was appointed a Member of the Order of the British Empire (MBE). Despite battling cancer, he continued working until his final days. Connor passed away at the age of 75 at his home in Harrow, Middlesex, on 28th November 1993. His body was cremated at Breakspear Crematorium in Ruislip, Greater London.

Kenneth Connor's comedic brilliance endured even beyond his passing, making its final mark in the posthumous airing of his last TV appearance in the 1994 episode "The Red Circle" from "The Memoirs of Sherlock Holmes." His contribution left an indelible legacy in the realm of British entertainment.

| Title | Year | Kenneth Connor |

Sergeant	1958	Horace Strong
Nurse	1959	Bernie Bishop
Teacher	1959	Gregory Adams
Constable	1960	Const. Charlie Constable
Regardless	1961	Sam Twist
Cruising	1962	Dr Arthur Binn
Cabby	1963	Ted Watson
Cleo	1964	Hengist Pod
Up the Jungle	1970	Claude Chumley
Henry	1971	Lord Hampton of Wick
Matron	1972	Mr. Tidey
Abroad	1972	Stanley Blunt
Girls	1973	Mayor Frederick Bumble
Dick	1974	Constable
Behind	1975	Maj. Leep
England	1976	Capt. S. Melly
That's Carry On!	1977	**Archive**
Emmannuelle	1978	Leyland/Voice of Harry Hernia

Stanley Unwin was born on 7th June 1911 in Pretoria, South Africa, before later relocating to England following his father's demise in 1914. By 1919, he found himself at the National Children's Home in Congleton, Cheshire. His foray into the media began with radio studies in the late 1920s at Regent Street Polytechnic in London. In 1937.

Unwin crafted his unique comedic language, "Unwinese," as showcased in Carry On Regardless, where it was amusingly referred to as "gobbledygook." Unwinese represented a whimsical distortion of the English language, with playful alterations to many words. For instance, it playfully described Elvis Presley and his contemporaries as possessing a "wasp-waist and swivel-hippy" demeanour. Unwin attributed the inspiration for Unwinese to his mother, recalling a humorous incident when she mentioned "falolloping (falling) over" and "grazing her kneeclabbers" on her way home.

Unwin's career gained momentum when he accidentally transmitted a Unwinese sketch, leading to collaborations with Frankie Howerd and Ted Ray. His ventures extended into the film industry by the late 1950s, and he narrated "Happiness Stan" for the Small Faces' album Ogdens' Nut Gone Flake (1968).

Unwin's career took a unique turn in 1969 when he appeared in Gerry Anderson's "Supermarionation" TV series, The Secret Service, showcasing Unwinese in both human and puppet form. Despite being retired in later years, he continued making occasional appearances in various projects, including collaborations with Suns of Arqa and a cameo in Rex the Runt (1998). Unwin's comedic language, Unwinese, reminiscent of Lewis Carroll's nonsense poetry, is hailed for its influence on John Lennon's literary works.

Stanley Unwin passed away on 12th January 2002, leaving behind a unique linguistic legacy and a lasting impact on British comedy.

Bill Owen born William John Owen Rowbotham, MBE 14th March 1914, was an English actor and songwriter who left an enduring mark on British television. Born in Acton Green, London, Owen's early film appearances in 1945 did not bring him lasting fame until 1973, when he assumed the role of William "Compo" Simmonite in the beloved British sitcom Last of the Summer Wine. Portraying a scruffy working-class pensioner, Compo endeared himself to audiences for 26 years until Owen's death. The sitcom, spanning from 1973 to 2010, holds the record as the world's longest-running comedy series.

Owen's versatility extended beyond acting; he served in the Royal Army Ordnance Corps during World War II, surviving an injury in battle training. In the 1960s, he enjoyed a successful second career as a songwriter, contributing to hits like "Marianne," recorded by Cliff Richard. His commitment to socialist ideals was evident in his support for the Labour Party, contributing to the Keep Sunday Special campaign and serving as the president of Arts for Labour. Owen's contributions to British television and his left-wing views shaped his legacy. Despite battling pancreatic and bowel cancer, he continued filming Last of the Summer Wine until his death in Westminster on 12th July 1999, aged 85. Bill Owen is buried in the churchyard of St John's Parish Church in Upperthong, near Holmfirth in Yorkshire, alongside his co-star Peter Sallis, who joined him in eternal rest in June 2017 at the age of 96.

CARRY ON CRUISING (1962)

Captain Crowther, preparing for a new cruise on the SS Happy Wanderer, faces unexpected challenges as five inexperienced and bumbling crew members join the voyage. The passengers, including single ladies Gladys and Flo, add to the eccentric mix.

While the crew's mishaps continue, Gladys and Flo become entangled in romantic misadventures, with the ship's PT instructor catching their attention. Ship's doctor Dr. Binn, smitten with Flo, faces challenges in expressing his feelings. A plot unfolds, orchestrated by Gladys and the First Officer, leading to a surprising romantic revelation.

Based on an original story by Eric Barker, Carry on Cruising extends its gratitude to P&O – Orient Lines in the credits. The cast includes regulars Sid James, Kenneth Williams, and Kenneth Connor, while notable figures Joan Sims and Charles Hawtrey are absent. Sims, falling ill just before filming, was swiftly replaced by Dilys Laye, making her Carry On debut with only four days' notice. Sims made a comeback two years later in "Carry On Cleo." Liz Fraser makes her second of four appearances, and Lance

Percival, appearing only in "Carry On Cruising," takes on the role of the ship's chef initially designated for Hawtrey. Vincent Ball, the Australian actor, makes his first of two Carry On appearances. Notably, this film is the last to have its screenplay written by Norman Hudis and stands out as the first in the series to be filmed in colour.

CAST:

Kenneth Williams as **First Officer Leonard Marjoribanks**
Sid James as Captain Wellington Crowther
Kenneth Connor as **Dr Arthur Binn**
Lance Percival as **Wilfred Haines, Ship's Cook**
Liz Fraser as **Glad Trimble**
Dilys Laye as **Flo Castle**
Esma Cannon as **Bridget Madderley**
Jimmy Thompson as **Sam Turner**
Ronnie Stevens as **Drunk**
Vincent Ball as **Jenkins**
Cyril Chamberlain as **Tom Tree**
Ed Devereaux as **Young officer**

The film ranked as the 12th most popular film at the British box office in 1962.

According to Kinematograph Weekly, it was considered a "money maker" at the British box office for the same year.

FACTS AND TRIVIA:

FILMING SCHEDULE

- Dates: 8th January – 16th February 1962
- Exteriors: Tibury Docks

PREMIERE

- Location: Southampton, England
- Event: The film's premiere took place on a cruise ship.

- Budget: £140,000

CASTING CHALLENGES

- The role of the ship's cook, Wilfred Haines, was originally meant for Charles Hawtrey but was rewritten for Lance Percival after a dispute led to Hawtrey quitting. This marks the only "Carry on..." movie without Hawtrey during his fourteen-year regular association with the series (from Carry on Sergeant in 1958 to Carry on Abroad in 1972).

MISC

- The "SS Happy Wanderer," including its interiors and deck scenes, is primarily a set constructed at Pinewood Studios. The set is affixed atop a hydraulic rig, presenting a life-sized mock-up with all the features of a real cruise ship.
- The exploding cake scene posed challenges, requiring multiple retakes. Lance Percival, portraying the ship's cook, Wilfred Haines, revealed that the cake explosion was achieved with a pressure pump underneath, leading to difficulties in capturing the desired scene.
- Percival mentioned that it took nine takes to get a scene lasting ten seconds due to the unpredictability of the exploding cake.

PROFILES:

Lance Percival, born John Lancelot Blades Percival on 26th July 1933 in Sevenoaks, Kent. In his younger years, Percival received his education at Sherborne School in Dorset, where he cultivated his skills in playing the guitar. Following this, he embarked on national service with the Seaforth Highlanders, serving as a lieutenant and being stationed in Egypt. In 1955, he made a significant move, emigrating to Canada, where he worked as an advertising copywriter, crafting jingles for radio. During this time, he also formed a calypso group under the moniker "Lord Lance," touring the United States and Canada.

Percival gained recognition in the early 1960s for his topical calypsos on television shows like "That Was The Week That Was," after catching the eye of Ned Sherrin at the Blue Angel Club in Mayfair. His distinctive appearance, characterised by a tall, thin frame, a crooked nose, and prominent ears, contributed to his comedic persona.

Throughout the 1960s, he made notable appearances in British comedy films, and his talents extended to the music scene, with a chart-topping cover of the calypso-style song "Shame and Scandal in the Family" in October 1965. He continued recording comedy songs, such as "The Beetroot Song" (1963) and "The Maharajah of Brum" (1967).

In the mid-1960s, Percival ventured into voice acting, providing the voices for both Paul McCartney and Ringo Starr in the cartoon series "The Beatles" (1965) and later voicing the central character "Old Fred" in the animated film "Yellow Submarine." His film career expanded, starring alongside Julie Andrews, Rock Hudson, and Jeremy Kemp in "Darling Lili" (1970) and appearing in other productions like "Too Late the Hero" (1970) and "Mrs. Brown, You've Got a Lovely Daughter" (1968).

However, tragedy struck on 14th December 1970, when Percival was involved in a fatal three-car crash on the A20, south of Farningham, Kent, known as Death Hill. After a challenging recovery, he faced legal consequences but was ultimately acquitted when evidence suggested a tyre on his car had likely deflated before the crash.

Percival made a successful return to film work, featuring in Frankie Howerd films and contributing to the Thames Television game show "Whodunnit!" between 1972 and 1978, which he co-wrote with Jeremy Lloyd. In the 1980s, he continued his presence in BBC Radio light entertainment programmes like "Just a Minute" and authored two books of verse, "Well-Versed Cats" and "Well-Versed Dogs," both illustrated by Lalla Ward.

Towards the later years of his life, Percival transitioned to writing and became renowned as an after-dinner speaker. He battled a long illness before passing away on 6th January 2015 at the age of 81. Lance Percival was cremated at Putney Vale Crematorium on 20th January 2015.

Liz Fraser, born Elizabeth Joan Winch on 14th August 1930 in Southwark, London, despite commonly citing her birth year as 1933, she revealed her true age during the audition for "I'm All Right Jack," a revelation prompted by the Boulting Brothers' preference for a younger actress. The disruption caused by the Second World War led to her evacuation, first to Westerham in Kent and later to Chudleigh, Devon. Tragically, her father passed away in May 1942 when Liz was just 11. She attended St Saviour's and St Olave's Grammar School for Girls. She pursued evening courses at Goldsmiths College, City of London College for Commerce, and the London School of Dramatic Art.

Liz Fraser's film career commenced with "Touch and Go" (1955) under her birth name. Notably, she worked with Peter Sellers for the first time in "The Smallest Show on Earth" (1957). Her breakthrough role came in "I'm All Right Jack" (1959), earning her a BAFTA nomination.

She was in several of the early Carry On films - **Carry On Regardless** (1961), **Carry On Cruising** (1962), and **Carry On Cabby** (1963), but was temporarily ousted by producer Peter Rogers due to her candid remarks about marketing. Fraser made a successful return to the series in **Carry On Behind** (1975) although it is reported that her salary was half of what it had been before.

Her filmography includes a diverse range of productions, such as "Two-Way Stretch" (1960), "The Americanization of Emily" (1964), "Up the Junction" (1968), and a series of sex comedies in the 1970s. Additionally, Fraser was a familiar face on British television, appearing in shows like "Hancock's Half Hour," "The Avengers," "Sixpenny Corner," and "Parsley Sidings."

In November 1958, Liz married Peter Yonwin, a travelling salesman, but the marriage ended in divorce. Her second marriage to TV director Bill Hitchcock took place in January 1965. Despite initially deciding not to work together, they collaborated on projects like "Albert!" and "Turnbull's Finest Half-Hour." Tragically, Hitchcock passed away from a pulmonary embolism in February 1974. Liz Fraser faced personal health challenges, being diagnosed with breast cancer in 1978 and 1979.

Liz Fraser's family included a half-brother, Philip, 11 years her senior, and she actively supported charities while being a patron of the London Repertory Company. An adept poker and bridge player, Liz Fraser breathed her last on 6th September 2018 at Royal Brompton Hospital, succumbing to complications following a surgical procedure.

CARRY ON CABBY (1963)

Charlie Hawkins, the hardworking owner of Speedee Taxis, neglects his wife Peggy. Peggy, feeling unappreciated, secretly starts a rival cab company, GlamCabs, using their joint funds.

The competition causes Speedee's decline, with Peggy's company thriving due to attractive drivers.

Charlie, oblivious to Peggy's involvement, struggles to save his business. Desperate, he suggests a merger, only to discover Peggy's ownership. The rivalry escalates, leading to comedic and dramatic events, ultimately testing their relationship.

Carry On Cabby marked the first screenplay by Talbot Rothwell, based on a story by Dick Hills and Sid Green, known for their work with Morecambe and Wise. The film features regulars Sid James, Hattie Jacques, Kenneth Connor, and Charles Hawtrey. Liz Fraser makes her third and final appearance for more than a decade, while Bill Owen and Esma Cannon make their last appearances.

Notably, Carry On Cabby introduces Carry On regular Jim Dale and is the first film in the series without Kenneth Williams, who declined a role due to script concerns. The character Allbright, initially offered to Williams, was scaled down and given to Norman Chappell.

Originally planned as a non-Carry On film titled "Call Me A Cab," the project transitioned midway into becoming part of the Carry On series. Distinguished from other films in the series, Carry On Cabby explores a dramatic plotline revolving around a troubled marriage.

CAST:

Sid James as **Charlie Hawkins**
Hattie Jacques as **Peggy Hawkins**
Charles Hawtrey as **Terry "Pintpot" Tankard**
Kenneth Connor as **Ted Watson**
Esma Cannon as **Flo Sims**
Liz Fraser as **Sally**
Bill Owen as **Smiley Sims**
Milo O'Shea as **Len**
Norman Chappell as **Allbright**
Judith Furse as **Battleaxe**
Renée Houston as **Molly**
Ambrosine Phillpotts as **Aristocratic lady**
Amanda Barrie as **Anthea**
Carole Shelley as **Dumb driver**

Cyril Chamberlain as **Sarge**
Peter Gilmore as **Dancy**
Jim Dale as **Expectant father** (credited as "Small man" and named "Jeremy" in the film)

FACTS AND TRIVIA:

FILMING SCHEDULE

- Filming dates: 25th March – 7th May 1963
- Exteriors: The streets of Windsor
- The scene in which "Pintpot" (Charles Hawtrey) drives a cab (PEG 1) round and round a roundabout was filmed at the junction of Goswell Road and Arthur Road, Windsor, with the railway arches of Windsor & Eton Central Station visible in the background. This area has changed considerably since 1963 with the building of King Edward Court and Ward Royal. Some filming was also undertaken in Farm Yard opposite Windsor & Eton Riverside Station.
- Budget: £149,986

RELEASE

- First screened to the trade (cinema distributors) on 22nd August 1963, the film went on general release across the UK later the same year on 7th November.

CHALLENGES

- Charles Hawtrey, being non-proficient in driving, received one-hour lessons thrice daily from the Pinewood Studios staff for a duration of three weeks. He successfully passed his driving test on the Friday just before the commencement of filming.

SEE ALSO

- Taxi! – contemporary TV series with Sid James in a similar role to Carry On Cabby

- The filming of Carry On Cabby is portrayed in the BBC drama Hattie, a dramatisation of the life of Hattie Jacques.

PROFILES

Hattie Jacques (born Josephine Edwina Jaques) on 7th February 1922, at Sandgate High Street, Sandgate, Kent. She was the youngest child of Robin Rochester Jaques and Mary Jaques (née Thorn). Her family, primarily non-theatrical, moved from Newton in Lincolnshire to London after her father's death in a flying accident in August 1923.

Jacques attended Lady Margaret Primary School in Chelsea and later the Godolphin and Latymer School in Hammersmith, where she also took dance classes at the Dean Sisters Academy. Despite leaving Godolphin and Latymer in 1939 with unremarkable grades, Jacques continued with amateur theatricals, participating in productions with the Curtain Club in Barnes in May 1939.

With the outbreak of World War II, Jacques joined the Voluntary Aid Detachment (VAD) as a nurse, serving in a mobile unit during the Blitz in London. In the summer of 1943, she became a welder in a north London factory until the end of the year. During this time, she became romantically involved with an American soldier, Major Charles Kearney, who later returned to his family after the war.

In 1944, after being auditioned by Leonard Sachs, Jacques made her professional theatrical debut at the Players' Theatre in London, adding a "c" to her birth name as Josephine Jacques. She became a regular performer with the company, appearing in music hall revues and playing the Fairy Queen in Victorian-style pantomimes.vJacques made her television debut in June 1946 while performing in a Late Joys revue. During this period, she adopted the nickname "Hattie." In the same year, she had a brief, uncredited role in the film Green for Danger.

In December 1946, Jacques joined the Young Vic Theatre Company, playing Smeraldina in The King Stag. In March 1947, she had her first credited big-screen role in Alberto Cavalcanti's film Nicholas Nickleby as Mrs Kenwick. During this time, she began a relationship with the actor John Le Mesurier.

In August 1947, Jacques auditioned for the BBC Home Service show It's That Man Again (ITMA) and joined the cast as the greedy schoolgirl Sophie Tuckshop. Her run in ITMA started in September 1947, marking the beginning of her prolific career in radio. Jacques went on to have a successful partnership with Tommy Handley on ITMA, Peter Brough on Educating Archie, and Tony Hancock on Hancock's Half Hour.

In 1948, Hattie Jacques continued her busy schedule, recording ITMA episodes for half the week and performing at the Players' Theatre in the evenings. During the spring, she recorded the role of Flora in No, No, Nanette for the BBC and appeared at the Whitehall Theatre in Bates Wharf with the Under Thirty Theatre Group. Later that year, Jacques showcased her singing talents at the Three Cripples Tavern in the David Lean film Oliver Twist. In September, she commenced recording her second series of ITMA. She returned to the Players' for the Christmas pantomime, The Sleeping Beauty in the Wood, receiving praise from The Times for her role as the Fairy Queen Antedota.

Tragedy struck in January 1949 when Tommy Handley, star of ITMA, passed away suddenly. The BBC, considering Handley integral to the show, promptly cancelled it. Jacques, deeply influenced by Handley, acknowledged him as one of the greatest radio performers. During the same year, after actor John Le Mesurier divorced his wife, Jacques proposed to him, and they married on 10th November at Kensington Registrar's Office, followed by a honeymoon in Southsea. She returned to the Players' to perform as Marrygolda in the Christmas pantomime Beauty and the Beast.

From 1950 to 1958, Hattie Jacques experienced increasing fame. In 1950, the film Chance of a Lifetime, a social and industrial relations drama, featured Jacques in a significant role as Alice, a welder. Her performance earned praise, with film critic Geoff Mayer highlighting her mock seductive dance scene. In June 1950, Jacques joined the radio show Educating Archie, playing Agatha Dinglebody. This collaboration marked her first work with Eric Sykes, who was impressed by her elegance on stage. They would later form a long-lasting professional partnership.

Throughout 1951, Jacques continued her diverse work, portraying Mrs Fezziwig in the film Scrooge and appearing in a second radio series Educating Archie. She also adapted and performed in the Christmas pantomime Ali Baba and the Thirty-nine Thieves at the Players' Theatre. In 1952, she took on the role of Mrs Jenks in the comedy horror film Mother Riley Meets the Vampire. Jacques showcased her versatility by balancing performances in film, radio, and pantomime during this period.

In 1952, Hattie Jacques faced a significant life event as she became pregnant. Despite her pregnancy, she continued to work diligently, participating in the Players' revue The Bells of St Martins from August to November 1952. The Times commended her performance, especially highlighting her concluding feat of sliding down a table and executing the splits. However, The Manchester Guardian remarked on her being "monumental of person but surprisingly thin of voice."

During the same period, Jacques worked on the third series of Educating Archie from September 1952 to June 1953. Additionally, she directed the Players' Christmas pantomime, Babes in the Wood, in 1952. In March 1953, just a few days after giving birth to her first son, Robin, Jacques returned to work to film Up to His Neck. Later in the year, she starred alongside John Le Mesurier in the "movie-masque" The Pleasure Garden, which won the Prix de Fantasie Poétique at the 1954 Cannes Film Festival. She continued her association with Educating Archie in series four from October 1953 to April 1954 and also appeared in and directed Cinderella at the Players'. Jacques continued her involvement in radio, featuring in Paradise Street and Archie in Goonland. She played Mrs Leathers in 18 episodes of Mrs Dale's Diary between February and April 1955. Notably, she produced and directed Twenty Minutes South, initially at the Players' Theatre and later for 105 performances at the St Martin's Theatre. In the same year, she appeared in seven episodes of The Granville Melodramas on ITV from October to December.

A second pregnancy in 1956 led to the birth of her son, Kim. In June 1956, Jacques made an appearance in an episode of The Tony Hancock Show on ITV, which paved the way for her role as Griselda Pugh in the BBC radio series Hancock's Half Hour. This collaboration marked a significant contribution to the success of the series. She continued to appear in Hancock's Half Hour, making 20 episodes between January and June 1958 and a special edition on Christmas Day 1958. Concurrently, Jacques spent much of 1958 at the London Palladium, undertaking 380 performances of the revue Large as Life alongside Terry-Thomas, Eric Sykes, and Harry Secombe.

The Carry On series became a pivotal part of Jacques's career from 1958 to 1963. She appeared in 14 films over a 15-year period, solidifying her status as a "Mother Hen" figure in the Carry On team. Jacques became known for her recurring role as a no-nonsense matron, featured in films like Carry On Nurse, Carry On Doctor, Carry On Again Doctor, Carry On Camping, and Carry On Matron. She formed close friendships with co-stars Kenneth Williams and Joan Sims, providing them with advice and practical help. Jacques's association with the Carry On series began in March 1958 with Carry On Sergeant, and her role as "Matron" in Carry On Nurse garnered widespread attention, especially for the memorable scene involving a daffodil and Wilfrid Hyde-White's buttocks. Her popularity continued to soar with various characterisations, including the formidable maths mistress Grace Short in Carry On Teacher (1959) and the friendly Police Sergeant Laura Moon in Carry On Constable (1960). Jacques's ability to triumph over juvenile material was noted by critics, securing her place as a beloved figure in the Carry On series.

On 29th January 1960, Hattie Jacques made her debut in the BBC comedy series Sykes and a…, appearing in the first episode alongside Eric Sykes as a pair of twins. Regulars in the cast included Richard Wattis and Deryck Guyler. Jacques portrayed the character Hattie (Hat) Sykes, a middle-class, slightly pretentious lady struggling to maintain her dignity amidst the men's foolishness. The show enjoyed considerable success, running for sixty episodes over nine series during the next five years. Media historian Graham McCann praised it as "one of the best-natured, least pretentious and most successful British sitcoms of the 1960s." The comedic partnership of Jacques and Sykes became ingrained in the public consciousness, leading to the release of a comedy album titled Eric and Hattie and Things!!!, although it did not achieve chart success.

In September 1960, Jacques starred in her second television series, Our House, alongside Charles Hawtrey, Bernard Bresslaw, and Joan Sims. She played the librarian Georgina Ruddy, a character forced to remain quiet at work and compensated by being extremely noisy at home. Later in the same year, she took on minor roles in two films: Watch Your Stern, featuring several Carry On regulars, and School for Scoundrels, opposite Ian Carmichael. Jacques's screen time increased with her role as

Nanette Parry in Make Mine Mink, co-starring with Terry-Thomas and Athene Seyler. She later considered this film her favourite.

In October 1961, Jacques appeared on Desert Island Discs, expressing her belief that she would feel too lonely on such a quiet island due to her temperament. By this time, the Carry On film franchise had become a phenomenon, with Carry On Regardless, the fifth film in the series released that year. Jacques received a fee of £100 for her small role as a disgruntled hospital sister, appearing briefly on screen alongside English character actor Kynaston Reeves. Although initially intended for a major part, Jacques's ill health prevented her from committing to a more extended role.

Her involvement in the Carry On series continued with Carry On Cabby in 1963, where she played "Peggy Hawkins," the emotionally neglected wife of taxi firm boss "Charlie," portrayed by Sid James. Jacques considered this film her favourite of the series, as it allowed her to shed her "battleaxe" persona and take on the romantic lead opposite James.

In 1963, Hattie Jacques's personal life took a complicated turn. The previous year, she encountered John Schofield, a cockney used car dealer, who became romantically involved with her after chauffeuring her to a Leukaemia Research Fund event. Schofield provided the attention and support that her then-husband, John Le Mesurier, did not. This led to Jacques deciding to move Schofield into the family home, prompting Le Mesurier to relocate to a separate room. Despite the challenges, he expressed his commitment to repairing the damage, stating, "I could have walked out, but whatever my feelings, I loved Hattie and the children, and I was certain—I had to be certain—that we could repair the damage."

During these personal upheavals, Jacques was unexpectedly featured on This Is Your Life in February 1963, approached by

Eamonn Andrews during the sixth series rehearsal of Sykes and a... While Le Mesurier did not disclose the marital situation to Andrews, his comment that for Jacques, "the home comes first" was considered by biographer Andy Merriman to have been said "rather pointedly." Despite the challenges in their marriage, both Jacques and Le Mesurier appeared in the 1963 Tony Hancock film The Punch and Judy Man. In 1964, Le Mesurier moved out of the marital home, making a conscious decision to shield Jacques from negative publicity. He allowed her to bring a divorce suit based on his own infidelity, ensuring that the press held him accountable for the break-up and portraying Jacques as the victim.

In 1964, amid her personal challenges, Jacques recorded four episodes of the radio show Housewives' Choice. Additionally, she starred in her own television series, Miss Adventure, playing the role of private investigator Stacey Smith. While Jacques had envisioned the series to be suspenseful, it turned out more comedic than expected, leaving her disappointed with the outcome. In August of that year, she portrayed Madame Arcati in an ITV production of Blithe Spirit. The play's writer, Noël Coward, praised Jacques for delivering a performance that wasn't overshadowed by Margaret Rutherford, who had originated the stage role in 1940 and played it in the 1945 film version.

In 1966, Jacques travelled to Rome to film The Bobo with Peter Sellers. Before the filming, she underwent a strict diet, losing five stone (32 kg), although she was disappointed that few people noticed the change. Despite the challenges, Jacques enjoyed the filming experience, describing it as "one of the loveliest things I've worked on." During her time in Italy, Schofield came to visit, started an affair with an Italian heiress, and ended his relationship with Jacques. Deeply upset, Jacques, who had struggled with weight issues since her teens, turned to comfort food, causing her weight to increase to nearly 20 stone (127 kg)

In the summer of 1967, Carry On producer Peter Rogers gathered the cast for the 15th film in the series Carry On Doctor. Initially considering Joan Sims for the role of the hospital matron, Rogers changed course as Sims believed that Jacques's portrayal in Carry On Nurse was unmatched. Consequently, Jacques was cast as Matron, with Sims taking on a smaller role as the timid assistant of the film's lead character, Francis Bigger, portrayed by Frankie Howerd. Building on her role in Carry On Nurse, Jacques's screen time was expanded in Carry On Doctor, which saw its release in December of that year, achieving considerable success.

Entering 1968, Jacques featured alongside Spike Milligan and Frank Thornton in thirteen episodes of the sketch show The World of Beachcomber, based on the Beachcomber column in the Daily Express newspaper and broadcast on the BBC from January to April. Following this series, she joined Frankie Howerd in his sketch show, Howerd's Hour, on ITV. In 1969, Jacques maintained a busy schedule, appearing in six films, including The Magic Christian alongside Peter Sellers, portraying a character named Ginger with an "insatiable lust for bestsellers on the atrocities of World War Two." She also appeared on television in Pickwick with Harry Secombe and Roy Castle and in Carry On Christmas, broadcast on Christmas Eve.

Despite a hectic 1969, 1970 proved relatively quiet for Jacques in terms of professional output. Apart from an episode of Catweazle, she featured alongside Willoughby Goddard in a six-episode series of Charley's Grants. The filming for Carry On Loving took place in May and June, and the film was released in September that year. Another Carry On film followed in 1971, Carry On at Your Convenience, where Jacques played Beattie Plummer, the housebound wife of Sid Plummer, portrayed by Sid James. In the same year, she completed another series with Sykes, titled Sykes and a Big, Big Show, a music and sketch programme with six episodes broadcast between February and April.

Two additional Carry On films followed in 1972: Carry On Matron, in which Jacques played the title role, and Carry On Abroad, portraying Floella, the fiery Spanish cook at a half-finished hotel. The latter marked a reduction in Jacques's screen time, with only one week spent filming her scenes. Post-production, concerns about her deteriorating health were raised by the film's insurers, expressing reluctance to insure her on set for any future film.

Throughout 1972, Jacques co-starred in the first series of Sykes, portraying Hattie Sykes as "the wide-eyed, less-knowing but remarkably patient sister-cum-mother-figure." At its height, Sykes attracted 17 million viewers. In February 1972, Jacques watched from home as her son Robin witnessed Le Mesurier winning the British Academy of Film and Television Arts "Best Television Actor" award for his role in Dennis Potter's television play Traitor. Jacques, emotionally moved, shared with her son the unhappiness she felt due to losing John and having no one to spend her life with.

In 1974, Jacques's house was searched by police, and in the same week, she received official notification of the intention to appoint her as an OBE. To shield her family from further press intrusion, particularly during court appearances, she declined the honour. Later that year, amidst filming the third series of Sykes, she suffered a cancer scare and lost a considerable amount of weight. Despite this, she refused to interrupt the busy production schedule. After completing filming on 5th December, she underwent surgery at Charing Cross Hospital, revealing the presence of benign tumours on her kidneys.

In 1976, Jacques participated in a promotional advertising film for British Rail, engaging in a race to London against racing driver Jackie Stewart. From 1976 onwards, she and Eric Sykes appeared together in the stage play A Hatful of Sykes, both in the UK and internationally. However, their relationship became strained during different tours, with Sykes adjusting the act to receive more acclaim than Jacques. Health issues surfaced in 1977 while performing in Blackpool, with Jacques suffering from arthritis and ulcerated legs. The strained relations persisted when the show moved to Rhodesia, and by 1979, the relationship had deteriorated significantly. Despite their differences, Jacques and Sykes filmed the seventh series of Sykes in 1979 and the television film Rhubarb Rhubarb in April 1980.

In 1980, Jacques's health declined, preventing her from travelling to Greece as planned. Advised against the trip by her doctor, she visited Ireland instead. During the return ferry crossing, she confided in her friend Bruce Copp about her anticipation of a shortened life. By October, her health deteriorated further, leading to her admission to Charing Cross Hospital. On 6 October 1980, at the age of 58, Hattie Jacques passed away in her sleep from a heart attack with complications from kidney failure.

Jacques's funeral, held at Putney Vale Crematorium, saw her ashes scattered, and notable figures like Kenneth Williams expressed deep sadness at her loss. A memorial service at St Paul's, Covent Garden followed a month later. In November 1995, a blue plaque was unveiled at her former house, 67 Eardley Crescent, Earls Court, London. In 2011, Jacques and Le Mesurier's marriage became the focus of a BBC Four biographical film titled Hattie, featuring Ruth Jones as Jacques.

Title	Year	Hattie Jacques
Sergeant	1958	Capt. Clark (medical officer)
Nurse	1959	Matron
Teacher	1959	Grace Short
Constable	1960	Sgt. Laura Moon
Regardless	1961	Frosty-faced sister

Cabby	1963	Peggy Hawkins
Doctor	1967	Matron
Camping	1969	Miss Haggerd, the Matron
Again Doctor	1969	Miss Soaper, the Matron
Loving	1970	Sophie Bliss/Plummett
At Your Convenience	1971	Beattie Plummer
Matron	1972	Matron
Abroad	1972	Floella
Dick	1974	Martha Hoggett
That's Carry On!	1977	Archive

Esma Cannon - Esma Ellen Charlotte Littmann (née Cannon), born on 27th December 1905, known as Esme or Esma Cannon, was an Australian-born character actress and comedian with a stature of 4 feet 7 inches (1.40 m). She relocated to Britain in the early 1930s, making a significant mark in British film productions from the 1930s to the 1960s.

Having commenced her journey at Minnie Everett's School of Dancing in Sydney, Cannon ventured into acting on stage at the tender age of four, debuting in Madama Butterfly. Her early roles included Ruth Le Page in Sealed Orders at the Theatre Royal in 1914 and the portrayal of Baby in an adaptation of Seven Little Australians the same year. She continued to secure children's roles well into adulthood. Percy Hutchinson, a theatrical impresario, played a pivotal role in her London debut in the play Misadventure.

In the 1930s, Cannon not only worked as an actress but also engaged in stage management and production. Her film debut came in an uncredited role in The Man Behind the Mask (1936), and she went on to feature in 64 films over the next 26 years. Notable performances include comedic roles and dramatic turns in films like Holiday Camp (1947) and Jassy (1947).

Towards the end of her career, Cannon appeared in various films, including Inn for Trouble (1960), Doctor in Love (1960), Raising the Wind (1961), What a Carve Up! (1961), Over the Odds (1961), We Joined the Navy (1962), On the Beat (1962), Nurse on Wheels (1963), and Hide and Seek (1964). She also graced the British television comedy series The Rag Trade (1961–1963) and featured in four Carry On films - **Carry On Constable** (1960), **Carry On Regardless** (1961), **Carry On Cruising** (1962) and **Carry On Cabby** (1963).

Esma Cannon married Ernst Littmann in London in 1945, and the couple had a son named Michael Anthony in 1946. Remaining married until her passing in 1972, Cannon officially retired in 1964 after featuring in the film Hide and Seek. She passed away at the age of 66 and was laid to rest at Saint-Benoît-la-Forêt in France. The news of her death became known only after a "Where are They Now?" feature appeared in 'Films and Filming' several years post her demise.

In the 2011 television drama "Hattie," centred around the career of Hattie Jacques, the character of Esma Cannon was portrayed by actress Marcia Warren. The play included several scenes depicting the two actresses on the set of "Carry On Cabby," marking Cannon's second-to-last role. In this portrayal, Cannon was portrayed as disenchanted with acting, contemplating the prospect of departing from the world of show business.

CARRY ON JACK (1963)

Meet Albert Poop-Decker, the freshly minted Midshipman who, in a feat that defies all expectations, took a leisurely 8 1/2 years to secure his qualification. Setting sail on the frigate Venus, his escapades lead him through the comedic chaos of Spanish waters, mutinies that could rival a sitcom, and encounters with pirates that are more laughable than fearsome. Accompanied by a Captain with a penchant for quirkiness, a sweetheart steeped in hilarity, and a best friend who's a perpetual source of amusement, the journey is a rib-tickling ride.

In a plot embroidered with mistaken identities and shipwrecks that could make even the staunchest stoic chuckle, the survival of this zany crew is nothing short of a comedic miracle. Brace yourself for a tale where maritime misadventures and uproarious antics collide, proving that in the world of Albert Poop-Decker, laughter is the best compass on the high seas!

In a departure from the familiar faces of the typical Carry On ensemble, "Carry On Jack" features the consistent presence of only Kenneth Williams and Charles Hawtrey on screen, with Jim Dale making a humorous cameo as a sedan chair carrier. Marking his debut in the Carry On series, Bernard Cribbins begins his comedic journey with this film, going on to make three appearances in total. Furthermore, "Carry On Jack" introduces Juliet Mills, Donald Houston, and Cecil Parker to the Carry On universe, each making their sole appearances in the franchise.

Noteworthy for being the second film in the series to embrace colour cinematography, "Carry On Jack" boldly ventures into a historical setting adorned with period costumes, a departure from the customary contemporary themes of the series. The film's comedic origins can be traced back to a non-Carry On project initially titled "Up the Armada," which underwent several title changes before seamlessly becoming part of the Carry On series.

CAST:

Bernard Cribbins as **Midshipman Albert Poop-Decker**
Kenneth Williams as **Captain Fearless**
Juliet Mills as **Sally**
Charles Hawtrey as **Walter Sweetley**

Percy Herbert as **Mr Angel**
Donald Houston as **First Officer Jonathan Howett**
Jim Dale as **Carrier**
Cecil Parker as **First Sea Lord**
Patrick Cargill as **Spanish Governor**
Ed Devereaux as **Hook**
Peter Gilmore as **Patch (Roger)**
George Woodbridge as **Ned**
Ian Wilson as **Ancient carrier**
Jimmy Thompson as **Nelson**
Anton Rodgers as **Hardy**
Michael Nightingale as **Town Crier**
Frank Forsyth as **Second Sea Lord**
John Brooking as **Third Sea Lord**
Barrie Gosney as **Coach driver**
Jan Mazurus as **Spanish Captain**
Viviane Ventura as **Spanish secretary**
Marianne Stone as **Peg**

FACTS AND TRIVIA:

- Budget: £152,000
- Filming dates: 2nd September – 26th October 1963
- The central plot concerning Sally appears to draw inspiration from episode 2 of the British TV series "Sir Francis Drake," which predates it by three years (1961). In that particular episode, a young girl, the daughter of a ship's gunner, clandestinely boards Drake's ship by disguising herself as a man.
- Filming Exteriors: Frensham Pond. The background to the scenes with HMS Venus on fire and "firing" on the other ships is Kimmeridge Bay, Dorset.

PROFILES:

Bernard Joseph Cribbins OBE was born on 29th December 1928 in the Derker area of Oldham, Lancashire, to John Edward Cribbins and Ethel (née Clarkson); Bernard grew up facing financial challenges alongside his two sisters. Leaving school at 13, he started as an assistant stage manager, later serving an apprenticeship at the Oldham Repertory Theatre. Cribbins began national service in the Parachute Regiment in Aldershot, Hampshire, in 1947.

Cribbins ventured into the entertainment scene with his West End debut in 1956, subsequently securing roles in films such as "Two-Way Stretch" (1960), "The Wrong Arm of the Law" (1963), and several Carry On films - **Carry On Jack** (1963), **Carry On Spying** (1964) and **Carry On Columbus** (1992). Beyond his acting prowess, Cribbins delved into narration, voicing Tufty in RoSPA road safety films and providing the voice of Buzby, the Post Office's animated mascot. He was also a familiar face on television, starring in series like "Cribbins" (1969–70) and hosting children's TV shows like "Star Turn" and "Star Turn Challenge."

During the swinging 1960s, Cribbins gained recognition in the UK for his hit novelty records, "The Hole in the Ground" and "Right Said Fred." His versatile screen roles encompassed playing astronaut Vincent Mountjoy in "The Mouse on the Moon" (1963), Albert Perks in "The Railway Children" (1970), barman Felix Forsythe in Alfred Hitchcock's "Frenzy" (1972), and the pretentious hotel guest Mr Hutchinson in the classic "Fawlty Towers" episode "The Hotel Inspectors" (1975). Cribbins also lent his talents to narrating for the BBC series "Jackanory" from 1966 to 1991, took on the role of narrator for "The Wombles" (1973–1975), and assumed the title character in the CBeebies series "Old Jack's Boat" (2013–2015).

In the realm of Doctor Who, Cribbins portrayed Tom Campbell in the 1966 film "Daleks' Invasion Earth 2150 A.D." and returned 41 years later as Wilfred Mott in the show's revival series, marking his final appearance in the 60th-anniversary special "Wild Blue Yonder" (2023).

Cribbins' later career encompassed stage roles, including Nathan Detroit in "Guys and Dolls" and Moonface Martin in "Anything Goes," along with numerous pantomime performances. His contributions to children's arts were recognised with a J. M. Barrie award in 2014, and he was named an Officer of the Order of the British Empire (OBE) in 2011.

In his personal life, Cribbins was married to Gillian McBarnet from 1955 until her passing in October 2021. They faced the loss of a child early in their marriage. Despite a prostate cancer diagnosis in 2009, Cribbins maintained good health, save for a persistent back condition. His autobiography, "Bernard Who? 75 Years of Doing Just About Anything," was published in 2018.

Bernard Cribbins passed away on 27th July 2022 at the age of 93, and his funeral was held at Woking Crematorium in Surrey on 14th September. His legacy endures through his contributions to the arts and the hearts of those he entertained over the years.

Juliet Maryon Mills was born on 21st November 1941 in London during World War II to actor Sir John Mills and playwright Mary Hayley Bell. Mills spent her early years surrounded by notable figures in the entertainment industry, with actress Vivien Leigh as her godmother and playwright Noël Coward as her godfather. She attended the Elmhurst Ballet School in Surrey.

As a child, Mills made early film appearances, including a role as a baby in the 1942 film "In Which We Serve," starring her father. Her major breakthrough came in 1958 with the role of Pamela

Harrington in the Peter Shaffer play "Five Finger Exercise," earning her a Tony Award nomination.

In the 1960s, Mills showcased her talent in both film and television, featuring in productions like "The Rare Breed" and TV series such as "The Man from U.N.C.L.E." and "12 O'Clock High." Her career pinnacle in film came with "Avanti!" (1972), directed by Billy Wilder, earning her a Golden Globe Award nomination. Mills became a naturalised United States citizen on 10th October 1975.

Mills is best known for her role in the American TV series "Nanny and the Professor," playing Phoebe Figalilly, a nanny with magical powers. Despite her Golden Globe-nominated performance, the series ran for only two seasons.

Her achievements continued with an Emmy Award for her supporting role in the miniseries adaptation of "QB VII" (1974) and recurring roles in TV series like "Born Free" (1974–75) and "Passions," securing a Daytime Emmy Award nomination.

Peter Gilmore was born John Peter Gilmore on 25th August 1931 in Leipzig, Germany. He spent his early years in Nunthorpe, North Riding of Yorkshire. Gilmore left school at 14 and embarked on his journey to become an actor. In 1952, he briefly attended the Royal Academy of Dramatic Art preparatory school Parada before being expelled.

Gilmore featured in various British movies, including The Great St Trinian's Train Robbery (1966), Oh! What a Lovely War (1969), The Abominable Dr. Phibes (1971), and Warlords of Atlantis (1978). His early career also involved appearances in stage musicals, such as Lock Up Your Daughters. In 1960, he released a single titled "Follow That Girl" (HMV POP 740). Gilmore played Macheath in a 1968 production of the Beggar's Opera, earning praise for his portrayal alongside Jan Waters as Polly.

His breakthrough came with the role of Captain James Onedin in the BBC television period drama The Onedin Line (1971–1980). Despite his success, Gilmore felt typecast as the rugged sea captain after gaining recognition for the character.

Later in his career, he appeared in a Doctor Who serial titled Frontios (1984), playing the character Brazen. Additionally, Gilmore made an appearance in a Heartbeat episode, "The Frighteners," during the Nick Berry era. His third wife, actress Anne Stallybrass, was a regular in the series.

Gilmore appeared in 11 Carry On films:

- Carry On Cabby (1963) as **Dancy**
- Carry On Jack (1963) as **Patch, Pirate Captain, aka Roger**
- Carry On Cleo (1964) as **Galley Master**
- Carry On Cowboy (1965) as **Henchman Curly**
- Carry On Don't Lose Your Head (1966) as **Citizen Robespierre**
- Carry On Follow That Camel (1967) as **Captain Humphrey Bagshaw**
- Carry On Doctor (1968) as **Henry**
- Carry On Up the Khyber (1968) as **Private Ginger Hale**
- Carry On Again Doctor (1969) as **Henry**
- Carry On Henry (1971) as **King Francis of France**
- Carry On Columbus (1992) as **Governor of the Canaries**

On the personal front, Peter Gilmore married three times. His first marriage was to actress Una Stubbs (1958–1969), with whom he adopted a child. He then married Jan Waters (1970–1976) and later actress Anne Stallybrass (1987–2013).

Peter Gilmore passed away in London on 3rd February 2013 at the age of 81. He was survived by his third wife, Anne Stallybrass, and a son, Jason, whom he had adopted during his first marriage.

CARRY ON SPYING (1964)

In the bustling world of espionage, the bumbling yet endearing Agent Simpkins finds himself leading a team of eccentric trainees on a mission of utmost importance. Their target? The nefarious STENCH (the Society for the Total Extinction of Non-Conforming Humans) who has stolen a top-secret chemical formula with world-altering potential.

Armed with an array of quirky gadgets and an undeniable flair for disguises, Agent Simpkins and his motley crew embark on a rollercoaster chase to thwart the sinister plans of STENCH.

Carry On Spying introduces the talented Barbara Windsor to the Carry On family, marking her inaugural appearance in the series. The ensemble cast includes stalwarts such as Kenneth Williams, Charles Hawtrey, and Jim Dale, ensuring the familiar and beloved faces of Carry On regulars grace the screen. Additionally, Bernard Cribbins makes his second of three appearances in the Carry On universe, with a notable return 28 years later in "Carry On Columbus." Eric Barker, a seasoned series contributor, makes his triumphant third entry, concluding his run in "Carry On Emmannuelle" 14 years down the line. Dilys Laye makes a comeback after her series debut in "Carry On Cruising," adding another layer of continuity and charm to the film.

"Carry On Spying" carries the distinction of being the last monochrome venture in the series. The film, underpinned by humour and espionage antics, showcases the endearing characters and comedic genius that became synonymous with the Carry On legacy.

CAST:

Kenneth Williams as **Desmond Simkins (codename Red Admiral)**
Barbara Windsor as **Daphne Honeybutt (codename Brown Cow)**
Charles Hawtrey as **Charlie Bind (codename Yellow Peril)**

Bernard Cribbins as **Harold Crump (codename Bluebottle)**
Jim Dale as **Carstairs**
Eric Barker as **The Chief**
Richard Wattis as **Cobley**
Dilys Laye as **Lila**
Eric Pohlmann as **The Fat Man**
Victor Maddern as **Milchmann**
Judith Furse as **Dr. Crow** (voiced by John Bluthal)

FACTS AND TRIVIA:

- Budget: £148,000
- Filming dates: 8th February – 13th March 1964
- Albert R. Broccoli, the mastermind behind the James Bond film series, raised objections to the proposed character name "James Bind agent 006½" intended for Charles Hawtrey, and he even threatened legal action. Faced with this challenge, producer Peter Rogers swiftly pivoted, renaming the character Charlie and adjusting the agent's code number to the clever and catchy "double 0 – ooh!" to maintain the film's playful spirit. In a parallel struggle, poster artist Tom Chantrell found himself modifying the film poster due to similar concerns about its resemblance to Renato Fratini's poster for "From Russia with Love."
- The film, a delightful satire on various spy films, with the James Bond series taking the lightest jab, cleverly incorporates elements from iconic movies like "The Third Man." Notably, Eric Pohlmann, who portrays The Fat Man, had a minor role in "The Third Man" and also lent his voice to SPECTRE No. 1 in "From Russia with Love." The sly humour extends to the female assistants of Dr Crow, some of whom sport hairstyles reminiscent of Modesty Blaise, a character whose adventures had just begun captivating readers in the London Evening Standard the year before.

- Carry On Spying garnered widespread critical acclaim, with particular praise directed towards its brisk pacing, satirical wit, and Kenneth Williams' standout performance, heavily influenced by his "Snide" persona from Hancock's Half Hour.
- Kinematograph Weekly lauded the film as a "money maker" for the year 1964, underlining its commercial success.
- The Monthly Film Bulletin offered a nuanced perspective, describing the film as a product fresh off the Carry On assembly line. While acknowledging the sporadic and somewhat feeble satirical attempts at James Bondery, the review notes a reliance on routine, blending a few bright gags within a sea of coy camp, female impersonation, and mildly smutty jokes. Bernard Cribbins earns praise for his humorous portrayal, especially in his disguise as an Oriental harridan in an Algiers bordello, delivering a comedic parody of Eastern music. The addition of newcomer Barbara Windsor is deemed a valuable asset, while Dilys Laye's performance as Lila is characterized as charming.
- The Radio Times Guide to Films awarded the production 3 out of 5 stars, characterising it as a spy spoof that mercilessly ribs the Bond movies and Graham Greene's espionage entertainments. The ninth instalment of the Carry On series introduces Barbara Windsor in her series debut as the resourceful member of a quartet of agents dispatched to Vienna to recover a secret formula. Though the Casbah scenes may slow down the narrative, the review highlights the escalating pace in STENCH's underground HQ, a brilliantly observed send-up of 007's domain.

PROFILES:

Dame Barbara Windsor, originally born Barbara Ann Deeks on 6th August 1937 in Shoreditch, London, hailed from humble beginnings. Her parents, John Deeks, a bus driver, and Rose

Deeks (née Ellis), a dressmaker, raised her on Angela Street. Notably, Barbara's maternal great-grandmother had Irish roots, having escaped the Great Famine of Ireland in the mid-19th century.

The onset of World War II in 1939 prompted Barbara and her mother to seek refuge from the war on Yoakley Road, Stoke Newington. During this time, she attended St Mary's Infants' School. Reluctantly initially, Barbara's mother agreed to evacuation after a tragic incident involving the loss of one of Barbara's school friends in a bomb raid. At the age of six, Barbara was sent to Blackpool, where she faced a traumatic incident but was later rescued by authorities.

Returning to London in 1944, Barbara resided with a school friend and her parents. Despite the challenges, her interest in performing blossomed when she attended Madame Behenna's Juvenile Jollities, a drama school. Her parents' divorce when she was 16, with her father cutting all contact post-divorce, added to the hurdles she faced.

Barbara's showbiz journey commenced with her uncredited film debut in 1954's "The Belles of St. Trinians." Subsequent television appearances and musical performances marked the beginning of her entertainment career. She adopted the stage name "Windsor" in 1953, inspired by the Coronation of Elizabeth II.

Despite passing her 11-plus exams with top marks and earning a scholarship to Our Lady's Catholic High School, Stamford Hill, Barbara faced challenges. Expelled for clashing with the reverend's mother over time off for a pantomime appearance, she then attended the Aida Foster School, Golders Green, taking elocution lessons.

Barbara's breakthrough came with Joan Littlewood's Theatre Workshop, where she gained prominence in productions like

"Fings Ain't Wot They Used T'Be" and the film "Sparrows Can't Sing." Her career flourished with appearances in comedy and thriller films, as well as TV sitcoms.

She became synonymous with the "good-time girl" persona in nine Carry On films between 1964 and 1974. Despite the success, her strong association with Carry On limited her roles in later years.

Barbara's stage success included Broadway stints and various stage productions. Notable performances include her Tony Award-nominated role in "Oh, What a Lovely War!" and playing Marie Lloyd in "Sing A Rude Song." She continued to dazzle on stage, participating in numerous pantomimes and theatre productions. In the latter part of her career, Barbara's roles diversified, including playing Kath in Joe Orton's "Entertaining Mr Sloane."

Windsor left an indelible mark on the entertainment industry, particularly through her iconic role as Peggy Mitchell in the long-running soap opera EastEnders. Joining the show in 1994, Windsor's portrayal of Peggy earned her the Best Actress award at the 1999 British Soap Awards. Despite a two-year hiatus between 2003 and 2005 due to the Epstein–Barr virus, she returned and continued her role until her departure in 2010 after a dramatic storyline involving a fire at the Queen Victoria pub.

Windsor made occasional returns to EastEnders in 2013, 2014, and for the 30th-anniversary episode in 2015. However, it was revealed in 2016 that her character, Peggy Mitchell, would be written off, marking her final appearance on 17th May 2016.

Beyond EastEnders, Windsor showcased her versatility in hosting the BBC documentary Disaster Masters in 2005 and lending her voice to the Dormouse in Disney's Alice in Wonderland (2010). She also ventured into radio presenting for BBC Radio 2 and reprised her role in Alice Through the Looking Glass (2016). In 2017, she appeared as herself in the BBC Television biopic "Babs," offering insights into her life and career.

Barbara Windsor's connection to the infamous Kray twins, Reggie and Charlie, adds a captivating layer to her life narrative. This association unfolded during a complex period in London's social and cultural history. The Kray twins, acting as criminal kingpins in the East End, exerted influence over various facets of London's underworld. Meanwhile, Barbara was navigating her ascent in the entertainment industry.

While Barbara's involvement with the Kray twins is acknowledged in her autobiography, "All of Me," the details of these relationships remain somewhat enigmatic. The book reveals that before her marriage to Ronnie Knight, Barbara Windsor had a connection with Reggie's older brother, Charlie Kray, illustrating the entanglement of the glamorous entertainment world with the gritty underworld of East End crime.

The relationship with Charlie Kray appears to have been more enduring, becoming a significant part of Barbara's personal history during her later Carry On films era. The narrative surrounding Barbara Windsor's ties to the Kray twins provides insight into the fascinating interplay between celebrity culture and the shadowy realms of London's criminal underworld during a specific era. These relationships, though intricate and occasionally controversial, contribute to the multifaceted nature of Barbara Windsor's life, adding depth to her compelling story.

Barbara Windsor's personal life involved three marriages and no children. Her health journey included a diagnosis of Alzheimer's disease in 2014, which became public in 2018. Despite her challenges, Windsor, along with her husband Scott Mitchell, actively supported dementia campaigns, participating in the London Marathon in 2019.

Barbara Windsor passed away on 10th December 2020 at the age of 83. Her death was acknowledged in the subsequent episode of EastEnders, and tributes poured in from co-stars, entertainers, politicians, and members of the Royal family.

Throughout her career, Windsor received numerous honours, including an MBE in 2000, the Freedom of the City of London in 2010, and a DBE in the 2016 New Year Honours for her contributions to charity and entertainment. Her legacy endures, with her being the first person inducted into the BBC Hall of Fame and receiving recognition on the Hackney Empire Walk of Fame in 2017.

Title	Year	Barbara Windsor
Spying	1964	Daphne Honeybutt
Doctor	1967	Nurse Sandra May
Camping	1969	Babs
Again Doctor	1969	Goldie Locks
Henry	1971	Bettina
Matron	1972	Nurse Susan Ball
Abroad	1972	Sadie Tomkins
Girls	1973	Hope Springs (Muriel Bloggs)
Dick	1974	Harriett / Harry
That's Carry On!	1977	Presenter

Eric Leslie Barker, born on 12th February stood as an illustrious English comedy actor, primarily etched in the memories of audiences for his roles in the beloved British Carry On films. While his major contributions align with the early films in the Carry On series, he made a noteworthy return for **Carry On Emmannuelle** in 1978.

Born in Thornton Heath, London, Barker emerged as the youngest of three children on 20th February 1912. Raised in Croydon, Surrey, he received his education at Whitgift School. Initially involved in his father's paper merchants' company,

Barker shifted his focus to full-time writing, with his debut novel, "The Watch Hunt," published at the age of eighteen. His literary pursuits expanded to short stories, plays, and eventually to lyrics, revues, and sketches for both stage and radio.

Barker found a significant breakthrough during World War II as part of the armed forces radio show "Merry Go Round," which he also contributed to writing. Post-war, the show persisted, featuring Barker and his wife, actress Pearl Hackney, in the Navy-themed instalment named "Waterlogged Spa." His catchphrase "Steady Barker" and his comedic stumbling over words starting with 'h' became iconic, contributing to the show's success and showcasing Barker's versatility in voice acting.

Transitioning to the 1950s, Barker ventured into television and films. His eponymous comedy sketch show, "The Eric Barker Half-Hour," aired on the BBC, featuring notable personalities like Nicholas Parsons and Deryck Guyler. The success of the show prompted Barker to pen his autobiography, "Steady Barker," in 1956.

Barker received acclaim for his film role as a barrister's clerk in "Brothers in Law" (1957), earning him a BAFTA as "Most Promising Newcomer." This recognition paved the way for a prolific film career spanning two decades, encompassing classics like three St Trinians films and four entries in the Carry On series. His knack for portraying busybodies or authority figures found its niche, exemplified in films like "**Carry On Constable**" (1960). He was one of only three actors (the others being Kenneth Williams and Kenneth Connor) to appear in both the first of the original series of Carry On films, **Carry On Sergeant** (1958), and the last, **Carry On Emmannuelle** (1978). Barker's other Carry On appearance was in **Carry On Spying** (1964).

Beyond acting, Barker showcased his writing prowess with several novels under different pen names, including "Sea

Breezes" as Christopher Bentley in the early 1930s and "Golden Gimmick" in 1958 under his own name. Notably, P. G. Wodehouse commended Barker's "real talent for humorous writing."

In his personal life, Barker married actress Pearl Hackney, with whom he frequently collaborated. Their union bore a daughter, Petronella Barker, who also ventured into films and television. In 1971, Eric Barker became the featured guest on the British ITV television programme "This Is Your Life."

Eric Barker passed away on 1st June 1990 at the age of 78. His resting place is in Canterbury, Kent, where he was interred in the churchyard of St. Mary's, Stalisfield Green, near Faversham—the place he had called home for a considerable number of years.

Dilys Laye was born Dilys Lay on 11th March 1934 in London, the daughter of Edward Charles Lay and Margaret Hewitt. Raised in Croydon, Surrey, she faced the challenges of the Second World War, enduring evacuation to Devon with her brother. Laye's return home marked the beginning of her mother's aspiration to transfer her thwarted theatrical dreams to her daughter. Educated at St Dominic's Sixth Form College, Harrow, Laye received stage training at the Aida Foster School.

Laye's stage debut in 1948 at the New Lindsey Theatre Club set the stage for her diverse early experiences, ranging from drama and pantomime to revue. Her first film role came in 1949 in "Trottie True." The 1950s witnessed her West End debut in "And So to Bed" and Broadway debut in "The Boy Friend." Notable films during this period included "The Belles of St Trinian's" and "Doctor at Large."

Laye made her mark in the Carry On film series, featuring in "**Carry On Cruising**," "**Carry On Spying**," "**Carry On Doctor**," and "**Carry On Camping**." In 1967, she had a cameo in Charlie Chaplin's "A Countess from Hong Kong." The 1970s marked Laye's collaboration with playwright Peter Barnes and her association with the Royal Shakespeare Company (RSC).

Laye continued her association with Barnes, co-writing the ITV comedy series "Chintz" in 1981. Her diverse roles included Lady Dunce in Barnes's radio adaptation of Thomas Otway's "The Soldier's Fortune" and performances in RSC productions. In the 1990s, she toured in various musicals, including "The Phantom of the Opera" and "Sweeney Todd." Her final stage appearance was in 2006, performing in the Chichester Festival Theatre's revival of the RSC's "Nicholas Nickleby."

Laye married three times, first to stuntman Frank Maher, then to actor Garfield Morgan, and finally to scriptwriter Alan Downer in 1972. Laye battled lung cancer, surpassing doctors' predictions by six months. She passed away at the age of 74, witnessing her son's marriage before her death.

CARRY ON CLEO (1964)

In this uproarious comedy, meet two unsuspecting Britons, Hengist and Horsa, whose lives take an unexpected turn when they are captured and enslaved by the invading Romans. Transported to the heart of Rome, Hengist finds himself thrust into the chaos of the eternal city.

In a hilarious twist of fate, Hengist's first encounter in Rome results in a case of mistaken identity. Due to a series of comical misunderstandings, Hengist is wrongly assumed to be a skilled fighter. He is promptly drafted into the prestigious Royal Guard, tasked with the monumental responsibility of protecting none other than the mighty Caesar himself.

The familiar ensemble of Sid James, Kenneth Williams, Kenneth Connor, Charles Hawtrey, and Jim Dale graces the screen, with Connor making his final appearance until his return in Carry On

Up the Jungle six years later. Joan Sims, absent since Carry On Regardless three years earlier, returns to the series, marking the beginning of her prolific presence in every Carry On film up to Carry On Emmannuelle in 1978, establishing her as the most featured actress in the series.

Jon Pertwee makes his debut in the Carry On universe, the first of his four appearances. Amanda Barrie, taking on the title role, marks her second and final appearance in the Carry On series. Notably, Carry On Cleo, alongside Carry On Sergeant and Carry On Screaming!, earned the honour of having its original posters reproduced on stamps by the Royal Mail. This recognition was part of the celebrations commemorating the 50th anniversary of the Carry On series in June 2008.

CAST:

Sid James as **Mark Antony**
Kenneth Williams as **Julius Caesar**
Charles Hawtrey as **Seneca**
Kenneth Connor as **Hengist Pod**
Joan Sims as **Calpurnia**
Jim Dale as **Horsa**
Amanda Barrie as **Cleopatra**
Victor Maddern as **Sergeant Major**
Julie Stevens as **Gloria**
Sheila Hancock as **Senna Pod**
Jon Pertwee as **Soothsayer**
Brian Oulton as **Brutus**
Michael Ward as **Archimedes**
Francis de Wolff as **Agrippa**
Tom Clegg as **Sosages**
Tanya Binning as **Virginia**
David Davenport as **Bilius**
Peter Gilmore as **Galley Master**

Ian Wilson as **Messenger**
Norman Mitchell as **Heckler**
Brian Rawlinson as **Hessian driver**
Gertan Klauber as **Marcus**
Warren Mitchell as **Spencius**
Michael Nightingale as **Caveman**

FACTS AND TRIVIA:

- Budget: £165,802
- Filming dates: 13th July – 28th August 1964
- The film's costumes and sets were initially designated for Cleopatra (1963) until the production relocated to Rome, necessitating the construction of new sets there.
- The original poster and promotional artwork, masterfully crafted by Tom Chantrell, faced a setback. They were pulled from circulation after 20th Century Fox successfully won a copyright infringement case against the distributor Anglo Amalgamated. The court ruled that the design was based on a painting by Howard Terpning, of which Fox owned the copyright. The artwork was originally created to promote the Cleopatra film, leading to the withdrawal of Carry On Cleo's promotional material.
- The film had its premiere at London's Warner cinema on 10th December 1964, later establishing itself as one of the 12 most beloved movies at the British box office in 1965.
- Colin McCabe, Professor of English at the University of Exeter, acclaimed this film, along with Carry On Up the Khyber, as among the best films ever made.
- In 2007, the memorable quip "Infamy, infamy, they've all got it in for me," delivered by Kenneth Williams, earned the title of the funniest one-line joke in film history. This iconic line, although not penned by Rothwell, was borrowed with

permission from a script by Frank Muir and Denis Norden for Take It from Here.

PROFILES:

Amanda Barrie was born as Shirley Anne Broadbent on 14th September 1935 in Ashton-under-Lyne, Lancashire, to Hubert and Connie Broadbent. Barrie underwent her education at St Anne's College, Lytham St Annes, followed by training at the Arts Educational School in London and the Bristol Old Vic Theatre School.

Barrie's initial foray into the entertainment world included pantomime performances as a child and a stint as a chorus girl in London's West End. Her breakthrough as an actress came at sixteen when she made her West End debut in 1961's Babes in the Wood. Throughout the 1960s, Barrie showcased her talent in various stage productions, including Cabaret, Private Lives, Hobson's Choice, and Aladdin. Her screen debut in the comedy film Operation Bullshine (1959) paved the way for roles in popular films like What a Whopper and Doctor in Distress.

Barrie starred in two Carry On films, playing a cab driver in **Carry On Cabby** (1963) and assuming the title role in **Carry On Cleo** (1964). Notably, she portrayed Alma Sedgewick (later Baldwin) in Coronation Street, transitioning from bit-player status in the early 1980s to a high-profile character until her departure in 2001. Her character's storyline involved a battle with cervical cancer, adding depth to her portrayal. Following her Coronation Street stint, Barrie continued her acting journey. Notable roles include Margo Phillips in the BBC medical soap opera Doctors and the character Bev Tull in the popular ITV1 prison series Bad Girls. She also took part in reality shows like Hell's Kitchen and Celebrity Big Brother.

Jon Devon Roland Pertwee, born on 7th July 1919, in Chelsea, London, belonged to a family with French Huguenot ancestry. The Pertwee surname, an Anglicisation of "Perthuis," traced its roots to the family's lineage as Counts descended from Charlemagne. His father, Roland Pertwee, served as a screenwriter and actor, while Avice Scholtz, his mother, separated from his father during his youth. Jon Pertwee's educational journey included Frensham Heights School in Surrey, Sherborne School in Dorset, and various other schools despite facing expulsions. Initially denied admission to the Central School of Speech & Drama due to a lisp, he later gained entry to the Royal Academy of Dramatic Art (RADA), graduating in 1939.

Before embarking on his acting career, Pertwee worked as a circus performer, showcasing his daredevilry on a motorcycle within the Wall of Death, accompanied by a toothless lion in the sidecar. Contracted with the BBC at the age of 18, he began his acting journey, later spending six years in the Royal Navy during World War II. Pertwee was involved in various activities, including crewing HMS Hood and serving in the top-secret Naval Intelligence Division alongside Ian Fleming.

From 1959 to 1977, Pertwee portrayed the conniving Chief Petty Officer Pertwee in The Navy Lark on BBC Radio. His versatility and comedic talents were evident in his ability to perform different voices and accents. Pertwee's contribution to the series extended beyond his initial role, filling in various additional characters after Ronnie Barker's departure. His radio career showcased his comedic skills with notable shows like Waterlogged Spa and Puffney Post Office.

Pertwee appeared in several Carry On films: **Carry On Cleo** (1964), as the soothsayer; **Carry On Cowboy** (1965) as Sheriff Earp; **Carry On Screaming!** (1966) as Dr. Fettle and **Carry On Columbus** (1992) as the Duke of Costa Brava.

In 1969, Pertwee transitioned to television, taking on the iconic role of the Third Doctor in Doctor Who. His portrayal marked a departure from the previous incarnations, reflecting influences from the James Bond film series. Pertwee played the Doctor as an active crusader with a penchant for action and stylish attire. He served as a scientific adviser to Brigadier Lethbridge-Stewart and UNIT, contributing to the show for five seasons until 1974. Pertwee's interpretation of the Doctor was characterised by confidence, articulateness, and warmth. His era was marked by a more action-oriented and scientifically minded Doctor.

After Doctor Who, Pertwee continued to leave a lasting impact on the entertainment industry, he hosted the murder-mystery game show Whodunnit? from 1974 to 1978. Following that, he took on the titular role in the television series Worzel Gummidge, based on the books by Barbara Euphan Todd. The show's success led to its continuation in New Zealand in 1987.

Pertwee married twice, first to Jean Marsh in 1955 (divorced in 1960) and then to Ingeborg Rhoesa in the same year. He had two children, Dariel and Sean, both of whom pursued acting careers. Pertwee authored two autobiographies, "Moon Boots and Dinner Suits" (1984), covering his life before Doctor Who, and "Doctor Who: I Am the Doctor – Jon Pertwee's Final Memoir" (1996), written posthumously.

Jon Pertwee continued his involvement with Doctor Who conventions until his death. He passed away in his sleep from a heart attack on 20th May 1996 at the age of 76. Pertwee's legacy endured through his contributions to Doctor Who, and his distinctive voice was posthumously used in audio productions. His death came shortly after the broadcast of the Doctor Who television film.

CARRY ON COWBOY (1965)

In the uproarious town of Stodge City, chaos ensues when a notorious outlaw runs amok. Enter Marshal P. Knutt, an unsuspecting sanitation engineer who is hilariously mistaken for a US Peace Marshal. Now tasked with restoring order, controlling the situation, and apprehending the wild outlaw, Marshal Knutt finds himself in a sidesplitting showdown between mop and mischief in this laugh-out-loud comedy.

Carry On Cowboy marks the debut of series regulars Peter Butterworth and Bernard Bresslaw, adding to the comedic ensemble. The familiar faces of Sid James, Kenneth Williams, Jim Dale, Charles Hawtrey, and Joan Sims grace the screen while Angela Douglas embarks on the first of her four appearances in the series. Even the usually critical Kenneth Williams couldn't help but praise the film, hailing it as 'a success on every level' in his diary, celebrating its blend of humour and pathos.

CAST:

Sid James as **Johnny Finger/The Rumpo Kid**
Kenneth Williams as **Judge Burke**
Jim Dale as **Marshal P. Knutt**
Charles Hawtrey as **Big Heap**
Joan Sims as **Belle Armitage**
Peter Butterworth as **Doc**
Bernard Bresslaw as **Little Heap**
Angela Douglas as **Annie Oakley**
Percy Herbert as **Charlie**
Sydney Bromley as **Sam Houston**
Edina Ronay as **Delores**
Lionel Murton as **Clerk**
Peter Gilmore as **Curly**
Davy Kaye as **Josh**
Jon Pertwee as **Sheriff Albert Earp**

Alan Gifford as **Commissioner**
Brian Rawlinson as **Stagecoach guard**
Michael Nightingale as **Bank manager**
Simon Cain as **Short**
Sally Douglas as **Kitikata**
Cal McCord as **Mex**
Garry Colleano as **Slim**
Arthur Lovegrove as **Old Cowhand**
Margaret Nolan as **Miss Jones**
Tom Clegg as **Blacksmith**
Larry Cross as **Perkins**

FACTS AND TRIVIA:

- Budget: £195,000
- Filming dates: 12th July – 3rd September 1965.
- Exteriors were filmed on Chobham Common, Surrey, and at Black Park, Fulmer, Buckinghamshire.
- Carry on Cowboy introduced the series' first sung main title theme.
- Angela Douglas performs a song, "This is the Night for Love," in a saloon bar scene.
- The Monthly Film Bulletin in 1966 noted some clever and amusing ideas but criticised the heavy reliance on outrageous puns and not particularly subtle double entendres. It considered the film the nearest-the-knuckle of the series.
- Allmovie has praised the film, calling it "one of the best of the long-running Carry On series."

PROFILES:

Jim Dale, born James Smith on 15th August 1935, in Rothwell, Northamptonshire, began his educational journey at Kettering Grammar School. Initially dedicating six years to dance training, he transitioned to become a stage comic in 1951, marking the commencement of his illustrious career.

Following two years of national service in the Royal Air Force, Dale ventured into the entertainment scene. At the age of 22, he collaborated with George Martin, head of Parlophone, making history as the first pop singer to do so. His hits on the UK Singles Chart in the late 1950s, including "Be My Girl" and "Sugartime," catapulted him to fame.

Despite his successful music career, Dale shifted focus from teen idol status to pursuing comedy aspirations. As a lyricist, he gained acclaim for "Georgy Girl," the theme for the 1966 film of the same name, earning nominations for prestigious awards.

Jim Dale's film debut in Break-In (1956) marked the beginning of a prolific career. His enduring legacy lies in eleven Carry On films, where he portrayed the hapless romantic lead. Notable performances include Carry On Cowboy (1965) and Carry On Screaming! (1966). Beyond Carry On, Dale took on diverse roles, from portraying Spike Milligan to featuring in Walt Disney's Pete's Dragon (1977).

Dale's stage career involved touring British variety music halls and, in 1970, joining the National Theatre Company under Sir Laurence Olivier. Notable performances include Scapino (1970) and The Card (1973). On Broadway, he earned acclaim for productions like Barnum (1980), A Day in the Death of Joe Egg (1985), and Me and My Girl (1986).

In the United States, Jim Dale achieved widespread recognition as the voice behind the Harry Potter audiobooks, narrating all seven novels. His narrations earned him two Grammy Awards and numerous other accolades, including Audie Awards and AudioFile Earphone Awards.

Jim Dale continued his multifaceted career, opening every episode of the ABC drama Pushing Daisies as the unseen narrator. His contributions extended to narrating audiobooks like Peter and the Starcatchers (2004) and the musical SPIN: The Rumpelstiltskin Musical (2018). In 2003, he received the MBE, acknowledging his significant contribution to promoting children's English literature.

Title	Year	Jim Dale
Cabby	1963	Expectant Father
Jack	1963	"Carrier"
Spying	1964	Carstairs
Cleo	1964	Horsa
Cowboy	1965	Marshall P Knutt
Screaming!	1966	Albert
Don't Lose Your Head	1966	Lord Darcy Pue
Follow That Camel	1967	Bertram Oliphant 'Bo' West
Doctor	1967	Dr. James Kilmore
Again Doctor	1969	Dr. Jimmy Nookey
That's Carry On!	1977	Archive
Columbus	1992	Christopher Columbus

Angela Douglas was born Angela McDonagh on 29th October 1940 in Gerrards Cross, Buckinghamshire. Her journey into the world of acting commenced as a teenager when she joined the Worthing, West Sussex repertory company. In 1958, Angela made her debut in London's West End theatre, marking the beginning of a prolific career.

Venturing into film, Angela Douglas initially appeared uncredited in the 1958 film Six-Five Special. She made her speaking film debut in The Shakedown (1959), sharing the screen with Tommy Steele in It's All Happening. However, it was in the 1960s that she gained prominence through her roles in several iconic Carry On Films, including **Carry On Cowboy** (1965), **Carry On Screaming!**

(1966), **Follow That Camel** (1967), and **Carry On Up the Khyber** (1968).

Beyond the Carry On series, Angela's filmography includes The Comedy Man (1964), Digby, the Biggest Dog in the World (1973), and The Four Feathers (2002).

Angela Douglas transitioned seamlessly into television, gracing shows like Gideon's Way, The Avengers, The Saint, Z-Cars, Dixon of Dock Green, Jason King, Casualty, Holby City, Coronation Street, and Doctor at Large.

However, her career took a temporary pause when her husband, Kenneth More, was diagnosed with Parkinson's disease. After More's death, Angela resumed her acting pursuits, featuring in Doctor Who, Peak Practice, Soldier, Soldier, and Cardiac Arrest.

In addition to her on-screen accomplishments, Angela Douglas delved into journalism and writing. She authored two books, including the autobiographical Swings and Roundabouts. In 2018, she ventured into fiction with her debut novel, "Josephine: An Open Book," drawing inspiration from her own experiences.

On a personal note, Angela's life intertwined with fellow actor Kenneth More in 1962, leading to their marriage on 17th March 1968, a union that endured until Kenneth More's passing on 12th July 1982. In 1988, Angela encountered Scottish playwright and director Bill Bryden, whom she later married in 2009. Sadly, Bill Bryden passed away on 5th January 2022. Angela Douglas's journey is a tapestry of artistic achievements, personal relationships, and a resilient return to the limelight after challenging life circumstances.

CARRY ON SCREAMING! (1966)

In this Edwardian-era comedy horror, lovebirds Doris and Albert stumble into a bizarre adventure when Doris is abducted by the monstrous Oddbod in Hocombe Woods. Detective Sergeant Sidney Bung and Detective Constable Slobotham join Albert in a quirky investigation, leading them to the eccentric Bide-A-Wee Rest Home, ruled by the enigmatic Valeria and her electrically charged brother, Dr. Orlando Watt; the mansion holds secrets that intertwine with the strange disappearances. As the detectives delve deeper, they find themselves entangled in a web of peculiarities and unexplained phenomena, leading to an unpredictable and eerie climax.

Carry On Screaming! was produced by Anglo-Amalgamated; it stands as the final contribution before the series transitioned to The Rank Organisation. The movie boasts the familiar faces of Kenneth Williams, Jim Dale, Charles Hawtrey, Joan Sims, Bernard Bresslaw, and Peter Butterworth, with notable appearances by Harry H. Corbett in his sole series role and Fenella Fielding in her second and final appearance. Angela Douglas, making the second of her four Carry On appearances, also graces the screen. In a playful nod to the popular Hammer horror films of the time, "Carry On Screaming!" is a comedic parody that captivates audiences with its hilarious take on the horror genre.

CAST:

Harry H. Corbett as **Detective Sergeant Sidney Bung**
Kenneth Williams as **Dr Orlando Watt**
Peter Butterworth as **Detective Constable Slobotham**
Jim Dale as **Albert Potter**
Fenella Fielding as **Valeria Watt**
Tom Clegg as **Oddbod**
Bernard Bresslaw as **Sockett**
Billy Cornelius as **Oddbod Junior**
Joan Sims as **Emily Bung**
Charles Hawtrey as **Dan Dann**
Angela Douglas as **Doris Mann**

Jon Pertwee as **Doctor Fettle**
Michael Ward as **Mr Vivian**
Norman Mitchell as **Cabby**
Frank Thornton as **Mr Jones**
Frank Forsyth as **Desk Sergeant**
Anthony Sagar as **Policeman**
Sally Douglas as **Girl**
Marianne Stone as **Mrs Parker**
Denis Blake as **Rubbatiti**
Gerald Thomas as **Voice of Oddbod Junior** (uncredited)

Filming for Carry On Screaming! took place from 10th January 1966 to 25th February 1966, with Pinewood Studios and locations in Berkshire and Buckinghamshire serving as the backdrop.

This instalment marked a departure for the series as it introduced a sung main title theme, Carry On Screaming!, credited to "Anon." Initially thought to be sung by Jim Dale, the film version was actually performed by Ray Pilgrim, a session singer for the Embassy label. Boz Burrell also released a 45 rpm version in 1966 (Columbia DB 7972). In the 2005 album "What a Carry On," Gary Williams sang the theme with the Royal Ballet Sinfonia conducted by Gavin Sutherland.

Deborah Kerr declined the role of Valeria, a character frequently mistaken for a vampire but more a parody of Morticia Addams. Initially written as Valeria's father, the character of Orlando Watt was altered at the request of Kenneth Williams, who wanted to play his age (39), making Orlando and Valeria siblings in the final version. Charles Hawtrey joined the cast last minute at the request of American distributors, replacing Sydney Bromley in the role of Dan Dann, offering him the unique distinction of a leading credit for under five minutes' screen time. Finally, Harry H. Corbett took over from Sid James, who was committed to a pantomime until June 1966.

FACTS AND TRIVIA:

- Budget: £197,500
- Filming Dates: 10th January – 25th February 1966
- Exteriors: Windsor, Berkshire & Fulmer, Buckinghamshire
- Harry H Corbett received £12,000 for his role as Detective Sergeant Sidney Bung, setting a record as the highest fee paid to a Carry On actor at that time.
- The Monthly Film Bulletin stated: "With the exception of an enthralling portrayal by Jim Dale (and some delightful squeaks from the monster Odbodd Junior) This film is rather sombre, even by Carry On standards. The regular cast members, especially Kenneth Williams, appear too disinterested to invest much enthusiasm; Harry H. Corbett exaggerates every line, and the horror clichés prove to be less amusing than the straightforward routines in some of Hammer's early epics.

PROFILES:

Harry H. Corbett OBE was born on 28th February 1925, the youngest of seven children, in Rangoon, Burma (now Myanmar), where his father, George Corbett, served as a company quartermaster sergeant in the South Staffordshire Regiment of the British Army. Corbett was sent to Britain after his mother, Caroline Emily, née Barnsley, died of dysentery when he was eighteen months old. He was then raised by his aunt, Annie Williams, in Earl Street, Ardwick, Manchester, and later on a new council estate in Wythenshawe. He attended Ross Place and Benchill Primary Schools, and although he passed the scholarship exam for entry to Chorlton Grammar School, he couldn't take up his place and instead attended Sharston Secondary School.

Corbett enlisted in the Royal Marines during the Second World War, serving in the Home Fleet on the heavy cruiser HMS Devonshire. After VJ Day in 1945, he was posted to the Far East, where he was involved in quelling unrest in New Guinea and reportedly killed two Japanese soldiers in hand-to-hand combat. He then deserted in Tonga, remaining in Australia before surrendering to the Military Police. His military service left him with a damaged bladder and a red mark on his eye, both untreated until late in his life.

Upon returning to civilian life, Corbett trained as a radiographer before pursuing acting as a career, joining the Chorlton Repertory theatre. In the early 1950s, he added the initial "H" to avoid confusion with the television entertainer Harry Corbett, known for his act with the glove-puppet Sooty. From 1958, Corbett began appearing regularly in films, gaining public attention as a serious performer. He appeared in television dramas such as The Adventures of Robin Hood and Police Surgeon (1960). He worked and studied Stanislavski's system at Joan Littlewood's Theatre Workshop at the Theatre Royal in Stratford, London.

In 1962, scriptwriters Galton and Simpson invited Corbett to appear in "The Offer," an episode of the BBC's Comedy Playhouse. He played Harold Steptoe, leading to the creation of the successful series Steptoe and Son, which continued until 1974. While the show made Corbett a star, it also typecast him, limiting serious acting opportunities. The production became stressful in its final years due to Wilfrid Brambell's (Albert Steptoe) alcoholism.

Corbett's involvement with Steptoe and Son extended to radio, where episodes were remade with the original cast. Despite the challenges, Corbett and Brambell reprised their roles for various projects, including a TV commercial for Kenco coffee in 1981.

Steptoe and Son led Corbett to comedy films, such as Ladies Who Do (1963), The Bargee (1964), The Magnificent Seven Deadly Sins (1971), and Jabberwocky (1977). He also appeared in two Steptoe and Son films and had roles in television series like Jackanory (1966), Mr. Aitch (1967), and Grundy (1980). Corbett recorded numerous records, including novelty songs based on the rag-and-bone character and sea shanties.

Corbett was married twice, first to actress Sheila Steafel (1958–1964) and then to actress Maureen Blott (stage name Crombie) (1969 until his death in 1982). They had two children, Jonathan and Susannah, the latter becoming an actress and author. Corbett was a Labour Party campaigner and appeared in a party-political broadcast. Prime Minister Harold Wilson wished to have him appointed an Officer of the Order of the British Empire (OBE), which happened in the 1976 New Year Honours.

A heavy smoker, Corbett had his first heart attack in September 1979. Despite health issues, he continued working in pantomime, TV series, and films. His final role was in an episode of Tales of the Unexpected, titled "The Moles," filmed shortly before his death and broadcast in May 1982. Corbett died of a heart attack on 21st March 1982 in Hastings, East Sussex, at the age of 57. He is buried at St Michael the Archangel church at Penhurst, East Sussex.

Fenella Fielding, OBE born Fenella Marion Feldman on 17th November 1927 in Hackney, London, to a Romanian Jewish mother, Tilly (née Katz; 1902–1977), and a Lithuanian Jewish father, Philip Feldman.

Fielding embarked on her acting journey in 1952, focusing on stage productions, including the Bromley Little Theatre. Her breakthrough came when she accompanied the then-unknown actor Ron Moody to an audition. Notably, her performance in Sandy Wilson's musical version of Valmouth propelled her to stardom in 1958. By 1959, she shared the stage with Kenneth Williams in the comedy revue Pieces of Eight, written by Harold Pinter and Peter Cook. Fielding's television career included guest appearances in shows like The Avengers, Danger Man, and four episodes of Morecambe and Wise Show between 1969 and 1972. She also starred in her own television programme, Izeena (1966). In the late 1960s, Federico Fellini approached Fielding to work on one of his films, but she declined due to prior commitments at the Chichester Festival Theatre.

Fielding featured in two Carry On films: initially in **Carry On Regardless** (1961) and later in **Carry On Screaming!** (1966).

Fielding continued to contribute to the entertainment industry, starring in the children's television series Uncle Jack from 1990 to 1993 as the notorious villainess, The Vixen. In 1999, she appeared in Rik Mayall and Adrian Edmondson's film Guest House Paradiso. Her later years saw her performing readings of English translations of Greek classics and publishing her memoir in 2017. She was appointed Officer of the Order of the British Empire (OBE) in the 2018 Birthday Honours for services to drama and charity.

Fielding lent her voice to various projects, including the 1972 English adaptation of the 1970 French film 'Dougal And The Blue Cat' and the video game Martian Gothic. In the 2000s, she collaborated with Savoy on readings of Colette, J. G. Ballard's Crash, and T. S. Eliot's Four Quartets. Fielding was also known for her cover songs album, featuring tracks like Robbie Williams's "Angels" and Kylie Minogue's "Can't Get You Out of My Head".

Despite a period of obscurity, Fielding experienced a career "renaissance in recent years," with praise for her storytelling abilities and a comparison to great raconteurs like Quentin Crisp. The Times lauded her performance as Hedda Gabler, considering it "one of the experiences of a lifetime".

Fielding is the subject of MetaFenella, a 2014 online artwork by artist Martin Firrell.

Fielding experienced a stroke on 25th August 2018 and succumbed two weeks later at Charing Cross Hospital in Hammersmith on 11th September 2018, at the age of 90. She remained unmarried and had no children.

Tom Clegg was an English actor who garnered recognition for his numerous small roles in film and television spanning the 1950s, 1960s, and 1970s.

Born in Leeds in 1927, Clegg initially served in the Household Cavalry and pursued a career as a professional boxer before transitioning to the world of films as a stuntman, showcasing his skills in productions like Ivanhoe (1952).

Clegg's imposing stature and tough persona secured him various film roles, including The Flanagan Boy (1953), The Fake (1953), John of the Fair (1954), The Stateless Man (1955), The Extra Day (1956), Moby Dick (1956), The Hideout (1956), Saint Joan (1957), Battle of the V-1 (1958), Mark of the Phoenix (1958), This Sporting Life (1963), and Thunderball (1965).

On the small screen, he portrayed toughs and henchmen in series such as Quatermass II, Sword of Freedom, The Four Just Men, Dixon of Dock Green, Adam Adamant Lives!, The Saint and The Sweeney.

Clegg's versatility extended to comedy, featuring in episodes of Hancock's Half Hour (The Cold, Football Pools, The Big Night, and The Two Murderers), The Benny Hill Show, Corrigan Blake, and Till Death Us Do Part. His comedic roles also translated to the big screen, with appearances in Raising the Wind (1961), Decline and Fall... of a Birdwatcher, and Great Catherine (both 1968).

Renowned for his contributions to comedy, Clegg became a semi-regular presence in the Carry On film series, showcasing his talents in **Carry On Regardless** (1961), **Carry On Spying** (1964), **Carry On Cleo** (1964), **Carry On Cowboy** (1965), **Carry On Loving** (1970) and **Carry On Screaming** (1966).

(CARRY ON) DON'T LOSE YOUR HEAD (1966)

The 'Carry On' ensemble playfully satirises the French Revolution, set in 1789 Paris, where two English aristocrats come to the aid of their French counterparts amidst the upheaval of the revolting masses and the looming threat of Madame Guillotine. Despite the elusive antics of the enigmatic 'Black Fingernail' and his trusty sidekick, the determined chief of police sets out on a mission to apprehend them, adding a comedic twist to the historical turmoil.

Don't Lose your Head features regular team members Sid James, Kenneth Williams, Jim Dale, Charles Hawtrey, and Joan Sims. Set in France and England in 1789 during the French Revolution, it is a parody of Baroness Orczy's "The Scarlet Pimpernel."

The first Carry On to be produced by the Rank Organisation, "Don't Lose Your Head" was not initially conceived as part of the series and was initially released without the Carry On prefix. However, the ongoing popularity of the series persuaded Rank to add the prefix to the titles of this and the following film, "Follow That Camel," when they were re-released. French actress Dany Robin makes her only Carry On appearance in this film.

CAST:

Sid James as **Sir Rodney Ffing/The Black Fingernail**
Kenneth Williams as **Citizen Camembert**
Jim Dale as **Lord Darcy Pue**
Charles Hawtrey as **Duc de Pommfrit**

Joan Sims as **Desiree Dubarry**
Peter Butterworth as **Citizen Bidet**
Dany Robin as **Jacqueline**
Peter Gilmore as **Maximilien Robespierre**
Marianne Stone as **Landlady**
Michael Ward as **Henri**
Leon Greene as **Malabonce**
Richard Shaw as **Captain**
David Davenport as **Sergeant**
Jennifer Clulow as **1st lady**
Valerie Van Ost as **2nd lady**
Jacqueline Pearce as **3rd lady**

FACTS AND TRIVIA:

- Budget: £215,152
- Filming Dates 12th September – 28th October 1966

INTERIORS:

- Marble Hall, Clandon House, Guildford, Surrey, England
- Pinewood Studios, Buckinghamshire

EXTERIORS:

- Clandon House, Guildford, Surrey, England
- Claydon Park, Claydon, Buckinghamshire, England
- Cliveden, Buckinghamshire, England, UK
- Waddesdon Manor, Waddesdon, Buckinghamshire, England, UK
- Black Park, Buckinghamshire, England, UK

PROFILES:

Peter William Shorrocks Butterworth, born on 4th February 1915 in Bramhall, Cheshire, was a British actor and comedian. He married actress and impressionist Janet Brown in 1946 at St Mary's, Bryanston Square, Marylebone. The couple had two children: a son named Tyler, who later became an actor and married actress Janet Dibley, and a daughter named Emma, born in 1962, who sadly passed away in 1996 at the age of 34.

During the Second World War, Butterworth served as a lieutenant in the Fleet Air Arm of the Royal Navy. On 21st June 1940, he was shot down during an attack on a German-occupied seaplane air base in the Netherlands. Captured and sent to Stalag Luft III, he formed a duo with Talbot Rothwell, performing in camp shows. His wartime experiences, including covering for escapers during the events portrayed in The Wooden Horse, shaped his later career.

Butterworth's acting career gained momentum with his first film appearance in "William Comes to Town" (1948). He formed a close friendship with director Val Guest and starred in several films together. His television success included the Terry-Thomas sketch show "How Do You View?" and children's programmes like "Whirligig" and "Butterworth Time." He appeared in films alongside Sean Connery, David Niven, and Douglas Fairbanks Jr.

Butterworth's association with the iconic Carry On film series began with "Carry On Cowboy" (1965). He became a key figure in the series, making sixteen film appearances, two Christmas specials, the 1975 television series, and participating in West End theatre productions. His characters were typically quiet and subtly eccentric, often serving as stooges for other characters.

After the Carry On films, Butterworth continued his career with appearances in Richard Lester's films, including "A Funny Thing Happened on the Way to the Forum" (1966) and "Robin and Marian" (1976). He also had roles in "The Ritz" and a special appearance in "Oliver!" (1968). In 1979, posthumously, he took on small parts in "The First Great Train Robbery" and Alan Bennett's play "Afternoon Off."

In 1979, while starring as Widow Twankey in the pantomime "Aladdin" at the Coventry Theatre, Butterworth passed away in his hotel room from a heart attack. He was buried in Danehill Cemetery, East Sussex. Following his death, Carry On films producer Peter Rogers described him as "a thoroughly nice bloke and a dear friend."

Title	Year	Peter Butterworth
Cowboy	1965	Doc
Screaming!	1966	Const. Slobotham
Don't Lose Your Head	1966	Citizen Bidet
Follow That Camel	1967	Simpson
Doctor	1967	Mr. Smith
Up the Khyber	1968	Brother Belcher
Camping	1969	Joshua Fiddler
Again Doctor	1969	"Shuffling Patient"
Loving	1970	"Sinister Client"
Henry	1971	Charles, Earl of Bristol
Abroad	1972	Pepe
Girls	1973	The Admiral
Dick	1974	Tom
Behind	1975	Barnes
England	1976	Maj. Carstairs
Emmannuelle	1978	Richmond

Marianne Stone was born on 23rd August 1922; she graced the silver screen from the early 1940s to the late 1980s, often portraying working-class roles such as barmaids, secretaries, and landladies. She also played supporting roles alongside comedian Norman Wisdom.

Stone's cinematic repertoire included notable films such as Brighton Rock (1947), Seven Days to Noon (1950), The 39 Steps (1959), Lolita (1962), Ladies Who Do (1963), Oh! What a Lovely War (1969), and the first two "Quatermass" films. In a departure from her usual roles, Stone took on the serious and arguably most dramatic character, Lena van Broecken, in three episodes of the BBC's Secret Army between 1977 and 1978.

Affectionately known as "Mugsie," Stone was initially credited in her early films as "Mary Stone" and has also been credited as "Marion Stone." She enjoyed a marriage spanning fifty years, from 1947 to 1997, to actor-turned-theatre-critic and film historian Peter Noble. The union blessed them with two children, including DJ Kara Noble. Stone graced a total of 201 films before retiring in the 1980s when the offers dwindled.

Stone featured in nine Carry On films and an episode of Carry On Laughing:

- Carry On Nurse (1959) as **Alice Able**
- Carry On Constable (1960) as **Miss Horton** *(voice only, for Lucy Griffiths)*
- Carry On Jack (1963) as **Peg**
- Carry On Screaming! (1966) as **Mrs Parker**
- Carry On Don't Lose Your Head (1967) as **Landlady**
- Carry On Doctor (1967) as **Mother**
- Carry On at Your Convenience (1971) as **Maud**
- Carry On Matron (1972) as **Mrs Putzova** *(scenes deleted)*
- Carry On Girls (1973) as **Miss Drew**
- Carry On Dick (1974) as **Maggie**
- Carry On Behind (1975) as **Mrs Rowan**
- Carry On Laughing: "The Case of the Screaming Winkles" (1975) as **Madame Petra**

Marianne Stone passed away on 21st December 2009 at the age of 87.

Michael Ward, originally named George William Everard Yoe Ward, was born on 9th April 1909 in Carnmenellis, Cornwall. He was the son of clergyman William George Henry Ward and Annie (née Dingle). Initially, Ward pursued a career in teaching but later retrained at the Central School of Speech and Drama. His debut film role came in 1947 when he portrayed Mr Trafford in Alexander Korda's "An Ideal Husband."

Throughout the period from 1947 to 1960, Ward showcased his talent in over 30 films, establishing himself as one of the UK's busiest and most recognisable character actors. Notably, he featured in five Carry On films, four Norman Wisdom films, and six productions by the Boulting brothers.

During the early 1960s, Ward transitioned to television. Until his retirement in 1978, he graced various shows, including "The Jack Benny Programme," "The Avengers," "The Morecambe and Wise Show," "Dixon of Dock Green," "The Two Ronnies," "Armchair Theatre," "Rising Damp," and "Sykes."

Ward's Carry On contributions include:

- Carry On Regardless (1961) as **Photographer**
- Carry On Cabby (1963) as **Man in Tweeds**
- Carry On Cleo (1964) as **Archimedes**
- Carry On Screaming! (1966) as **Mr Vivian**
- Carry On Don't Lose Your Head (1966) as **Henri**

After featuring in the 1978 film "Revenge of the Pink Panther," Ward experienced a stroke that prompted his retirement. By 1986, he encountered difficulties with mobility and, at the age of 88, passed away on 8th November 1997 at St Mary's Hospital in London. Ward, a multifaceted individual, never completely recovered from the loss of his mother in the late 60s. Furthermore, he openly acknowledged his gay identity from the late 1960s, confronting challenges associated with his sexual orientation. Described as a sensitive man, Ward sought regular reassurance throughout his life.

(CARRY ON) FOLLOW THAT CAMEL (1967)

In this hilarious comedy, we follow the misadventures of a dashing young English aristocrat who finds himself in a pickle when he's falsely accused of cheating. Determined to prove his innocence and win back the heart of his beloved, he hatches a harebrained scheme to join the Foreign Legion.

Much like its predecessor, "Don't Lose Your Head," this film intriguingly strays from the customary "Carry On" naming tradition; however, for international audiences, it graced screens under the alternate titles of "Carry On In The Legion".

This comedic masterpiece playfully lampoons the timeless classic "Beau Geste" by PC Wren, along with a slew of other French Foreign Legion films. Notably, it served as producer Peter Rogers's bold endeavour to conquer the American market. Phil Silvers, in his sole appearance in the Carry On series, steals the show with his uproarious portrayal, reminiscent of the iconic Sergeant Bilko. Silvers joins the esteemed ranks of Carry On regulars such as Kenneth Williams, Jim Dale, Charles Hawtrey, Joan Sims, Peter Butterworth, and Bernard Bresslaw.

Angela Douglas shines in her third out of four appearances in the Carry On universe. At the same time, Anita Harris makes her unforgettable debut in the first of her two Carry On outings.

CAST:

Phil Silvers as **Sergeant Ernie Nocker**
Jim Dale as **Bertram Oliphant "Bo" West**
Peter Butterworth as **Simpson**
Kenneth Williams as **Commandant Maximilian Burger**
Charles Hawtrey as **Captain Le Pice**
Joan Sims as **Zig-Zig**
Angela Douglas as **Lady Jane Ponsonby**
Bernard Bresslaw as **Sheikh Abdul Abulbul**

Anita Harris as **Corktip**
John Bluthal as **Corporal Clotski**
Peter Gilmore as **Captain Bagshaw**
William Mervyn as **Sir Cyril Ponsonby**
Julian Holloway as **Ticket collector**
David Glover as **Hotel manager**
Larry Taylor as **Riff**
William Hurndell as **Raff**

FACTS AND TRIVIA:

- Budget: £288,366
- Location filming took place in early 1967, with scenes set in the Sahara being shot at Camber Sands near Rye, East Sussex, England.
- Filming encountered challenges as shooting had to be paused multiple times due to snow on the sands.
- Additional shots were captured at Birkdale beach near Southport, Lancashire.
- Interestingly, some of the town sets used in this film were repurposed the following year for the production of "Carry On Up the Khyber."

PROFILES:

Phil Silvers –was the youngest of eight children, born to Russian Jewish immigrants Saul and Sarah Silver. His upbringing in New York was influenced by his father, a sheet metal worker involved in constructing early skyscrapers.

Silvers' entertainment career began at a young age, singing in theatres to compensate for film projector breakdowns. He transitioned into vaudeville and burlesque comedy, eventually making his Broadway debut in 1939. Silvers' talent shone in various productions, earning critical acclaim and paving the way for his entry into the film industry. His film career flourished with notable appearances in movies like "All Through the Night" (1942) and "Summer Stock" (1950), alongside Gene Kelly and Judy Garland. His versatility was evident in roles ranging from comedic to character-driven performances.

Silvers' Broadway achievements included starring roles in "Top Banana" (1952) and "Do Re Mi" (1960), earning him accolades and nominations. Though initially declining the lead role in "A Funny Thing Happened on the Way to the Forum", he later participated in the stage revival, securing another Tony Award.

In 1955, Silvers skyrocketed to fame with his portrayal of Sergeant Ernest G. Bilko in the television series initially titled "You'll Never Get Rich", later rebranded as "The Phil Silvers Show". This military comedy quickly captivated audiences as the cunning Bilko outwitted his way through various challenges. By 1958, CBS repositioned the show to air on Friday nights and relocated the setting to Camp Fremont in California. However, just a year later, the series disappeared from the schedule.

During the 1963–1964 television season, Silvers returned to CBS screens as Harry Grafton, a factory foreman dabbling in get-rich-quick schemes reminiscent of his earlier Bilko character. This 30-episode stint in "The New Phil Silvers Show" featured an ensemble cast including Stafford Repp, Herbie Faye, Buddy Lester, Elena Verdugo as his sister Audrey, and her children portrayed by Ronnie Dapo and Sandy Descher.

In later years, Silvers continued to charm audiences through television appearances and guest roles, displaying his enduring comedic prowess. However, his personal life was marked by struggles with gambling and depression. Despite health challenges, Silvers remained dedicated to his craft until his passing in 1985.

Julian Holloway was born 24th June 1944 in Watlington, Oxfordshire, England; his education journey took him through Ludgrove School, Harrow School, and the prestigious Royal Academy of Dramatic Art.

In his personal life, Holloway has experienced the complexities of relationships. He briefly dated Tessa Dahl in 1976, resulting in the birth of their daughter Sophie Dahl. Subsequently, he married Zena Walker in 1971, which ended in divorce shortly after. Later, in 1991, he married voice-over artist and actress Debbie Wheeler, but their union dissolved in 1996. Moreover, Holloway is connected to the esteemed English architect and scenic designer Oliver Percy Bernard, adding another layer to his rich family history.

During the 1962–63 television season of "Our Man Higgins", Holloway embarked on his inaugural major acting role as Quentin, featuring in four episodes.

In an episode titled "Big Spender" of the 1970s British police drama "The Sweeney", Holloway portrayed John Smith, the mastermind behind an organised crime family embroiled in an intricate fraud scheme with two unscrupulous employees of a car park company.

His extensive television credits encompass diverse productions such as the Uncle Silas television dramatisations, "Elizabeth R", "Remember WENN", "Whatever Happened To The Likely Lads", "Beverly Hills, 90210", "Minder", "The Professionals", "The New Avengers", "Z-Cars", "The World of Wodehouse", and the 1989 Doctor Who story "Survival". Additionally, his filmography boasts notable titles like "Young Winston" (1972), "Porridge" (1979), "The Great Rock 'n' Roll Swindle" (1980), "A Christmas Carol" (2009), and "The Rum Diary" (2011).

Holloway has earned acclaim as a proficient voice actor, particularly in the United States. Notable roles include Captain Zed in "Captain Zed and the Zee Zone" (1991), Bradford Milbanks in "James Bond Jr.", Siegfried Fischbacher in "Father of the Pride" (2004), Prime Minister Almec in several episodes of "Star Wars: The Clone Wars" (2008-2020), and the primary antagonist Odlaw in the "Where's Waldo?" (1991 series). Furthermore, he has contributed his vocal talents to video games such as "Pirates of the Caribbean: At World's End" and "Medal of Honor: European Assault". Notably, he voiced Death in the Cartoon Network animated series "Regular Show" (2010–2017).

Holloway has appeared in eight Carry On films, alongside a memorable appearance in one of the Carry On Christmas TV specials.

- Carry On Follow That Camel (1967) as **Ticket Collector**
- Carry On Doctor (1967) as **Simmons**
- Carry On Up the Khyber (1968) as **Major Shorthouse**
- Carry On Camping (1969) as **Jim Tanner**
- Carry On Loving (1970) as **Adrian**
- Carry On Henry (1971) as **Sir Thomas**
- Carry On at Your Convenience (1971) as **Roger**
- Carry On England (1976) as **Major Butcher**

Television:

- **Carry On Christmas** (1973) as **Captain Rhodes**

CARRY ON DOCTOR (1967)

Dr. Kilmore finds himself in a sticky situation when he's caught in a compromising position on the roof of the nurses' home and gets the sack. But fear not! His loyal patients refuse to let him go without a fight. With their zany antics and determination, they square off against the formidable Dr. Tinkle and the domineering

Matron, all in a bid to keep their beloved doctor at the helm. Get ready for a sidesplitting showdown that proves laughter truly is the best medicine!

Carry On Doctor features a stellar cast including Sid James, Kenneth Williams, Jim Dale, Charles Hawtrey, Joan Sims, Peter Butterworth, and Bernard Bresslaw, while introducing Frankie Howerd in his debut appearance in the series, bringing his trademark humour to the screen.

Fans will delight in the return of familiar faces, with Hattie Jacques making a comeback for the first time since Carry On Cabby four years prior and Barbara Windsor reprising her role after her debut in Carry On Spying three years earlier. Additionally, Anita Harris graces the screen for her second and final appearance in the series.

CAST:

Frankie Howerd as **Francis Kitchener Bigger**
Kenneth Williams as **Doctor Kenneth Tinkle**
Sid James as **Charlie Roper**
Charles Hawtrey as **Mr Barron**
Jim Dale as **Doctor Jim Kilmore**
Hattie Jacques as **Lavinia, the Matron**
Peter Butterworth as **Mr Smith**
Bernard Bresslaw as **Ken Biddle**
Barbara Windsor as **Nurse Sandra May**
Joan Sims as **Chloe Gibson**
Anita Harris as **Nurse Clarke**
June Jago as **Sister Hoggett**
Derek Francis as **Sir Edmund Burke**
Dandy Nichols as **Mrs Roper**
Peter Jones as **Chaplain**
Deryck Guyler as **Surgeon Hardcastle**
Gwendolyn Watts as **Mrs Mildred Barron**

Dilys Laye as **Mavis Winkle**
Peter Gilmore as **Henry**
Harry Locke as **Sam**
Marianne Stone as **Mother**
Jean St. Clair as **Mrs Smith**
Valerie Van Ost as **Nurse Parkin**
Julian Orchard as **Fred**
Brian Wilde as **Cox & Carter man**
Lucy Griffiths as **Miss Morrison**
Gertan Klauber as **Wash orderly**
Julian Holloway as **Doctor Simmons**

FACTS AND TRIVIA:

- Budget: £214,000
- Filming Dates 11th September - 20th October 1967

INTERIORS:

- Marble Hall, Clandon House, Guildford, Surrey, England
- Pinewood Studios, Buckinghamshire

EXTERIORS:

- Maidenhead, where the Town Hall doubled for the hospital
- Masonic Hall, Uxbridge
- Westbourne Street, London WC2

Carry On Doctor emerged as a cinematic sensation, ranking as the third highest-grossing general release in the British box office, surpassed only by "The Jungle Book" and "Barbarella." Kinematograph Weekly reports a notable British presence in the top ten general releases of the year, with "Up the Junction," "Poor Cow," "Here We Go Round the Mulberry Bush," and, of course, Carry on Doctor, all making their mark on audiences nationwide.

PROFILES:

Bernard Bresslaw's journey began on 25th February 1934 in Stepney, London, as the youngest of three boys in a Jewish family. His father, a tailor's cutter, sparked his early interest in acting through visits to the Hackney Empire. Education at the Coopers' Company's School in Tredegar Square and a scholarship from the London County Council led him to the Royal Academy of Dramatic Art, where he earned the Emile Littler Award as the most promising actor.

Launching his acting career with roles in radio and television, including "Educating Archie" and "The Army Game," Bresslaw's towering 6 ft 7 in (2.01 m) stature set him apart on screen. He achieved widespread recognition in the Carry On film franchise, featuring in 14 films. Notably, he portrayed the lead villain, Varga, in the 1967 Doctor Who story "The Ice Warriors."

Known for his catchphrase "I only arsked" in a strong Cockney accent, originating in "The Army Game" and revived in "Carry On Camping" (1969), Bresslaw became a distinctive comedic figure.

Beyond acting, Bresslaw embraced diverse interests. As a member of the Grand Order of Water Rats, he served as its "King Rat" in 1988. He was also a Freemason and part of Chelsea Lodge 3098. From 1985 to 1987, he portrayed 'Gorilla' in Yorkshire TV's 'The Giddy Game Show.'

Bresslaw's parody song "You Need Feet" gained recognition in the Rutles' TV special and the Yoko Ono film parody "A Thousand Feet of Film." Initially omitted, the song was later restored in subsequent DVD releases.

In the late 1980s, Bresslaw, alongside Miriam Margolyes, joined English comedienne Maureen Lipman in British Telecom advertisements. Playing Gerald and Dolly, a jittery couple, they interacted with Lipman's character, Beatrice "Beattie" Bellman, and her husband Harry.

Besides his entertainment contributions, Bresslaw displayed his creative side in the privately published poetry volume "Ode to the Dead Sea Scrolls."

In 1959, Bernard Bresslaw tied the knot with dancer Betty Wright, and together they welcomed three sons into their family: James, Mark, and Jonathan.

Tragically, on 11th June 1993, Bernard Bresslaw suffered a sudden heart attack in his dressing room at the Open Air Theatre in Regent's Park, London, as he prepared for "Taming of the Shrew." Following his passing, his cremation took place at Golders Green Crematorium, and his ashes found their final resting place on 17th June 1993.

Title	Year	Bernard Bresslaw
Nurse	1959	Ted York's feet (uncredited)
Cowboy	1965	Little Heap
Screaming!	1966	Sockett
Follow That Camel	1967	Sheikh Abdul Abulbul
Doctor	1967	Ken Biddle
Up the Khyber	1968	Bungdit Din
Camping	1969	Bernie Lugg
Up the Jungle	1970	Upsidasi
Loving	1970	Gripper Burke
At Your Convenience	1971	Bernie Hulke
Matron	1972	Ernie Bragg
Abroad	1972	Brother Bernard
Girls	1973	Peter Potter
Dick	1974	Sir Roger Daley
Behind	1975	Arthur Upmore
That's Carry On!	1977	Archive

Lucy Griffiths was born 24th April 1919 in Birley, Herefordshire. She became a household name through her memorable performances in a plethora of Hammer horror films, starring alongside icons like Peter Cushing in "Frankenstein and the Monster from Hell" and Christopher Lee in "The Two Faces of Dr. Jekyll."

On the small screen, Griffiths showcased her versatility with appearances in popular television programmes including "On the Buses," "Mind Your Language," "All Creatures Great and Small," "Secret Army," and "Z-Cars."

Her talent wasn't confined to the spotlight, as she also contributed to the classic British film "Genevieve," albeit in a small, uncredited role. Griffiths continued to leave her mark with various other uncredited parts in numerous British productions throughout her illustrious career.

Her Carry On contributions include:

- Carry On Nurse (1959) as **Trolley Lady**
- Carry On Constable (1960) as **Miss Horton** - (voice dubbed by Marianne Stone)
- Carry On Regardless (1961) as **Auntie** (uncredited)
- Carry On Doctor (1967) as **Miss Morris - Elderly Patient**
- Carry On Again Doctor (1969) as an **Old Lady wearing Headphones**
- Carry On Loving (1970) as **Woman** (scenes deleted)
- Carry On Behind (1975) as **Lady with Hat** (uncredited)

Griffiths passed away on 29th September 1982, at the age of 63, in London, England.

CARRY ON UP THE KHYBER (1968)

In the comedic adventure, we find Sir Sidney Ruff-Diamond in charge of the hilariously mismanaged British outpost nestled near the eccentric Khyber Pass. With the bumbling protection of the kilt-wearing soldiers from the Third Foot and Mouth regiment, one would expect a bit of safety. However, their peace is threatened when the mischievous Khazi of Kalabar devises his outrageous schemes.

Carry On Up the Khyber features familiar faces such as Sid James, Kenneth Williams, Charles Hawtrey, Joan Sims, Bernard Bresslaw, and Peter Butterworth. Wanda Ventham makes her second and final appearance in the Carry On franchise (following her appearance in Carry On Cleo), while Roy Castle debuts in his sole Carry On role, typically portrayed by Jim Dale.

Angela Douglas bows out of the series after her fourth appearance, and Terry Scott returns to the fold following a minor role in the inaugural film Carry On Sergeant a decade prior. Carry On Up the Khyber cleverly satirises Kiplingesque depictions of British Raj life in both contemporary and Hollywood eras. The title itself, a nod to the risqué Carry On humour, employs wordplay with "Khyber" (derived from "Khyber Pass") as rhyming slang for "arse."

CAST:

Sid James as **Sir Sidney Ruff-Diamond**
Kenneth Williams as **The Khasi of Kalabar**
Charles Hawtrey as **Private James Widdle**
Roy Castle as **Captain Keene**
Joan Sims as **Lady Joan Ruff-Diamond**
Bernard Bresslaw as **Bungdit Din**
Peter Butterworth as **Brother Belcher**
Terry Scott as **Sergeant Major MacNutt**

Angela Douglas as **Princess Jelhi**
Cardew Robinson as **The Fakir**
Peter Gilmore as **Private Ginger Hale**
Julian Holloway as **Major Shorthouse**
Leon Thau as **Stinghi**
Michael Mellinger as **Chindi**
Wanda Ventham as **The Khasi's First Wife**
Alexandra Dane as **Busti**

Talbot Rothwell penned the screenplay for the film. Impressed by Rothwell's work on "Carry On Jack," producer Peter Rogers recruited him as the official writer for the Carry On series. Rothwell went on to write an additional nineteen Carry On films.

The movie features a fictional Highland infantry regiment of the British Army known as the 3rd Foot and Mouth Regiment. Nicknamed "the Devils in Skirts," these Highlanders have a tradition of going commando under their kilts. To outfit the 3rd Foot and Mouth Regiment, the production team rented tartans and bonnet badges originally designed for the Highland regiment in the 1960 film "Tunes of Glory." Additionally, pith helmets and webbing were borrowed from the 1964 war classic "Zulu."

FACTS AND TRIVIA:

- Budget: £235,637
- Filming Dates 8th April – 31st May 1968
- Filming of scenes set on the North West Frontier took place beneath the summit of Snowdon in North Wales.
- The lower section of the Watkin Path doubled as the Khyber Pass, complete with garrison and border gate.
- In September 2005, a plaque was revealed in Snowdonia to commemorate the filming location of the movie.

- In 1969, "Carry On Up the Khyber" ranked as the second most popular film at the UK box office.
- Carry On Up the Khyber is often hailed as the top instalment in the Carry On series.
- Colin MacCabe, Professor of English at the University of Exeter, praised this film along with Carry On Cleo as among the finest films ever made.
- In 1999, it secured the 99th position on the BFI's roster of the greatest British films in history.

PROFILES:

Roy Castle OBE was born on 31st August 1932 in Scholes, near Holmfirth, West Riding of Yorkshire; Castle displayed his tap-dancing skills from a young age and honed his talent at Nora Bray's school of dance. He commenced his professional career in entertainment after leaving Holme Valley Grammar School, initially performing in amateur concert parties.

During the 1950s, Castle resided in Cleveleys near Blackpool, where he began his career as a stooge for entertainers Jimmy Clitheroe and Jimmy James. His talent swiftly gained recognition, leading to appearances at prestigious venues such as the Royal Variety Show by 1958. Castle also ventured into the music scene, releasing a charting single, "Little White Berry", in 1960.

Castle's television and film career flourished, with notable appearances in productions like the Morecambe and Wise series and the film "Dr. Who and the Daleks". He starred in productions such as the TV musical "Pickwick". Castle's versatility extended to hosting and performing on various television shows, including "The Generation Game" and "The Good Old Days".

However, Castle's most enduring role was as the host of the long-running children's series "Record Breakers", which he presented for over two decades. His association with the show led to numerous world records, including the fastest tap-dance and the longest wing walk. Castle's dedication to charity was exemplified by his fundraising efforts, such as tap-dancing to raise £1 million for charity in 1985.

Outside of his entertainment career, Castle was a devoted family man, and a committed Christian. He married dancer Fiona Dickson in 1963, and they had four children together. Despite his fame, Castle remained a humble supporter of Liverpool Football Club, attending matches even during his illness.

Tragically, Castle's battle with lung cancer, which was diagnosed in 1992, ended with his passing on 2nd September 1994, at the age of 62, in Gerrards Cross, Buckinghamshire, England. Castle's funeral was attended by luminaries from the entertainment industry, reflecting the profound impact he had on his colleagues and audiences alike.

CARRY ON CAMPING (1969)

Two mischievous chaps concoct a cunning plan to whisk their unsuspecting girlfriends off to what they believe is a nudist colony for a bit of cheeky fun. However, their scheme takes an unexpected turn when they arrive at the location, only to discover it's actually a family-friendly campsite. Despite their initial disappointment, the lads decide to make the most of the situation and stay put.

As they settle into the campsite, the boys find themselves drawn into a series of hilarious escapades, especially when a busload of teenage schoolgirls descends upon the site. With mischief abound, our intrepid heroes seize the opportunity for more laughs and antics, much to the amusement of the campsite's other residents.

CAST:

Sid James as **Sid Boggle**
Kenneth Williams as **Doctor Kenneth Soaper**
Joan Sims as **Joan Fussey**
Charles Hawtrey as **Charlie Muggins**
Terry Scott as **Peter Potter**
Barbara Windsor as **Babs**
Bernard Bresslaw as **Bernie Lugg**
Hattie Jacques as **Miss Haggard/Matron**
Peter Butterworth as **Joshua Fiddler**
Brian Oulton as **Mr Short, camping store manager**
Valerie Leon as **Miss Dobbin, camping store assistant**
Julian Holloway as **Jim Tanner**
Dilys Laye as **Anthea Meeks**
Betty Marsden as **Harriet Potter**
Sandra Caron as **Fanny**
Trisha Noble as **Sally**
Amelia Bayntun as **Mrs Fussey**
Patricia Franklin as **Farmer's daughter**
Derek Francis as **Farmer**
Michael Nightingale as **Man in cinema**

FACTS AND TRIVIA:

- Budget: £208,354
- Filming Dates: 7th October – 22nd November 1968

EXTERIORS:

- Pinewood Studios' orchard doubled for Paradise Camp
- Chayste Place school, also known as Heatherden Hall at Pinewood Studios, featured in several Carry On films such as Carry On Nurse, Carry On Up the Khyber, Carry On Again Doctor, Carry On at Your Convenience, Carry On Behind, and Carry On England)

- Pinewood Green in Iver Heath housing estate, Buckinghamshire
- Everyman Cinema in Gerrards Cross, Buckinghamshire
- Maidenhead High Street
- Black Park, Buckinghamshire

RECEPTION:

- The film topped the UK box office in 1969
- Voted as the nation's favourite Carry On film in a 2008 survey by the Daily Mirror

PROFILES:

Owen John "Terry" Scott, born on 4th May 1927 in Watford, Hertfordshire, England, was the youngest of three children. Tragically, his only surviving brother, Aubrey, passed away when Terry was six. After completing National Service in the Navy at the end of World War II, he briefly pursued studies in accounting.

Terry Scott's acting career commenced with radio appearances, notably on shows like Workers Playtime, followed by ventures into television. Joining the Whitehall Theatre Company provided him with opportunities in farce. He partnered with Bill Maynard at Butlin's Holiday Camp in Skegness and co-starred in the TV series Great Scott - It's Maynard! During the 1960s, he collaborated with Hugh Lloyd in Hugh and I (1962–1967) and played Ugly Sisters in pantomime at The London Palladium.

Scott ventured into music with the novelty record "My Brother" in 1962 and later featured in TV commercials for Curly Wurly caramel bars during the 1970s, where he amusingly portrayed a schoolboy. His contribution to the Carry On film series began with Carry On Sergeant in 1958, and he returned in 1968 for Carry On Up the Khyber, eventually taking on main roles in six later films.

He teamed up with June Whitfield, starring in the comedy series Happy Ever After and its successor Terry and June. Despite both having multiple Carry On appearances, they never appeared together in the same film. Additionally, they worked on the sketch show Scott On (1968) and had supporting roles in the film Bless This House. From 1981 to 1992, Terry Scott lent his voice to Penfold the hamster in the animated series Danger Mouse. His later career included diverse roles, showcasing his versatility in the entertainment industry.

In 1979, Scott faced a life-threatening brain haemorrhage, requiring a life-saving operation. He battled creeping paralysis, necessitating a neck brace. The actor's health further deteriorated when he was diagnosed with cancer in 1987. Despite these challenges, he continued to maintain his sense of humour, expressing reluctance to give up vices like alcohol and cigarettes.

Terry Scott passed away from the effects of cancer at his family home in Witley, Surrey, on 26th July 1994 at the age of 67. His life concluded with a quote reflecting his characteristic wit: "I know it would be better to give up the booze, fags and birds, but life would be so boring, wouldn't it?"

Title	Year	Terry Scott
Sergeant	1958	Sgt. Paddy O'Brien
Up the Khyber	1968	Sgt. Maj. Macnutt
Camping	1969	Peter Potter
Up the Jungle	1970	Cecil the Jungle Boy
Loving	1970	Terence Philpot
Henry	1971	Cardinal Wolsey
At Your Convenience	1971	Mr Allcock (scenes deleted)
Matron	1972	Dr. Prodd
Abroad	1972	Irate Wundatours Customer (scenes deleted)
That's Carry On!	1977	Archive

CARRY ON AGAIN DOCTOR (1969)

In a hilarious twist of fate, Doctor Nookey stumbles upon a witch doctor's weight-reducing potion during his stint on a mission in the South Seas. Recognising the goldmine potential of this concoction, he hastily makes his way back to England, determined to turn his newfound discovery into a money-making scheme that could finally bring him the fortune he's always dreamed of.

Carry On Again Doctor debuted in December 1969, joining the ranks of its predecessors with a humorous take on healthcare. The ensemble cast includes beloved regulars such as Sid James, Kenneth Williams, Charles Hawtrey, Joan Sims, Barbara Windsor, and Hattie Jacques. Notably, this film marked Jim Dale's departure from the series for 23 years until his return in Carry On Columbus. Additionally, it introduced Patsy Rowlands to the franchise, who went on to appear in a further eight Carry On films.

The initial script of "Carry On Again Doctor" encountered issues with Rank's legal adviser, who raised concerns about its similarity to an earlier 'Doctor' script submitted by Talbot Rothwell, the writer of "Carry On Again Doctor," to producer Betty Box. Notably, both scripts revolved around the concept of a medical mission and a slimming potion. However, since Box had not pursued Rothwell's 'Doctor' script, it was determined that there were no legal impediments to incorporating similar ideas into this film.

CAST:

Sid James as **Gladstone Screwer**
Jim Dale as **Doctor Jimmy Nookey**
Kenneth Williams as **Doctor Frederick Carver**
Charles Hawtrey as **Doctor Ernest Stoppidge/Lady Puddleton**
Barbara Windsor as **Goldie Locks (real name Maud Boggins)**

Joan Sims as **Ellen Moore**
Hattie Jacques as **Miss Soaper, the Matron**
Patsy Rowlands as **Miss Fosdick**
Peter Butterworth as **Shuffling patient**
Lucy Griffiths as **Old lady with headphones**
Valerie Leon as **Deirdre Filkington-Battermore**
Patricia Hayes as **Mrs Beasley**
Alexandra Dane as **Stout woman**
Pat Coombs as **New Matron**
William Mervyn as **Lord Paragon**
Valerie Van Ost as **Out-Patients Sister**
Wilfrid Brambell as **Mr Pullen**
Elizabeth Knight as **Nurse Willing**
Peter Gilmore as **Henry**
Harry Locke as **Porter**
Gwendolyn Watts as **Night sister**
Frank Singuineau as **Porter**

FACTS AND TRIVIA:

- Budget: £219,000
- Filming Dates: 17th March – 2nd May 1969

EXTERIORS:

- Maidenhead: The town hall was used as the hospital, as previously seen in "Carry On Doctor".
- Pinewood Studios: Heatherden Hall served as the exterior for the Moore-Nookey Clinic.
- Windsor, Berkshire: Dr Nookey's consulting rooms were filmed here, the same location used in "Carry On Regardless" and "Carry On Loving".

RELEASE:

- When the film premiered in New York by American International Pictures in February 1973, it was titled "Carry on Doctor".
- The sequence where Dr Nookie causes a short circuit in the hospital's electrical system, and the ensuing chaos was featured as an introduction to the 1980s compilation show "Carry On Laughing".
- According to Empire, the fast-paced plot and varied locations contribute to making this film one of the more successful entries in the series.

PROFILES:

Patricia Amy Rowlands was born on 19th January 1931 in Palmers Green, Middlesex. She attended the Sacred Heart convent school at Whetstone, where an elocution teacher recognised her acting potential and encouraged her to pursue a career in the field.

At the age of fifteen, Rowlands won a scholarship to the Guildhall School of Music and Drama. Her early career included performances in Annie Get Your Gun's chorus and a summer season in Torquay. She spent several years with the Players' Theatre in London before making her West End debut in Sandy Wilson's musical Valmouth. During this time, she met her future husband, the composer Malcolm Sircom, with whom she later divorced in 1967.

Other notable West End theatre credits encompassed roles in Semi-Detached, Shut Your Eyes and Think of England, The Seagull, Ben Travers's The Bed Before Yesterday, and When We Are Married. She also starred in Cameron Mackintosh's revival of Oliver! in the mid-1990s and played Jack's mother in the original London cast of Sondheim's Into the Woods. Her final appearance was as Mrs Pearce in the National Theatre's production of My Fair Lady.

Rowlands made frequent early television appearances, including roles in Gert and Daisy, Danger Man, and The Avengers. From 1969 to 1991, she became a regular in the Carry On films, making her debut in Carry On Again Doctor. She played various roles in nine Carry On films, including Carry On Loving, Carry On Henry, and Carry On Matron.

Between 1971 and 1976, Rowlands played Betty in the ITV sitcom Bless This House. She also appeared in other television series such as For the Love of Ada, Hallelujah! (1980s), and an episode of Zorro in 1991. She participated in screen adaptations of Frances Hodgson Burnett's works, appearing in Little Lord Fauntleroy (1980) and A Little Princess (1986).

In her later years, Patricia Rowlands appeared in revivals of major musicals such as Oliver! and My Fair Lady. Her television credits included The Cazalets, The Canterbury Tales, The Cater Street Hangman, Get Well Soon, Vanity Fair, Murder Most English, and Bottom for the BBC. In 2002, she appeared as a guest on the paranormal series Most Haunted. In 2003, Rowlands participated in numerous DVD audio commentaries alongside fellow surviving stars from the Carry On films.

Unfortunately, Rowlands developed breast cancer and abandoned her plans to become an acting teacher. She quietly retired and passed away in an East Sussex hospice three days after her 74th birthday on 22nd January 2005. Patricia Rowlands was survived by her only son, Alan.

Title	Year	Patsy Rowlands
Again Doctor	1969	Miss Fosdick
Loving	1970	Miss Dempsey
Henry	1971	Queen

At Your Convenience	1971	Hortence Withering
Matron	1972	Evelyn Banks
Abroad	1972	Miss Dobbs
Girls	1973	Mildred Bumble
Dick	1974	Mrs. Giles
Behind	1975	Linda Upmore

CARRY ON 70'S

CARRY ON UP THE JUNGLE (1970)

The beloved `Carry On' troupe embarks on a wild safari to track down a rare bird. However, their journey takes a hilarious turn as they stumble into the wrong tents, inadvertently disrupt a tranquil jungle, and hilariously navigate through unexpected encounters. Along the way, they encounter headhunters, stumble upon an all-female tribe in search of companionship, and even find themselves in the path of a lustful gorilla with an eye for comedy. With each twist and turn, this zany safari becomes a laugh-out-loud escapade filled with mishaps and mayhem.

In this uproarious escapade, we witness Frankie Howerd's comedic brilliance in his second and final appearance in the franchise. Alongside him are the familiar faces of Sid James, Charles Hawtrey, Joan Sims, Terry Scott, and Bernard Bresslaw, bringing their trademark humour to the jungle setting. Kenneth Connor rejoins the cast after a six-year hiatus since Carry On Cleo, becoming a staple in the series until Carry On Emmannuelle in 1978. Jacki Piper also makes her debut in the franchise, marking the beginning of her four-film run.

This rib-tickling tale playfully mocks the timeless Tarzan escapades (penned by Edgar Rice Burroughs), injecting a surprising dose of darkness as our hapless heroes find themselves entangled with a cannibalistic tribe deep in the heart of the jungle. But fear not! Amidst the peril, the laughter flows freely, offering a comedic escape from the chaos. Carry On Up the Jungle gleefully pokes fun at Hammer Film Productions' "Cavegirl" series, cheekily referencing classics like "One Million Years B.C." (1966) and "Slave Girls" (1967).

In a charming behind-the-scenes tale, Bernard Bresslaw diligently studied Swahili for his native orders, unaware that the "African" extras hailed from the Caribbean and struggled with the language. Nevertheless, Sid James, drawing from his South African roots, acknowledged Bresslaw's efforts with warm congratulations.

The film's whimsy extends to the festive season, as showcased in the Christmas Special Carry On, where our characters opt for an unconventional Oozlum bird over the traditional turkey for their holiday feast.

Adding to the hilarity, Charles Hawtrey, portraying Walter Bagley, amusingly assumes the role of father to Ugg/Cecil Bagley, played by Terry Scott, despite a comically slim twelve-and-a-half-year age gap. Meanwhile, Joan Sims charms as Lady Bagley, despite being three years younger than her on-screen offspring.

Behind the scenes, Kenneth Williams was custom-fit for the role of Professor Tinkle, while Jungle Boy was earmarked for Jim Dale. However, Williams' commitment to "The Kenneth Williams Show" and Dale's reservations about the character's sparse dialogue led to a delightful reimagining of their roles.

CAST:

Frankie Howerd as **Professor Inigo Tinkle**
Sid James as **Bill Boosey**
Charles Hawtrey as **Walter Bagley/King Tonka**
Joan Sims as **Lady Evelyn Bagley**
Kenneth Connor as **Claude Chumley**

Bernard Bresslaw as **Upsidasi**
Terry Scott as **Ug the Jungle Boy/Cecil Bagley**
Jacki Piper as **June**
Valerie Leon as **Leda**
Reuben Martin as **Gorilla**
Edwina Carroll as **Nerda**
Danny Daniels as **Nosha Chief**
Yemi Ajibadi as **Witch Doctor**
Lincoln Webb as **Nosha with girl**

FACTS AND TRIVIA:

- Budget: £210,000
- Filming Dates: 13th October - 21st November 1969.

LOCATIONS:

- Maidenhead Library: Served as the setting for Professor Tinkle's lecture. The original building, now demolished, stood directly opposite Maidenhead Town Hall, also featured in "Carry On Doctor," "Carry On Again Doctor," and "Carry On Behind."
- Clarence Crescent, Windsor: The very final scene of the movie was filmed here.

BOX OFFICE SUCCESS:

- The film ranked among the top eight most popular movies at the UK box office in 1970.

KENNETH WILLIAMS' REACTION:

- In his diary entry dated Saturday, 3rd April 1976, Kenneth Williams expressed positive sentiments about the film after watching it on television. He found it quite funny, even laughing aloud at one point. Williams particularly praised the performances of Kenneth Connor and Terry Scott, though he was less enthusiastic about Sid James.

PROFILES:

Francis Alick Howard OBE, better known by his stage name Frankie Howerd, was born on 6th March 1917. Howerd was born in York, England to Edith Florence Howard and soldier Francis Alfred William. Raised in the Hartoft Street area, he later moved to Eltham, London, attending Shooter's Hill Grammar School.

Although initially aspiring to be a serious actor, Howerd found success in comedy during his World War II service in the British Army. He debuted on BBC radio in 1946 and gained popularity with his distinctive style, featuring catchphrases like "titter ye not". Howerd's career spanned stage, radio, and television, including notable roles in films like "The Runaway Bus" (1954) and "Up Pompeii!" (1969–70).

Despite societal norms of the time, Howerd concealed his homosexuality, maintaining a discreet relationship with Dennis Heymer, who also served as his manager. His struggles with his sexuality and mental health were evident, influencing his comedic style.

Howerd died on the 19th of April 1992, at the age of 75, in Fulham, London, England; however, his comedic legacy endures, with biographical dramas and tributes honouring his contributions to British comedy. His former homes and venues bear plaques commemorating his life and career. Barry Cryer described his career as a series of comebacks, highlighting his enduring impact on comedy.

Jacki Piper, born Jacqueline Crump on 3rd August 1946, is a distinguished English actress recognised for her roles as the female lead in numerous British film comedies, including **Carry On Up the Jungle** (1970), **Carry On Loving** (1970), **Carry On at Your Convenience** (1971), and **Carry On Matron** (1972).

Originally from Birmingham, Piper received her training at the Birmingham Theatre School. Her acting journey commenced on the stage in the mid-1960s, performing in repertory theatre in Rhyl, Wales, under the name Jackie Crump. She made her film debut alongside Roger Moore in "The Man Who Haunted Himself" in 1970. Piper's other notable film appearances include "Doctor in Trouble" (1970) and "The Love Ban" (1973). Opting for a stage name for her film endeavours, she adopted the moniker Jacki Piper.

In addition to her film career, Piper has graced various television series, such as "Z-Cars", the sitcom "The Fall and Rise of Reginald Perrin" (in which she portrayed the recurring character Esther Pigeon), and "Dangerfield".

Her television credits extend to series like "Thriller", where she portrayed the Bride in the episode "Night Is the Time for Killing" (18th January 1975); "Return of the Saint", appearing as Sally in the episode "Tower Bridge Is Falling Down" (10th December 1978); "Backup", in which she played Jury Foreman in the episode "Touched" (11th June 1997); "Barbara", portraying Angela Croft in the episode "Neighbours" (2nd March 2003); and "Wire in the Blood", embodying the character Mrs Davis in the episode "Still She Cries" (19th January 2004). Piper's theatrical prowess shines through in numerous West End productions and tours across the UK and internationally.

CARRY ON LOVING (1970)

In this hilarious comedy, pandemonium erupts when the mischievous 'Carry On' crew take charge of a phoney marriage agency. Meet Sid and Sophie Bliss, the wily duo behind the operation, determined to pair up the most improbable of couples imaginable. But there's a twist - they're masquerading as a married couple themselves, adding a delightful layer of deception to their chaotic matchmaking antics.

The ensemble cast includes familiar faces like Sid James, Kenneth Williams, Charles Hawtrey, Joan Sims, Hattie Jacques, Terry Scott, and Bernard Bresslaw, alongside newcomers Richard O'Callaghan (in his debut Carry On role) and Imogen Hassall (in her sole appearance in the series). Departing from the subtle innuendos of earlier films, the dialogue here embraces a more direct, bawdy humour. The film amusingly features fictional locales with suggestive names such as 'Much-Snogging-On-The-Green', 'Rogerham Mansions', and 'Dunham Road'.

CAST:

Sid James as **Sidney Bliss**
Kenneth Williams as **Percival Snooper**
Charles Hawtrey as **James Bedsop**
Hattie Jacques as **Sophie Bliss**
Joan Sims as **Esme Crowfoot**
Bernard Bresslaw as **Gripper Burke**
Terry Scott as **Terry Philpott**
Jacki Piper as **Sally Martin**
Richard O'Callaghan as **Bertrum Muffet**
Imogen Hassall as **Jenny Grubb**
Patsy Rowlands as **Miss Dempsey**
Bill Pertwee as **Barman**
Julian Holloway as **Adrian**
Janet Mahoney as **Gay**
Joan Hickson as **Mrs Grubb**
Mike Grady and Valerie Shute as **The Lovers**
Patricia Franklin as **Mrs Dreery**
Bill Maynard as **Mr Dreery**
Peter Butterworth as **Sinister client**
Amelia Bayntun as **Corset lady**

Ann Way as **Victoria Grubb**
Anthony Sagar as **Hospital Patient**
Kenny Lynch as **Bus Conductor**

FACTS AND TRIVIA:

- Budget: £215,000
- Filming Dates 6th April – 15th May 1970

EXTERIORS:

- The streets of Windsor, Berkshire.
- The building at the corner of Park Street and Sheet Street doubled for the Wedded Bliss Agency (previously used for the Helping Hands Agency in "Carry On Regardless")

BOX OFFICE:

- Ranked as the fourth-most-popular film at the British box office in 1971.

RECEPTION:

- The Sunday Sun described it as "no worse or better than its many predecessors".
- The Daily Mail suggested, "All you have to do is sit back and have a good old snigger".
- The Evening Standard remarked, "by now it's all a mite bit mechanical".
- David Parkinson's retrospective review for Radio Times awarded the film 2 out of 5 stars, criticising its focus on other clients of the bureau rather than the proprietors and characters played by Joan Sims and Kenneth Williams.

PROFILES:

Imogen Hassall, born on the 25th of August 1942, was named after Shakespeare's Cymbeline heroine. She hailed from a financially prosperous family of artists and businessmen in

Woking, Surrey. Her grandfather, John Hassall, and aunt, Joan Hassall, were both renowned illustrators, while her father, Christopher Hassall, distinguished himself as a poet, dramatist, and lyricist. Imogen had a brother named Nicholas. It is said that her godfather was the composer Ivor Novello, with whom her father collaborated extensively. However, conflicting sources are suggesting that this distinction might have belonged to Sir William Walton, a claim disputed by Lady Walton.

Hassall's journey into the arts began at Elmhurst Ballet School in Camberley from 1952 to 1954, followed by the Royal Ballet School at White Lodge in Richmond Park from 1955 to 1958. At 16, she furthered her studies in New York City before returning to London to pursue acting. After attending the London Academy of Music and Dramatic Art from 1960 to 1962, she joined the Royal Shakespeare Company for a season.

Her career flourished with notable appearances in both theatre and television, including roles in renowned British TV series like "The Saint", "The Avengers", and "The Persuaders!". Hassall's film career blossomed with significant roles in productions such as "The Long Duel" (1967), "When Dinosaurs Ruled the Earth" (1970), and "Incense for the Damned". In 1973, she starred in "White Cargo" alongside David Jason.

Hassall married actor Kenneth Ives, with whom she had a daughter, Melanie Ives Hassall, who tragically passed away shortly after birth in 1972. She later married actor Andrew Knox, but their marriage was short-lived, and she suffered a miscarriage. Hassall's private life often attracted tabloid attention due to her provocative film roles and revealing attire at premieres, earning her the moniker "Countess of Cleavage".

Her role in "Carry On Loving" inspired playwright Terry Johnson to include her character in the play "Cleo, Camping, Emmanuelle and Dick", which premiered at the Royal National Theatre in 1998.

Gina Bellman portrayed Hassall, and the play received the Olivier Award for Best New Comedy in 1999. Johnson later adapted the play into a television film titled "Cor, Blimey!" in 2000, although Hassall's character was omitted from the TV version, which underwent significant changes from the original play.

Following personal struggles, including failed relationships, the loss of her child, and career setbacks, Hassall battled depression. On 16th November 1980, she was found deceased in her Wimbledon home, having reportedly taken an overdose of Tuinal tablets. She was scheduled to depart on holiday with actress Suzanna Leigh that day. Hassall was laid to rest in Gap Road Cemetery, Wimbledon, London.

CARRY ON HENRY (1971)

Henry VIII finds himself in a dilemma due to his wife, Marie de Normandy's, chronic garlic breath. While the scent repulses him, his faithful equerry, Sir Roger de Loggerley, is oddly captivated and begins a steamy affair with her. Meanwhile, the lustful king, eager for a new wife, colludes with his conniving advisors, Thomas Cromwell and Cardinal Wolsey, to remove Marie from the equation.

Carry On Henry revolves around a fictionalised narrative featuring Sid James as Henry VIII, who pursues Barbara Windsor's character, Bettina. Alongside James and Windsor, the film stars regulars Kenneth Williams, Charles Hawtrey, Joan Sims, Terry Scott, and Kenneth Connor. Notably, this marked the reunion of Williams and Connor since their appearance together in Carry On Cleo seven years prior.

Originally, the film was titled "Anne of a Thousand Lays," a playful nod to the Richard Burton movie "Anne of the Thousand Days." Sid James even dons the same cloak worn by Burton in that film. Initially, there were considerations for Harry Secombe to portray

Henry VIII due to doubts about Sid James' availability, as he was committed to a lengthy engagement in South Africa. However, James adjusted his schedule upon learning about the film's production and returned just in time for shooting.

The promotional tagline, "A Great Guy With His Chopper," cleverly plays on the slang term "chopper," which was becoming popular due to the rising trend of modified motorcycles. The film's opening theme features a rendition of "Greensleeves" arranged by Eric Rogers.

CAST:

Sid James as **King Henry VIII**
Kenneth Williams as **Thomas Cromwell**
Charles Hawtrey as **Sir Roger de Lodgerley**
Joan Sims as **Queen Marie of Normandy**
Terry Scott as **Cardinal Wolsey**
Barbara Windsor as **Bettina**
Kenneth Connor as **Lord Hampton of Wick**
Julian Holloway as **Sir Thomas**
Peter Gilmore as **Francis, King of France**
Julian Orchard as **Duc de Poncenay**
Gertan Klauber as **Bidet**
David Davenport as **Major-domo**
Peter Butterworth as **Charles, Earl of Bristol (uncredited)**
Margaret Nolan as **Buxom lass**
William Mervyn as **Physician**
Norman Chappell as **1st plotter**
Derek Francis as **Farmer**
Bill Maynard as **Fawkes**
Douglas Ridley as **2nd plotter**
Leon Greene as **Torturer**
David Prowse as **Torturer**
Monica Dietrich as **Catherine Howard**

Billy Cornelius as **Guard**
Marjie Lawrence as **Serving maid**
Patsy Rowlands as **Queen**
Alan Curtis as **Conte di Pisa**

FACTS AND TRIVIA:

- Budget: £214,500
- Filming Dates 12th October – 27th November 1970

EXTERIORS:

- Windsor Great Park, Berkshire
- The Long Walk, Windsor Castle, Berkshire
- Knebworth House, Hertfordshire
- Two comedic madrigals originally composed for the film but left unused were eventually showcased in the 1972 Carry On Christmas special and later performed in the 1973 stage production Carry On London.

PROFILES:

Bill Maynard, born Walter Frederick George Williams on 8th October 1928, originally from Farnham, Surrey, eventually made Sapcote, Leicestershire his home. He married Muriel Linnett in 1949, and together they had two children before her passing in 1983. Later in life, Maynard entered matrimony with actress and singer Tonia Bern, though they divorced in 1998.

Maynard ventured into television during the 1950s, notably featuring alongside Terry Scott in "Great Scott – It's Maynard!" (1955–56). Throughout the 1970s and 1980s, he graced the screen in popular British sitcoms such as "Oh No It's Selwyn Froggitt" and "The Gaffer". Maynard also made appearances in five films within the Carry On series:

- Carry On Loving (1970) as **Mr. Dreery**
- Carry On Henry (1971) as **Guy Fawkes**

- Carry On at Your Convenience (1971) as **Fred Moore**
- Carry On Matron (1972) as **Freddy**
- *Carry On Abroad (1972) as **Mr. Fiddler** (scene deleted)*
- Carry On Dick (1974) as **Bodkin**

Following a break from television in the late 1980s, he endeared himself to audiences as Claude Jeremiah Greengrass in the long-running series "Heartbeat" from 1992 to 2000, reprising the role in the spin-off "The Royal" in 2003.

In March 1984, Maynard ventured into politics, contesting against Tony Benn in the Chesterfield by-election as an Independent Labour candidate. Maynard battled health issues later in life, using a mobility scooter due to multiple strokes. He passed away in the hospital on 30th March 2018, following a fall and hip fracture.

CARRY ON AT YOUR CONVENIENCE (1971)

A laid-back union representative finds himself in a hilarious clash with the management of a toilet factory. To add to his woes, his daughter is romantically involved with the boss's son. However, his spirits soar when he uncovers an unexpected talent in his previously silent pet budgie - the ability to predict winning racehorses.

Carry On at Your Convenience stands out as the first box office disappointment in the franchise's history. Critics suggest that its departure into political themes, particularly its portrayal of union activists as inept and absurd, failed to resonate with the traditional working-class audience.

Internationally titled "Carry On Round the Bend," the film only recouped its production costs in 1976 through various sales, including international and television deals. The ensemble cast includes familiar faces such as Sid James, Kenneth Williams,

Charles Hawtrey, Joan Sims, Hattie Jacques, Bernard Bresslaw, and introduces Kenneth Cope in his inaugural Carry On role.

CAST:

Sid James as **Sid Plummer**
Kenneth Williams as **WC Boggs**
Charles Hawtrey as **Charles Coote**
Hattie Jacques as **Beattie Plummer**
Joan Sims as **Chloe Moore**
Bernard Bresslaw as **Bernie Hulke**
Kenneth Cope as **Vic Spanner**
Jacki Piper as **Myrtle Plummer**
Richard O'Callaghan as **Lewis Boggs**
Patsy Rowlands as **Hortense Withering**
Davy Kaye as **Benny**
Bill Maynard as **Fred Moore**
Renée Houston as **Agatha Spanner**
Marianne Stone as **Maud**
Margaret Nolan as **Popsy**
Geoffrey Hughes as **Willie**
Hugh Futcher as **Ernie**
Simon Cain as **Barman**
Amelia Bayntun as **Mrs Spragg**
Leon Greene as **Chef**
Harry Towb as **Film Doctor**
Shirley Stelfox as **Bunny Waitress**
Larry Martyn as **Rifle Range Owner**
Peter Burton as **Hotel Manager**
Julian Holloway as **Roger**

FACTS AND TRIVIA:

- Budget: £218,805
- Filming Dates 22nd March – 7th May 1971

EXTERIORS:

- Brighton Palace Pier. The West Pier in Brighton was used two years later for Carry On Girls.
- Brighton – Clarges Hotel. The same location was also used in Carry On Girls.
- Pinewood Studios. The studio's wood storage area was used as the exterior of W.C. Boggs' factory.
- Pinewood Green, Pinewood Estate. The Plummers' house and the Moores' house.
- The Red Lion, Shreding Green, Buckinghamshire
- Kings Head, Albourne, West Sussex
- Cricketers Inn
- Royal Naval Arms
- The Seagull
- The Trout Inn
- The Man In Space
- Odeon Cinema, Uxbridge, Middlesex (demolished in September 1984)
- Heatherden Hall, Pinewood Studios
- Black Park Country Park, Iver Heath, Buckinghamshire

Following criticism of Sid James's character for his lecherous behaviour towards girls in "Carry On Henry" (1971), his role underwent a transformation to embody a beleaguered family man, reminiscent of his character in the television sitcom "Bless This House." In the subsequent film, "Carry On Matron" (1972), his character was depicted as being preoccupied with thievery while still making peculiar suggestive remarks to nurses, including one portrayed by Jacki Piper, who coincidentally played his daughter in the preceding film. However, James's woman-chasing persona returned in full force for the following instalments in the series.

PROFILES:

Margaret Ann Nolan was born on 29th October 1943 in Hampstead, London; Nolan's early life saw her parents relocate to County Waterford in Ireland during World War II, before returning to London post-war. Initially training as a teacher, Nolan's path veered towards acting after being encouraged by her then-boyfriend, actor Tom Kempinski.

Nolan's career commenced in modelling under the alias Vicky Kennedy, swiftly transitioning to acting under her birth name. She showcased her talent across various mediums, from television to theatre to film. Notable highlights included her portrayal of Dink in the James Bond classic "Goldfinger," where she famously adorned a gold bikini; her Carry On contributions include:

- Carry On Cowboy (1965) as **Miss Jones**
- Carry On Henry (1971) as **Buxom Lass**
- Carry On at Your Convenience (1971) as **Popsy**
- Carry On Matron (1972) as **Mrs Tucker**
- Carry On Girls (1973) as **Dawn Brakes**
- Carry On Dick (1974) as **Lady Daley**

Nolan's versatility extended to serious theatre, where she often engaged with political themes. Her contributions to comedy were honoured in 2011 when her name was featured on Gordon Young's Comedy Carpet installation, situated in front of Blackpool Tower. Additionally, after nearly three decades away from the screen, Nolan made a triumphant return in 2011. She took on a role tailor-made for her by Ann Cameron in Yvonne Deutschman's "The Power of Three."

In 2019, Margaret Nolan was selected by Edgar Wright for a role in his 2021 film "Last Night in Soho." This marked Nolan's last appearance.

In her personal life, Nolan shared a marriage with playwright Tom Kempinski, and together they welcomed two sons. Bravely confronting her battle with cancer, she peacefully passed away on 5th October 2020 at the age of 76 at her residence in Belsize Park, London, England.

CARRY ON MATRON (1972)

A mischievous gang devises a zany plan to swipe a large stockpile of birth-control pills from a maternity hospital. Their scheme takes an unexpected twist when one of the gang members disguises themselves as a nurse to infiltrate the hospital, only to become the target of a doctor's passionate advances.

Carry On Matron showcases a stellar cast, including stalwarts such as Sid James, Kenneth Williams, Charles Hawtrey, Joan Sims, Hattie Jacques, Bernard Bresslaw, Barbara Windsor, and Kenneth Connor. Notably, this marked Terry Scott's farewell to the Carry On franchise after his appearance in seven films, while it was also Kenneth Cope's final outing in the series.

Distinguished by its ensemble of regulars, "Carry On Matron" and its successor, "Carry On Abroad," boast the highest number of core Carry On team members. Notably absent are Jim Dale and Peter Butterworth. However, Dale would make a belated return for "Carry On Columbus" in 1992, while Butterworth reclaimed a prominent role in "Abroad" the subsequent year. Butterworth's intended portrayal of Freddy was relinquished due to prior commitments.

CAST:

Sid James as **Sid Carter**
Kenneth Williams as **Sir Bernard Cutting**
Charles Hawtrey as **Doctor Francis A Goode**
Hattie Jacques as **Matron**

Joan Sims as **Mrs Tidey**
Bernard Bresslaw as **Ernie Bragg**
Barbara Windsor as **Nurse Susan Ball**
Kenneth Connor as **Mr Tidey**
Terry Scott as **Doctor Prodd**
Kenneth Cope as **Cyril Carter**
Jacki Piper as **Sister**
Bill Maynard as **Freddy**
Patsy Rowlands as **Evelyn Banks**
Derek Francis as **Arthur**
Amelia Bayntun as **Mrs Jenkins**
Valerie Leon as **Jane Darling**
Brian Osborne as **Ambulance driver**
Gwendolyn Watts as **Frances Kemp**
Valerie Shute as **Miss Smethurst**
Margaret Nolan as **Mrs Tucker**
Michael Nightingale as **Doctor Pearson**
Wendy Richard as **Miss Willing**
Zena Clifton as **Au pair girl**

FACTS AND TRIVIA:

- Budget: £220,257
- Filming Dates 11th October – 26th November 1971

Exteriors:
- Heatherwood Hospital, Ascot, Berkshire
- The White House, Denham, Buckinghamshire
- St Mary's Church, Denham, Buckinghamshire

PROFILES:

Kenneth Charles Cope was born on 14th April 1931 in Liverpool (at the time Lancashire, now Merseyside), England. Cope began his journey in the entertainment industry by portraying character roles in films from the mid-1950s.

Between 1961 and 1966, Cope gained prominence for his portrayal of the shady Jed Stone in "Coronation Street", a role he reprised in 2008. His stint on the show led to the recording of a novelty pop single, "Hands Off, Stop Mucking About", with Tony Hatch. Although not a commercial success, it earned him a regular slot as a disc jockey on Radio Luxembourg.

Cope's career spanned across various mediums. He appeared in the satirical series "That Was the Week That Was" and released a single titled "Hands Off, Stop Mucking About". His film credits include roles in "Genghis Khan" (1965) and "Dateline Diamonds" (1965). Cope also featured in television series such as "The Avengers" and "The Adventures of Black Beauty". He gained prominence as Marty Hopkirk in "Randall and Hopkirk (Deceased)" (1969–1970).

In addition to his acting prowess, Cope took on leading roles in two Carry On films: **"Carry On at Your Convenience"** (1971) and **"Carry On Matron"** (1972).

Cope's career continued with appearances in "Minder", "Doctor Who", "Casualty", "Juliet Bravo", "The Bill", "Waking the Dead", "A Touch of Frost", and "Kavanagh QC". In 1984, Cope starred in "Bootle Saddles", a sitcom centred around a failing themed 'cowboy village'. Despite its unique premise, the series was cancelled after one season.

His later work includes roles in "Out of the Blue" (1995), "A Touch of Frost" (1997), and Channel 4's soap opera "Brookside" (1999–2002). Cope's Coronation Street character, Jed Stone, made a comeback to the show in 2008 after a 42-year absence, marking Cope's final acting role.

Cope married actress Renny Lister in 1961, whom he met during her time on "Coronation Street". They had two sons, Nick and Mark, who formed the rock band The Candyskins, and a daughter,

Martha, who followed in her parents' footsteps as an actress. In 1997, Lister retired from acting.

In 1974, Cope and his wife opened a restaurant named Martha's Kitchen in Watlington, Oxfordshire, after their daughter. In 2000, Cope was diagnosed with mesothelioma, later discovered to be a misdiagnosis, but he now battles chronic obstructive pulmonary disease.

CARRY ON ABROAD (1972)

The beloved cast of 'Carry On' sets off on a package holiday to the sunny Spanish resort of Elsbels. However, upon arrival, they discover that the Palace Hotel, where they're supposed to stay, is far from regal. In fact, it's still under construction, leaving the holidaymakers in a state of hilarity and chaos.

The ensemble cast includes familiar faces such as Sid James, Kenneth Williams, Joan Sims, Bernard Bresslaw, Barbara Windsor, Kenneth Connor, Peter Butterworth, and Hattie Jacques. Notably, it marks the final appearance of Charles Hawtrey, while June Whitfield makes a return after her last Carry On appearance in Carry On Nurse, 13 years prior. Additionally, Jimmy Logan and Carol Hawkins make their debut in the series.

This film, alongside its predecessor Carry On Matron, boasts the highest number of regular Carry On team members. Terry Scott was also part of the cast, though his scene as an irate Wundatours customer was ultimately cut from the final edit. Jim Dale, absent from this film, had departed from the series by this point but would later return for Carry On Columbus in 1992. Interestingly, Dale and Scott never shared the screen in a Carry On film together.

CAST:

Sid James as **Vic Flange**

Kenneth Williams as **Stuart Farquhar**
Charles Hawtrey as **Eustace Tuttle**
Joan Sims as **Cora Flange**
Peter Butterworth as **Pepe**
Kenneth Connor as **Stanley Blunt**
June Whitfield as **Evelyn Blunt**
Bernard Bresslaw as **Brother Bernard**
Barbara Windsor as **Sadie Tomkins**
Gail Grainger as **Moira Plunkett**
Jimmy Logan as **Bert Conway**
Sally Geeson as **Lily Maggs**
Carol Hawkins as **Marge Dawes**
Derek Francis as **Brother Martin**
Ray Brooks as **Georgio**
John Clive as **Robin Tweet**
David Kernan as **Nicholas Phipps**
Hattie Jacques as **Floella**
Patsy Rowlands as **Miss Dobbs**
Jack Douglas as **Harry**
Amelia Bayntun as **Mrs Tuttle**
Olga Lowe as **Madame Fifi**

FACTS AND TRIVIA:

- Budget: £225,000
- Filming Dates 17th April – 26th May 1972

LOCATIONS:

- Bagshot, Surrey: The setting for the road leading to the airport scenes in the film.
- High Street, Slough: Location of the Wundatours travel agency shop, later redeveloped into Cornwall House.
- Pinewood Studios: Served as the backdrop for various key scenes, including the Elsbels airport terminal building, the

Whippit Inn pub, and both interior and exterior shots of the Elsbels hotel.
- Fun fact: The hotel was actually constructed on the studio backlot, with a matte added to depict upper floors and sections of scaffold.
- In the opening credits, 'Sun Tan Lo Tion' hilariously appears as the 'Technical Director' of the film.
- Olga Lowe, portraying the brothel keeper, shares a historical connection with Sid James, having been one of the first actresses he collaborated with upon his arrival in the UK in 1946. Interestingly, Lowe was also on stage with James on the tragic night he passed away in Sunderland.

PROFILES:

June Rosemary Whitfield was born in Streatham, London on 11th November 1925, to John Herbert Whitfield and Bertha Georgina née Flett. Her parents, both amateur actors, fostered her love for performance from an early age. Despite the disruptions of World War II, Whitfield pursued her passion, eventually graduating from the Royal Academy of Dramatic Art in 1944.

Whitfield's career blossomed in the 1940s, with notable stage and radio work alongside personalities like Wilfred Pickles. Her transition to television in the 1950s marked the beginning of her iconic presence in British entertainment. Memorable roles in "The Glums" segment of "Take It from Here" showcased her comedic prowess.

Her breakthrough came with a leading role in the radio comedy "Take It from Here" on the BBC Light Programme in 1953. This paved the way for numerous television roles, including collaborations with Tony Hancock. Whitfield's versatility shone in various genres, from sitcoms like "Beggar My Neighbour" (1966) to appearances in the renowned "Carry On" film series:

- Carry On Nurse (1959) as **Meg**
- Carry On Abroad (1972) as **Evelyn Blunt**
- Carry On Girls (1973) as **Augusta Prodworthy / Paula Perkins (voice)**
- Carry On Columbus (1992) as **Queen Isabella**

Married to Timothy John Aitchison in 1955, Whitfield balanced her career with family life, raising a daughter, Suzy Aitchison, who followed in her footsteps. Despite her immense talent, Whitfield remained humble, attributing her success to love, laughter, and a touch of luck.

In 1968, she formed a successful television partnership with Terry Scott, starring in "Happy Ever After" (1974–1979) and "Terry and June" (1979–1987). Notably, from 1992 to 2012, she portrayed Edina Monsoon's mother in Jennifer Saunders' "Absolutely Fabulous". Whitfield also left her mark on radio, notably as Miss Marple in dramatisations of Agatha Christie's novels. Her contributions to comedy were recognised with awards and honours, including a DBE in 2017.

In December 2017, Whitfield revealed that she had moved into a care home. She passed away in London on 29th December 2018 at the age of 93. Her funeral took place at All Hallows Church in Tillington, near Petworth in West Sussex, on 18th January 2019. The service was attended by many of her co-stars and close friends.

Jennifer Saunders, her co-star from Absolutely Fabulous, praised Whitfield's "extraordinary grace" and expressed how much she would miss her dear friend. Julia Sawalha hailed her as a "great source of inspiration", while Jane Horrocks fondly remembered her as a "wonderful lady", noting her versatility, humour, and generosity.

CARRY ON GIRLS (1973)

A shrewd local entrepreneur pitches an extravagant proposal to the town council of a quaint seaside town: hosting a beauty pageant. He cunningly convinces them that it will attract unparalleled publicity. However, his grand plan faces fierce resistance from the formidable leader of the local Women's Liberation group, a formidable female councillor.

Carry On Girls stars familiar faces such as Sid James, Barbara Windsor, Joan Sims, Kenneth Connor, Bernard Bresslaw, and Peter Butterworth. Notably, neither Kenneth Williams nor Charles Hawtrey appear in this entry, with Williams occupied by stage commitments and Hawtrey omitted from the series.

Patsy Rowlands returns for the seventh time in the series, with Robin Askwith making his only appearance. Jack Douglas assumes a significant role in his third performance, while Valerie Leon completes her involvement after starring in six Carry On films. Jimmy Logan also makes his second and final appearance in the series, having first appeared as Bert Conway in **Carry on Aboard.**

The film presented a somewhat bolder approach, featuring increased nudity and openly sexual humour compared to its predecessors. Modifications made by the BBFC (primarily to suggestive dialogue and the hotel altercation scene involving contestants clad in bikinis portrayed by Barbara Windsor and Margaret Nolan) allowed the film to secure the commercially preferable A certificate (suitable for families) rather than the more restrictive AA certificate, which prohibited entry for those under fourteen.

In an earlier version of the script, Kenneth Williams was initially slated to portray Mayor Bumble, a role eventually taken on by Kenneth Connor in the final production. Williams, engaged in a

West End production of "My Fat Friend," was unavailable. The character of Cecil Gaybody was originally intended for Charles Hawtrey, but due to his unreliability, he was replaced. The part was then offered to Kenneth Williams, who declined due to prior stage commitments. Valerie Leon's character's voice in the film was dubbed by co-star June Whitfield.

Clarges Hotel, a setting in the film, later came under the ownership of actress Dora Bryan, known for her appearance in the first Carry On film, Carry On Sergeant. The hotel had previously featured (externally only) in the 1971 movie Carry On at Your Convenience.

CAST:

Sid James as **Sidney Fiddler**
Barbara Windsor as **Hope Springs (real name Muriel Bloggs)**
Joan Sims as **Connie Philpotts**
Kenneth Connor as **Mayor Frederick Bumble**
Bernard Bresslaw as **Peter Potter**
Peter Butterworth as **Admiral**
June Whitfield as **Augusta Prodworthy**
Jack Douglas as **William**
Patsy Rowlands as **Mildred Bumble**
Patricia Franklin as **Rosemary**
Valerie Leon as **Paula Perkins**
Robin Askwith as **Larry**
Margaret Nolan as **Dawn Brakes**
Angela Grant as **Miss Bangor**
Joan Hickson as **Mrs Dukes**
Sally Geeson as **Debra**
Jimmy Logan as **Cecil Gaybody**
Wendy Richard as **Ida Downes**
David Lodge as **Police Inspector**
Arnold Ridley as **Alderman Pratt**

Bill Pertwee as **Fire chief**
Marianne Stone as **Miss Drew**
Brenda Cowling as **Matron**
Zena Clifton as **Susan Brooks**

FACTS AND TRIVIA:

- Budget: £205,962
- Filming Dates 16th April – 25th May 1973

EXTERIORS:

- Brighton's West Pier. (The Palace Pier had been used a couple of years earlier in Carry On at Your Convenience)
- Slough Town Hall, Slough, Berkshire
- Clarges Hotel, Brighton
- Brighton Beach, Brighton
- Marylebone Railway Station, London

PROFILES:

Valerie Therese Leon was born on 12th November 1943 in Hampstead, London to Henry and Daphne Leon (née Ehrmann); she is the eldest of four children. Her father directed a textile company, while her mother, who trained at RADA, gave up her acting career to focus on motherhood. After attending the Channing School for Girls, she pursued a career as an au pair in Paris before returning to England.

Leon initially worked as a trainee fashion buyer at Harrods before transitioning into acting. She began her acting career as a chorus girl in a touring production of "The Belle of New York". Leon gained substantial publicity through her appearance in Hai Karate television adverts during the 1970s, earning global recognition as a sex symbol due to her glamorous looks and attractive figure, often being likened to the "English Raquel Welch".

She notably appeared in two James Bond films, "The Spy Who Loved Me" (1977) and "Never Say Never Again" (1983), alongside Roger Moore and Sean Connery, respectively. Her career also includes roles in prominent films such as "The Italian Job" (1969), "The Wild Geese" (1978), "Revenge of the Pink Panther" (1978), and a leading role in the Hammer horror film "Blood from the Mummy's Tomb" (1971).

Leon's Carry On appearances include:

- Carry On Up the Khyber (1968) as **Hospitality Girl**
- Carry On Camping (1969) as **Miss Dobbin**
- Carry On Again Doctor (1969) as **Deirdre**
- Carry On Up the Jungle (1970) as **Leda**
- Carry On Matron (1972) as **Jane Darling**
- Carry On Girls (1973) as **Paula Perkins**

Robin Mark Askwith, born on the 12th of October 1950, encountered adversity in his early life in Southport, Lancashire, notably contracting polio as a child and undergoing a lengthy recovery period. Despite this, his passion for acting flourished, influenced by experiences like watching film productions at Pinewood Studios and engaging in amateur dramatics.

His cinematic journey commenced after catching the eye of director Lindsay Anderson, leading to his breakout role as Keating in the renowned film if.... (1968), a role he later revisited in Britannia Hospital (1982). Following this success, Askwith balanced television appearances with notable film roles, including Otley (1969), Alfred the Great (1969), Scramble (1970), Nicholas and Alexandra (1971), and The Canterbury Tales (1972), Tower of Evil (1972), The Flesh and Blood Show (1972), and Horror Hospital (1973). He also showcased his comedic talent in films like Bless This House (1972) and No Sex Please, We're British

(1973), but it was his portrayal of Timothy Lea in the Confessions film series that truly propelled him to stardom.

On the small screen, Askwith has left his mark with memorable roles such as Fred Pickering in Beryl's Lot (1973–1975), Dave Deacon in Bottle Boys (1984–1985), and Ritchie de Vries in Coronation Street (2013–2014).

In 1975, Askwith earned acclaim at Drury Lane's New London Theatre, winning "Most Promising Newcomer – Male" at the Evening Standard British Film Awards. His recent television ventures include appearances in Emmerdale, Benidorm and a prominent role in The Madame Blanc Mysteries.

Beyond acting, Askwith is an accomplished stage performer, showcasing his talents in productions ranging from farces to pantomimes. His personal life has seen its share of ups and downs, including marriages and relocations, with Askwith now residing in Gozo, near Malta.

CARRY ON DICK (1974)

In this rollicking comedy, the infamous highwayman Dick Turpin adopts the guise of Reverend Flasher to evade capture. With his motley crew, he sets out to hilariously wreak havoc across the countryside, leaving a trail of laughter in their wake.

Carry On Dick marked a poignant moment for the series, serving as the final curtain call for some beloved Carry On stalwarts. Sid James, who graced the screen in nineteen previous films, gave his last memorable performance before his untimely passing from a heart attack two years later. Similarly, Hattie Jacques, with fourteen appearances, and Barbara Windsor, with nine, bid adieu to the film series, though all three would later feature in the Carry On Laughing TV spin-off. Windsor even co-hosted a film retrospective, That's Carry On!

Sam Kelly made his debut in the Carry On universe with this film, while Margaret Nolan and Bill Maynard concluded their runs, having appeared in six and five films, respectively. Notably, Carry On Dick also marked the 20th and final script penned by the series' long-time writer, Talbot Rothwell.

The ensemble cast, including Kenneth Williams, Bernard Bresslaw, Joan Sims, Kenneth Connor, Peter Butterworth, and Jack Douglas, delivered their trademark comedic performances, adding to the film's enduring charm.

CAST:

Sid James as **The Reverend Flasher/Dick Turpin**
Kenneth Williams as **Captain Desmond Fancey**
Barbara Windsor as **Harriett**
Hattie Jacques as **Martha Hoggett**
Bernard Bresslaw as **Sir Roger Daley**
Joan Sims as **Madame Desiree**
Peter Butterworth as **Tom**
Kenneth Connor as **Constable**
Jack Douglas as **Sergeant Jock Strapp**
Marianne Stone as **Maggie**
Patsy Rowlands as **Mrs Giles**
Bill Maynard as **Bodkin**
Margaret Nolan as **Lady Daley**
John Clive as **Isaak**
David Lodge as **Bullock**
Patrick Durkin as **William**
Sam Kelly as **Sir Roger's coachman**
George Moon as **Mr Giles**
Michael Nightingale as **Squire Trelawney**
Brian Osborne as **Browning**
Anthony Bailey as **Rider**
Billy Cornelius as **Tough man**

FACTS AND TRIVIA:

- Budget: £212,948
- Filming Dates 4th March – 11th April 1974

EXTERIORS:

- Countryside/Woodland - Black Park, Iver Heath, Buckinghamshire
- The Jolly Woodman Pub, Iver Heath, Buckinghamshire
- Stoke Poges Manor, Stoke Poges, Buckinghamshire
- St Mary's Church, Burnham, Buckinghamshire

PROFILE:

John Douglas Roberton, known professionally as Jack Douglas or Jack D. Douglas, was born on 26th April 1927 in Newcastle upon Tyne. He hailed from a theatrical family, with his father being a theatre producer and his brother, Bill Roberton, becoming a theatre director. Despite the family's London settlement, Douglas's mother was insistent on him being a Geordie and even travelled to Newcastle for his and his brother's births. Douglas spent his early years on a farm in Meriden before the family moved to Blackpool to escape the bombings during the Second World War.

Despite a desire to work in theatre, Douglas left home at the age of 14 to pursue his passion. Initially hired as an "Opposite Prompt Lime Boy" at Feldman's Theatre, he persevered through challenging tasks assigned by his father, eventually directing a Cinderella pantomime at the Empire Theatre in Sunderland. Douglas, along with Joe Baker, embarked on a successful ten-year global tour, performing in Australia, New Zealand, and South Africa. They then entered the realm of television with the popular children's TV show Crackerjack, followed by stints at the Windmill Theatre and the Glasgow Empire.

After Baker left for America, Douglas, longing to be a comedian, was initially discouraged by his agent, Leslie Grade. He then left show business, opened a restaurant in Blackpool, and, unexpectedly, returned to performing when approached by Des O'Connor. Douglas's character "Alf Ippititimus" was born during an improvised performance, leading to several years of collaboration with Des O'Connor. He gained recognition in the United States through appearances on NBC's Kraft Music Hall variety series.

Douglas's agent secured him a part in Carry On Matron, marking the beginning of his association with the iconic series. Despite not receiving payment, he accepted the role and received a luxurious gift of Dom Pérignon champagne. He appeared in the last seven Carry On films, progressing from cameo roles to leading roles, including Carry On Emmannuelle and the revival film Carry On Columbus (1992).

Following the Carry On films, Douglas participated in the stage show Carry On London at the Victoria Palace Theatre. He released a novelty record titled "Don't Forget The Beer, Dear" in 1978 and made guest appearances in various shows like The Goodies and The Shillingbury Blowers.

In December 2001, Douglas shared his life experiences on the BBC radio show That Reminds Me. He celebrated his 80th birthday on 26th April 2007, and after a period of ill health, he succumbed to pneumonia on the Isle of Wight on 18th December 2008 at the age of 81.

Title	Year	Jack Douglas
Matron	1972	"Twitching Father"
Abroad	1972	Harry
Girls	1973	William
Dick	1974	Sgt. Jock Strapp
Behind	1975	Ernie Bragg

England	1976	Bombardier Ready
That's Carry On!	1977	-
Emmannuelle	1978	Lyons
Columbus	1992	Marco the Cereal Killer

CARRY ON BEHIND (1975)

Elke Sommer plays a dazzling Russian belle who finds herself teaming up with Kenneth Williams, a quirky British archaeology professor. The unlikely duo joined forces on a Roman excavation over the festive holiday period. Expect plenty of mishaps, cultural clashes, and laugh-out-loud moments as they navigate ancient ruins and modern misunderstandings.

Unlike its predecessors, Carry On Behind was not penned by Talbot Rothwell, marking the first deviation from his writing since Carry On Cruising 13 years earlier. The film features the familiar faces of Kenneth Williams, Kenneth Connor, Jack Douglas, Joan Sims, Peter Butterworth, Bernard Bresslaw, and Patsy Rowlands.

Carry On Behind marked a final appearance for many actors:

- Bernard Bresslaw (marking his fourteenth film)
- Liz Fraser (fourth appearance after a twelve-year hiatus)
- Patsy Rowlands (ninth Carry On contribution)
- Carol Hawkins (second appearance after Carry On Abroad)

By this stage, Sid James, Terry Scott, Hattie Jacques, and Charles Hawtrey had already concluded their roles in the Carry On films.

In supporting roles, the film includes Sherrie Hewson, Ian Lavender, Adrienne Posta, George Layton, Larry Dann, Larry Martyn, and David Lodge. While these actors were largely known for their comedy work at the time, they were not long-standing members of the Carry On troupe. Carry On Behind also served as the debut for Windsor Davies, who would later appear in Carry On England.

CAST:

Elke Sommer as **Professor Anna Vooshka**
Kenneth Williams as **Professor Roland Crump**
Bernard Bresslaw as **Arthur Upmore**
Kenneth Connor as **Major Leap**
Jack Douglas as **Ernie Bragg**
Joan Sims as **Daphne Barnes**
Windsor Davies as **Fred Ramsden**
Peter Butterworth as **Henry Barnes**
Liz Fraser as **Sylvia Ramsden**
Patsy Rowlands as **Linda Upmore**
Ian Lavender as **Joe Baxter**
Adrienne Posta as **Norma Baxter**
Patricia Franklin as **Vera Bragg**
Donald Hewlett as **The Dean**
Carol Hawkins as **Sandra**
Sherrie Hewson as **Carol**
David Lodge as **Landlord**
Marianne Stone as **Mrs Elsie Rowan**
George Layton as **Doctor**
Brian Osborne as **Bob**
Larry Dann as **Clive**
Georgina Moon as **Sally**
Diana Darvey as **Maureen**

FACTS AND TRIVIA:

- Budget: £217,000
- Filming Dates 10th March – 18th April 1975
- Sims portrayed the mother of Rowlands on screen despite being only eight months older than her co-star.

EXTERIORS:

- Pinewood Studios: the Orchard doubled for the caravan site, as it had for the campsite in Carry On Camping.
- Maidenhead, Berkshire: the town hall doubled for the university seen at the start of the film. It had previously been used for the hospital exteriors in Carry On Doctor and Carry On Again Doctor.
- Farnham Common, Buckinghamshire

The chilly spring conditions during filming resulted in the clear visibility of bare trees, muddy fields, and actors' icy breath, despite the film portraying a summer caravanning holiday. This mirrors a similar challenge faced by the cast and crew during the filming of Carry On Camping. The signage in Fred Ramsden's butcher's shop indicates the closure for the Easter holidays, which can occur as early as March.

During the production of Carry On Behind, Bernard Bresslaw and Joan Sims were also involved in filming One of Our Dinosaurs Is Missing at Pinewood Studios.

In 2023, actor Larry Dann devoted a chapter in his autobiography, "Oh, What A Lovely Memoir," to recount his experiences during the making of Carry On Behind.

PROFILES:

Elke Sommer, born Elke Schletz on 5th November 1940 in Berlin to Baron Peter von Schletz, a Lutheran minister, and Renata von Schletz (née Topp), Elke's family was evacuated to Niederndorf, near Erlangen, during World War II. She attended a gymnasium from 1950 but left in 1957 after her father's passing. In the same year, she moved to London to work as an au pair and study English.

During a holiday in Italy, Sommer was discovered by film director Vittorio De Sica, leading to her film debut in 1958. That year, she also changed her surname to Sommer. She gained fame as a sex symbol and moved to Hollywood in the early 1960s. Sommer's popularity soared, and she appeared in publications like Playboy and became a sought-after pin-up.

Sommer established herself as a leading actress with roles in films such as The Prize (1963), A Shot in the Dark (1964), and The Art of Love (1965). She won a Golden Globe for Most Promising Newcomer Actress in 1964 for her role in The Prize.

Sommer was a frequent guest on television shows like The Dean Martin Show and The Tonight Show Starring Johnny Carson. She also participated in Bob Hope specials and was a panellist on Hollywood Squares from 1973 to 1980.

During the 1970s, Sommer starred in films like Zeppelin (1971), Ten Little Indians (1974), and House of Exorcism (1975). She became the Carry On films' joint highest-paid performer, at £30,000; this was an honour that she shared with Phil Silvers (who starred in Carry On Follow That Camel).

In the 1980s, Sommer hosted a programme called The Exciting World of Speed and Beauty. Later, she shifted her focus to painting and art, drawing inspiration from her travels and knowledge of languages. Sommer had a longstanding feud with Zsa Zsa Gabor, resulting in a multimillion-dollar libel suit in 1993. She received a Golden Palm Star on the Palm Springs Walk of Stars in 2001.

She was first married to Hollywood columnist Joe Hyams from 1964 to 1981. In 1993, she married Wolf Walther, the managing director of Essex House in New York City. They met while Sommer was performing in Tamara on Broadway. As of May 2017, Sommer resides in Los Angeles, California.

CARRY ON ENGLAND (1976)

In a hilarious twist, the crew of an anti-aircraft battery are far more engrossed in romantic entanglements than in battling the enemy. Enter Captain S Melly, a well-meaning but clumsy officer tasked with bringing order to the chaos. His mission? To quash the flirtatious banter and put a stop to their whimsical notion of "making love, not war".

The film featured only a handful of familiar faces from the Carry On ensemble. While Kenneth Connor took on a leading role, Joan Sims and Peter Butterworth, both long-time regulars, had minor supporting parts.

Windsor Davies, who had a prominent role in the previous film Carry On Behind, returns in a significant capacity, essentially reprising his Sergeant-Major character from the BBC sitcom "It Ain't Half Hot Mum". He is joined by Melvyn Hayes as his contrasting, effeminate counterpart. Judy Geeson and Patrick Mower, established actors new to the Carry On series, also play major roles.

The Brigadier's character was initially penned for series regular Kenneth Williams, and Private Easy's role was intended for Barbara Windsor. However, Williams was engaged in the stage play "Signed and Sealed", while Windsor was committed to "The Mike Reid Show".

Sid James, another series regular, was absent from the film due to his involvement in the stage play "The Mating Season". Tragically, on the play's opening night at Sunderland Empire Theatre on 26th April 1976, James suffered a fatal heart attack on stage at the age of 62.

In 2023, actor Larry Dann devoted a chapter in his autobiography "Oh, What A Lovely Memoir" to recount his experiences during the film's production.

Initially certified as AA by the British Board of Film Censors, which would have limited audiences to those aged fourteen and over, the film was later re-rated to an unrestricted A certificate. This change involved toning down scenes of topless nudity and removing a comedic reference to the word "fokker". Despite these adjustments, the film flopped commercially and was pulled from some cinemas after just three days.

The following actors make their second and final appearance in the Carry On series:

- Windsor Davies (Behind)
- Diane Langton (Teacher – although she also appeared in Carry On Laughing)
- Peter Jones (Doctor)
- Patricia Franklin makes her fifth and last appearance (Camping, Loving, Girls and Behind)
- Julian Holloway makes his eighth and final outing (Doctor, Up the Khyber, Camping, Loving, Henry and At your Convenience)

CAST:

Kenneth Connor as **Captain S Melly**
Windsor Davies as **Sergeant Major "Tiger" Bloomer**
Patrick Mower as **Sergeant Len Able**
Judy Geeson as **Sergeant Tilly Willing**
Jack Douglas as **Bombardier Ready**
Peter Jones as **Brigadier**
Diane Langton as **Private Alice Easy**
Melvyn Hayes as **Gunner Shorthouse**
Peter Butterworth as **Major Carstairs**
Joan Sims as **Private Jennifer Ffoukes-Sharpe**
Julian Holloway as **Major Butcher**
David Lodge as **Captain Bull**
Larry Dann as **Gunner Shaw**

Brian Osborne as **Gunner Owen**
Johnny Briggs as **Melly's driver**
Patricia Franklin as **Corporal Cook**
Linda Hooks as **Nurse**
John Carlin as **Officer**
Vivienne Johnson as **Freda**
Michael Nightingale as **Officer**

FACTS AND TRIVIA:

- Budget: £250,000
- Filming Dates 3rd May – 4th June 1976

EXTERIORS:

- Pinewood Studios. The orchard was utilised once again as it was for the camping and caravan sites in Carry On Camping and Carry On Behind.
- Black Park, Iver Heath, Buckinghamshire

PROFILES:

Windsor Davies was born on 28th August 1930 in Canning Town, East London. He attended Ogmore Grammar School and initially worked as a coal miner before serving with the East Surrey Regiment in Libya and Egypt from 1950 to 1952 during his National Service. After his military service, Davies undertook teacher training at Bangor Teacher Training College. Subsequently, he taught English and Maths in Leek, Staffordshire, followed by a position in Elephant and Castle, south London.

An active participant in amateur dramatics, Davies honed his acting skills at Bromley Little Theatre and completed a drama course with a Kew theatre company. He transitioned to professional acting at 31, joining the Cheltenham repertory theatre in 1961.

Davies' most iconic role was as Battery Sergeant Major Williams in "It Ain't Half Hot Mum". His character was inspired by real-life sergeant-majors he encountered during his National Service. Known for his booming catchphrases like "Shut Up!!" and "Oh dear, how sad, never mind", Davies' performance was hailed by many, including Spike Milligan, who considered it the funniest comic performance he had ever seen.

His television credits also include roles in "The Onedin Line", "Special Branch", "Callan", and "Never the Twain". In the realm of science fiction, he appeared in "Doctor Who" and voiced Sergeant Major Zero in "Terrahawks". He was also featured in "This Is Your Life" in 1976 and played George Vance in the BBC Two comedy series "The New Statesman" in 1985.

On the big screen, Davies portrayed Mog in "Grand Slam" (1978). He reprised his role as Sergeant Major Williams in the Royal Air Force training film "Hazardous Ops" in 1989.

In 1992-1993, Davies appeared as Baron Hardup in the pantomime "Cinderella" in Bournemouth.

Davies lent his distinctive voice to commercials for Pink Batts, Cadbury's Wispa, and Heinz Curried (Baked) Beans. He also narrated BBC Radio 4's "Morning Story", the audiobook for "Treasure Island", and voiced characters in Paul McCartney's "Rupert and the Frog Song".

In 1957, Davies married Eluned Lynne Evans, with whom he had four daughters and a son. Eluned passed away in September 2018. A resident of the south of France and an avid birdwatcher and amateur organist, Davies passed away on 17th January 2019 at the age of 88, just four months after his wife.

THAT'S CARRY ON! (1977)

Kenneth Williams and Barbara Windsor, two iconic figures from the "Carry On" series, present a delightful compilation showcasing some of the most memorable scenes from the extensive collection of "Carry On" films. Their witty banter and vibrant personalities add a touch of charm and nostalgia to the presentation, making it a treat for both long-time fans and newcomers alike.

As they guide viewers through the clips, Kenneth's sharp wit and Barbara's infectious energy bring each scene to life, highlighting the unique blend of humour, innuendo, and British eccentricity that the "Carry On" films are renowned for; the compilation offers a wonderful journey through the beloved series.

Whether it's the iconic moments that have become part of British pop culture or lesser-known gems that deserve to be rediscovered, this compilation curated by Kenneth Williams and Barbara Windsor is sure to entertain and evoke fond memories of the "Carry On" legacy.

The concept for the film was influenced by Metro-Goldwyn-Mayer's well-received That's Entertainment! Documentary series. It was launched in 1977 as a companion piece to the Richard Harris movie Golden Rendezvous.

The release of "That's Carry On" took 10 months, making it the film with the longest post-production period in the series. Filming concluded in April 1977, and the film was eventually released in February 1978. The budget for this projected amounted to £30,000.

CARRY ON EMMANNUELLE (1978)

In this comedic spoof inspired by the sultry 'Emmanuelle' films of the 1970s and the cheeky spirit of the 'Carry On' series, we follow the misadventures of a French diplomat's wife in high-society London. Despite her best efforts, she struggles to spark any passion in her husband. Determined to reignite the flames of desire, she embarks on a hilarious journey of seduction, charming her way through London's elite. However, her escapades don't go unnoticed, and a jealous lover spills the beans to the national press, turning her romantic exploits into headline news.

Carry On Emmannuelle marked the final appearance for regulars like Kenneth Williams, Kenneth Connor, Joan Sims, and Peter Butterworth. Jack Douglas was the only one to continue to 'Carry On Columbus'. Newcomers Beryl Reid, Henry McGee, and Suzanne Danielle joined for their only roles in the series.

The film took a more risqué turn, embracing a style reminiscent of the X-rated 'Confessions...' comedies and the 'Emmanuelle' films it parodies. Despite this, it was only certified AA by the British Board of Film Censors, limiting it to audiences aged 14 and over. This was a departure from the usual U or PG ratings of the series.

Carry On Emmannuelle faced widespread criticism, with many considering it even worse than its predecessor, Carry On England, and its successor, Carry On Columbus. Film critic Philip French dubbed it "morally and aesthetically offensive," while Christopher Tookey described it as "embarrassingly feeble". Kenneth Williams himself later admitted to finding the jokes repulsive.

The film flopped at the box office and was relegated to late-night TV slots in the UK for decades. Author Adrian Rigelsford remarked that it's likely the least-watched of all 'Carry On' films.

Despite the enduring popularity of other Carry On' films, Carry On Emmannuelle remains poorly regarded. Reviews have often criticised its lack of dignity and humour, with Suzanne Danielle's Lolita-esque performance being labelled as "unintentionally creepy". Some critics even blame it for the decline of the entire series.

In a 2018 retrospective on the series, the British Film Institute named Carry On Emmannuelle as one of the series' five worst films, joining the ranks of Carry On Girls, Carry On England, That's Carry On!, and Carry On Columbus.

In his 2023 autobiography, "Oh, What A Lovely Memoir", actor Larry Dann recounted the film's troubled production, recalling audiences walking out before the credits even rolled.

CAST:

Kenneth Williams as **Émile Prévert**
Suzanne Danielle as **Emmannuelle Prévert**
Kenneth Connor as **Leyland**
Jack Douglas as **Lyons**
Joan Sims as **Mrs. Dangle**
Peter Butterworth as **Richmond**
Larry Dann as **Theodore Valentine**
Beryl Reid as **Mrs. Valentine**
Henry McGee as **Harold Hump**
Victor Maddern as **Man in Launderette**
Dino Shafeek as **Immigration Officer**
Eric Barker as **Ancient General**
Joan Benham as **Cynical Lady**
Albert Moses as **Doctor**
Robert Dorning as **Prime Minister**
Steve Plytas as **Arabian Official**
Michael Nightingale as **Police Commissioner**
Bruce Boa as **U.S. Ambassador**
Llewellyn Rees as **Lord Chief Justice**
Jack Lynn as **Admiral**

Claire Davenport as **Blonde in Pub**
Norman Mitchell as **Drunken Husband**
Tricia Newby as **Nurse in Surgery**
James Fagan as **Concorde Steward**
Malcolm Johns as **Sentry**
Howard Nelson as **Harry Hernia**
Tim Brinton as **BBC Newscaster**
Corbett Woodall as **ITN Newscaster**
Marianne Maskell as **Nurse in Hospital**

FACTS AND TRIVIA:

- Budget: £349,302
- Filming Dates 10th April – 15th May 1978

EXTERIORS:

- Wembley, London
- Trafalgar Square, London
- Oxford Street, London
- London Zoo, London

PROFILE:

Suzanne Danielle, formerly known as Suzanne Morris, was born on 14th January 1957 in England.

She received her dance training at the Bush Davies School of Theatre Arts in Romford, Essex, and also attended Bedfords Park Community School in Harold Hill. At 16, Danielle made her West End debut in the musical "Billy" (1974) alongside Michael Crawford. This led to an invitation to perform as a dancer on Bruce Forsyth's show "Bruce and More Girls". Inspired by Cyd Charisse, she joined the dance group "The Younger Generation" after leaving school.

Danielle's screen debut was as "Pretty Girl" in an episode of "The Professionals" ("Killer with a Long Arm"), aired in January 1978.

Her first film appearance was in "The Wild Geese" (1978), followed by her credited role in "Carry On Emmannuelle" (1978), a reviewer noted her athletic and long-legged presence, likening her to Kenneth Williams. In 1979, she starred in "The Golden Lady" alongside Ina Skriver and appeared as a dancer performing a belly dance in "Arabian Adventure". Her final film was "The Trouble with Spies" (1987), filmed in 1984, where she acted alongside Donald Sutherland and Michael Hordern.

During the late '70s and early '80s, Danielle was known for playing attractive and promiscuous characters. She graced British television screens regularly from 1979 to 1983. Danielle was a team member on the game show "Give Us a Clue" and featured in various light entertainment programmes, including a 1984 Christmas episode of "Blankety Blank". As an actress, she appeared in "Doctor Who" (Destiny of the Daleks), "Hammer House of Horror", "Morecambe and Wise", and "Tales of the Unexpected". She also frequently appeared on the ITV series "Mike Yarwood", portraying Diana, Princess of Wales, opposite Yarwood's Prince Charles.

In 1980, Danielle took to the stage in a touring production of John Murray's comedy "The Monkey Walk", co-starring Patrick Mower. This tour extended to Singapore and New Zealand. In 1983, she was featured in an exercise instruction album titled "Shape Up and Dance". In 1985, Danielle played the lead role in a Christmas pantomime of "Jack and the Beanstalk" in Richmond, Surrey, with support from Jimmy Edwards, Kenneth Connor, and Joan Sims.

Danielle was in a relationship with actor Patrick Mower for seven years. In 1986, she met golfer Sam Torrance, who proposed to her in 1987 aboard a Concorde flight to Columbus, Ohio, for the Ryder Cup. They married on 14th February 1995 at Skibo Castle and have four children.

CARRY ON 90'S

CARRY ON COLUMBUS (1992)

In this comedy, overconfident Christopher Columbus seeks funding from the King and Queen of Spain for his Eastward expedition. Meanwhile, the Sultan of Turkey and his clumsy assistant, Fatima, plot to foil his journey. As Columbus sets sail with his quirky crew, the Sultan's bumbling schemes hilariously unravel. Will Columbus discover new lands, or will the Sultan's antics sink his plans?

The release of Carry On Columbus in 1992 coincided with the 500th anniversary of Christopher Columbus' voyage to the Americas. While two more serious films on Columbus were released that year, "1492: Conquest of Paradise" and "Christopher Columbus: The Discovery," this comedy offered a lighter take on the explorer's journey.

The mainstays of the Carry On series gracing "Carry On Columbus" include Jim Dale and Peter Gilmore, both in their eleventh Carry On films, alongside Bernard Cribbins (third appearance), Leslie Phillips (fourth), Jon Pertwee (fourth), and June Whitfield (fourth). Jack Douglas was the sole actor bridging the gap between "Carry On Columbus" and the previous film, marking his eighth appearance.

Frankie Howerd was set to play the King of Spain but sadly passed away before filming. The role was initially offered to Bernard Bresslaw, an original series regular, who declined. Eventually, Leslie Phillips took the part, starring opposite June Whitfield as the Queen, roles previously declined by Joan Sims and Barbara Windsor. Kenneth Connor, another Carry On veteran, declined the role of the Duke of Costa Brava, stating, "I want to be remembered as a Carry On star, not a Carry On bit-player."

The producers successfully enlisted alternative comedians like Peter Richardson, Alexei Sayle, Rik Mayall, Julian Clary, and Nigel Planer from The Comic Strip to join the cast.

Carry On Columbus received largely negative reviews from critics. Michael Dwyer of The Irish Times labelled it a "flaccid, feeble comeback effort" and criticised it as "wretched and pathetically unfunny". Despite this, the film outperformed the other two Columbus-themed movies released in 1992, "Christopher Columbus: The Discovery" and "1492: Conquest of Paradise", at the UK box office, earning £1,667,249. All three films, however, were considered box office flops. Notably, Carry On Columbus was made on a much tighter budget of £2.5 million, compared to the respective budgets of $45 million and $47 million for the other two.

CAST:

Jim Dale as **Christopher Columbus**
Bernard Cribbins as **Mordecai Mendoza**
Maureen Lipman as **Countess Esmerelda**
Peter Richardson as **Bart Columbus**
Alexei Sayle as **Achmed**
Rik Mayall as **The Sultan**
Sara Crowe as **Fatima**
Julian Clary as **Don Juan Diego**
Keith Allen as **Pepi the Poisoner**
Leslie Phillips as **King Ferdinand**
Jon Pertwee as **the Duke of Costa Brava**
Richard Wilson as **Don Juan Felipe**
Rebecca Lacey as **Chiquita yes**
June Whitfield as **Queen Isabella**
Nigel Planer as **The Wazir**
Larry Miller as **The Chief**
Jack Douglas as **Marco the Cereal Killer**

Andrew Bailey as **Genghis**
Burt Kwouk as **Wang**
Philip Herbert as **Ginger**
Tony Slattery as **Baba the Messenger**
Martin Clunes as **Martin**
David Boyce as **Customer with ear**
Sara Stockbridge as **Nina the model**
Holly Aird as **Maria**
James Faulkner as **Tomas de Torquemada**
Don Maclean as **Inquisitor with ham sandwiches**
Dave Freeman as **Inquisitor**
Duncan Duff as **Inquisitor**
Jonathan Tafler as **Inquisitor**
James Pertwee as **Inquisitor**
Perry Cree as **Inquisitor**
Toby Dale as **Inquisitor**
Michael Hobbs as **Inquisitor**
Peter Grant as **Cardinal**
Su Douglas as **Countess Joanna**
John Antrobus as **Manservant**
Lynda Baron as **Meg**
Allan Corduner as **Sam**
Nejdet Salih as **Fayid**
Mark Arden as **Mark**
Silvestre Tobias as **Abdullah**
Daniel Peacock as **Tonto the Torch**
Don Henderson as **The Bosun**
Harold Berens as **Cecil the Torturer**
Peter Gilmore as **Governor of the Canaries**
Marc Sinden as **Captain Perez**
Charles Fleischer as **Pontiac**
Chris Langham as **Hubba**
Reed Martin as **Poco Hontas**

Prudence Solomon as **Ha**
Peter Gordeno as **The Shaman**

FACTS AND TRIVIA:

- Budget: £2.5 million
- Filming Dates 21st April - 27th May 1992
- Exterior: Frensham Common (previously used nearly 30 years earlier for Carry On Jack)
- In a 2004 survey of British film professionals, Carry On Columbus was voted the worst British film ever made.
- Sadly, Carry On Columbus marked the final film directed by Gerald Thomas, who passed away on 9th November 1993.

A FESTIVE FARCE: THE HILARIOUS ANTICS OF CARRY ON CHRISTMAS (1969-1973)

The Carry On Christmas Specials were four unique specials produced for Thames Television, airing in 1969, 1970, 1972, and 1973. These specials featured much of the cast and the comedic style characteristic of the Carry On films. Barbara Windsor was the only performer to appear in all four Carry On Christmas specials. In contrast, Kenneth Williams, who starred in twenty-six Carry On films (the highest number of any Carry On actor), did not participate in any of the Christmas specials.

In 1983, Kenneth Williams and Barbara Windsor presented Carry On Laughing's Christmas Classics, highlighting some of the funniest moments from the festive specials in a format reminiscent of That's Carry On!

CARRY ON CHRISTMAS (1969)

The first special, Carry On Christmas, was broadcast in 1969. Filmed shortly after the completion of Carry On Up the Jungle, it featured the same main cast from that film. Scripted by long-term Carry On author Talbot Rothwell, the story is an irreverent take on Charles Dickens' A Christmas Carol, with Sid James as Scrooge.

In the 'Christmas Past' sequence, Scrooge fails to invest in the schemes of Dr. Frank N. Stein, who, assisted by his servant Count Dracula, attempts to create a mate for Barbara Windsor's Monster. The 'Christmas Present' sequence details Robert Browning's struggles to elope with Elizabeth Barrett without funds due to Scrooge's unwillingness to lend. The 'Christmas Future' sequence retells the story of Cinderella.

CAST:

Sid James as **Ebenezer Scrooge**
Terry Scott as **Dr Frank N Stein, Convent Girl, Mr Barrett, Baggie**
Charles Hawtrey as **Spirit of Christmas Past, Angel, Convent Girl, Buttons**
Hattie Jacques as **Elizabeth Barrett, Nun, Passer-by**
Barbara Windsor as **Cinderella, Fanny, Spirit of Christmas Present**
Peter Butterworth as **Count Dracula, Beggar, Convent Girl, Haggie**
Bernard Bresslaw as **Bob Cratchit, Frankenstein's Monster, Spirit of Christmas Future, Convent Girl, Town Crier, Policeman**
Frankie Howerd as **Robert Browning, Fairy Godmother**

CARRY ON AGAIN CHRISTMAS (1970)

The second special, Carry On Again Christmas, was broadcast the following year. Although Talbot Rothwell did not script this episode, Sid Colin, who had co-written Carry On Spying with Rothwell, collaborated with Dave Freeman, who would later script Carry On Behind, several episodes of the Carry On Laughing television series, and co-wrote the 1992 film Carry On Columbus. This special, based on Robert Louis Stevenson's Treasure Island, marked the Carry On debut of Wendy Richard, who later had small roles in Carry On Matron and Carry On Girls.

Despite the 1969 special being broadcast in colour, the 1970 special was shown in black and white due to a technicians' strike that led Thames Television to broadcast all their Christmas shows in black and white that year.

CAST:

Sid James as **Long John Sil**

Terry Scott as **Squire Treyhornay**
Charles Hawtrey as **Old Blind Pew, Night Watchman, Nipper the Flipper**
Kenneth Connor as **Dr Livershake**
Barbara Windsor as **Jim Hawkins**
Bernard Bresslaw as **Rollicky Bill**
Bob Todd as **Ben Gunn, Shipmate**
Wendy Richard as **Kate**

CARRY ON CHRISTMAS (OR CARRY ON STUFFING) (1972)

In 1972, a new Christmas special titled Carry On Christmas (or Carry On Stuffing) was produced. Talbot Rothwell fell ill while writing the script and was unable to complete it. Dave Freeman was brought in to finish the script, but the two did not collaborate directly. Charles Hawtrey withdrew from the special at short notice. Having taken third billing behind Sid James and Terry Scott in the previous two shows, Hawtrey demanded top billing in their absence. However, Carry On producer Peter Rogers refused and gave top billing to Hattie Jacques instead. As a result, Hawtrey's role was hastily recast and split between Norman Rossington and Brian Oulton, both of whom had appeared in cameo roles in several Carry On films. The special featured a collection of historical sketches loosely linked around an 18th-century banquet.

It included a performance of two madrigals originally written for Carry On Henry. These songs later reappeared in the 1973 stage show Carry On London.

CAST:

Hattie Jacques as **Maid, Miss Molly Coddle, Lady Fiona, Harriet, The Good Fairy**
Joan Sims as **Maid, Lady Rhoda Cockhorse, Mother, Esmeralda, Princess YoYo**

Barbara Windsor as **Maid, Eve, Virginia, Aladdin**
Kenneth Connor as **Sir Henry, Lieutenant Banghem, Hanky Poo**
Peter Butterworth as **Sir Francis Fiddler, Captain Dripping, Lieutenant Trembler, Hole in One**
Jack Douglas as **Mr Perkin, Adam, Tomkins, Ringworm, King of the Underworld**
Norman Rossington as **General Sir Ffingham Clodhopper, Genie**
Brian Oulton as **Oriental Orator**
Billy Cornelius as **Waiter**
Valerie Leon as **Serving Wench**
Valerie Stanton as **Demon King's Vision**

CARRY ON CHRISTMAS (1973)

Talbot Rothwell returned to write the fourth and final annual Christmas special, with Sid James reprising his role as a cheeky Santa in a department store grotto. He reflects on how Christmas has been celebrated through the ages, with the team performing sketches set in prehistoric, Georgian, World War I, and Robin Hood times. The special also includes a dance routine that's a real nutcracker.

CAST:

Sid James as **Sid Belcher (Santa), Seedpod, Sir Henry, Sergeant Ball, Robin Hood**
Joan Sims as **Mother, Sennapod, Bishop's Wife, Adelle, Salvation Army Woman, Maid Marion, Traffic Warden**
Barbara Windsor as **Virginia, Crompet, Lady Frances, Fifi**
Kenneth Connor as **Shop Manager, Anthro Pod, The Bishop, Private Parkin, Will Scarlet**
Peter Butterworth as **Carol Singer, Old Man, Darts Player, 2nd German Soldier, Friar Tuck**
Bernard Bresslaw as **Peapod, Camp Aristocrat, Darts Player, Captain Ffingburgh, Much, Policeman**

Jack Douglas as **Carol Singer (2001 BC), Crapper, 1st German Soldier, Ballad Singer**
Julian Holloway as **Captain Rose**
Laraine Humphrys as **Bed Customer**

CARRY ON LAUGHING (1975)

Carry On Laughing was created to revitalise the Carry On franchise amidst declining cinema audiences; it brought many original cast members to the small screen.

The show had two series: the first consisted of six half-hour episodes and the second of seven episodes. The episode "Orgy and Bess" marked the final Carry On performances of Sid James and Hattie Jacques.

Despite its connection to the popular film series, the TV series did not achieve the same level of recognition and is less frequently aired on British television.

The series was developed after the departure of key Carry On figures: writer Talbot Rothwell and actor Charles Hawtrey. Kenneth Williams also chose not to participate. Regulars like Sid James, Hattie Jacques, and Bernard Bresslaw appeared sporadically, with James featured in the first four episodes, Jacques in just one, and Bresslaw only in the second series.

With Rothwell gone, new writers were recruited. Lew Schwarz and veteran Carry On writer Dave Freeman wrote six episodes each, while Barry Cryer and Dick Vosburgh contributed "Orgy and Bess."

Episodes parodied well-known TV series, films, or books. Three episodes included a character based on Lord Peter Wimsey, named Lord Peter Flimsy. Two episodes parodied Upstairs, Downstairs, featuring characters Clodson (a spoof of Hudson the butler) and Mrs. Breeches (a parody of Mrs. Bridges the cook).

The series offered David Lodge, usually a minor player in the later Carry On films, the chance to play leading roles.

ATV previously brought the Carry On series to television in 1973 with What A Carry On, a special hosted by Shaw Taylor. It featured clips from the stage play Carry On London and interviews with stars like Sid James, Barbara Windsor, Bernard Bresslaw, Kenneth Connor, Peter Butterworth, and Jack Douglas. This footage is believed to be lost from the archives.

The BBC also used the title What A Carry On for a series showcasing classic clips from the films.

CARRY ON LAUGHING – SERIES ONE

EPISODE 1: THE PRISONER OF SPENDA

A cheeky parody of The Prisoner of Zenda, where cunning plots threaten to prevent the heir-apparent from being crowned king in a distant land. A hapless, newlywed couple on their honeymoon is unwittingly swept up in the schemes.

CAST:

Sid James as **Prince Rupert**
Barbara Windsor as **Vera Basket**
Peter Butterworth as **Count Yerackers**
Joan Sims as **Madame Olga**
Kenneth Connor as **Nickoff**
Jack Douglas as **Colonel Yackoff**
David Lodge as **Duke Boris**
Diane Langton as **Tzana**
Ronnie Brody as **Waiter**
Rupert Evans as **Major**

EPISODE 2: THE BARON OUTLOOK

Marie, posing as the French knight Sir Gaston, is seized and held captive in the castle of Baron Hubert and Lady Isobel, awaiting a ransom demand.

CAST:

Sid James as **Baron Hubert**
Joan Sims as **Lady Isobel**
Barbara Windsor as **Marie**
Kenneth Connor as **Sir William**
Peter Butterworth as **Friar Roger**
Diane Langton as **Griselda**
David Lodge as **Sir Simon de Montfort**
Brian Osborne as **Gaston**
John Carlin as **Ethelbert**
Linda Hooks as **Rosie**
Anthony Trent as **Herald**
John Levene as **Soldier (uncredited)**

EPISODE 3: THE SOBBING CAVALIER

Sir Jethro faces an impossible choice: stay loyal to Cromwell and risk execution by the Royalist Cavaliers, or support King Charles and face death from the Parliamentarian Roundheads. To complicate matters, his Cavalier brother-in-law, Lovelace, is secretly hiding in his home.

CAST:

Sid James as **Lovelace**
Barbara Windsor as **Sarah**
Joan Sims as **Lady Kate**
Jack Douglas as **Sir Jethro**
Peter Butterworth as **Oliver Cromwell**
David Lodge as **Colonel**

Bernard Holley as **Captain**
Brian Osborne as **Cavalier**

EPISODE 4: ORGY AND BESS

Queen Elizabeth I, faced with England on the brink of war with Spain, called upon Sir Francis Drake to help defuse the escalating tension.

CAST:

Sid James as **Sir Francis Drake**
Hattie Jacques as **Queen Elizabeth I**
Barbara Windsor as **Lady Miranda**
Jack Douglas as **Master of the Rolls...**
Kenneth Connor as **King Philip**
John Carlin as **Sir Walter Raleigh**
Norman Chappell as **Lord Burleigh**
Victor Maddern as **Todd**
MacDonald Hobley as **Quaker Reporter**
Simon Callow as **First Crew Member**
Brian Osborne as **Second Crew Member**

EPISODE 5: ONE IN THE EYE FOR HAROLD

England stands surrounded as William, Duke of Normandy, readies his forces to invade and claim the crown from King Harold. However, the English have a secret weapon up their sleeve.

CAST:

Jack Douglas as **Ethelred**
Joan Sims as **Else**
Kenneth Connor as **Athelstan**
David Lodge as **William the Conqueror**
Norman Chappell as **King Harold**

John Carlin as **Egbert**
Diane Langton as **Isoloe**
Patsy Smart as **Old Hag**
Brian Osborne as **Herald**
Paul Jesson as **Messenger**
Jerold Wells as **Black Cowl**
Linda Hooks as **Nellie**
Billy Cornelius as **Pikeman**
Nosher Powell as **Pikeman**

EPISODE 6: THE NINE OLD COBBLERS

Renowned detective Lord Peter Flimsey is summoned to investigate the mysterious death of Mr Longhammer, whose body has been discovered concealed behind the stage curtain in the village hall.

CAST:

Jack Douglas as **Lord Peter Flimsy**
Joan Sims as **Amelia Forbush**
Kenneth Connor as **Punter**
David Lodge as **Inspector Bungler**
John Carlin as **Vicar**
Victor Maddernas **Charlie**
Patsy Rowlands as **Miss Dawkins**
Barbara Windsor as **Maisie**
Sam Harding as **Pianist** (uncredited)

CARRY ON LAUGHING – SERIES TWO

EPISODE 1: UNDER THE ROUND TABLE

King Arthur brings together his knights to form the Round Table, intending to protect and govern a united England. The only problem? They are utterly inept!

CAST:

Joan Sims as **Lady Guinevere**
Bernard Bresslaw as **Sir Pureheart**
Jack Douglas as **Sir Gay**
Kenneth Connor as **King Arthur**
Peter Butterworth as **Merlin**
Oscar James as **Black Knight**
Victor Maddern as **Sir Osis**
Norman Chappell as **Sir William**
Desmond McNamara as **Minstrel**
Valerie Walsh as **Lady Ermintrude**
Ronnie Brody as **Shortest Knight**
Billy Cornelius as **Man-at-arms**
Brian Capron as **Trumpeter**

EPISODE 2: THE CASE OF THE SCREAMING WINKLES

Master detective Lord Peter Flimsy, accompanied by his butler, Punter, is summoned to a lavish country hotel to investigate the mysterious death of a guest.

CAST:

Jack Douglas as **Lord Peter Flimsy**
Kenneth Connor as **Punter**
Joan Sims as **Mrs. MacFlute**
Peter Butterworth as **Admiral Clanger**
David Lodge as **Inspector Bungler**
Sherrie Hewson as **Nurse Millie Teazel**
Norman Chappell as **Potter**
Marianne Stone as **Madame Petra**
Melvyn Hayes as **Charwallah Charlie**
John Carlin as **Major Merridick**
Michael Nightingale as **Colonel Postwick**

EPISODE 3: AND IN MY LADY'S CHAMBER

Sir Henry Bulgeon-Plunger's son, Willy, has returned from his expedition to the Amazon basin, bringing along a few unexpected surprises!

CAST:

Kenneth Connor as **Sir Harry**
Barbara Windsor as **Lottie**
Joan Sims as **Mrs. Breeches**
Jack Douglas as **Clodson**
Bernard Bresslaw as **Starkers**
Andrew Ray as **Willie**
Peter Butterworth as **Silas**
Carol Hawkins as **Lilly**
Sherrie Hewson as **Virginia**
Vivienne Johnson as **Teeny**

EPISODE 4: SHORT KNIGHT, LONG DAZE

Back at King Arthur's court, Sir Point of No Return, the treasurer of the Round Table, has gone missing. In search of guidance and comfort, Arthur consults Merlin, who foretells the arrival of a remarkable knight: Lancelot.

CAST:

Joan Sims as **Lady Guinevere**
Bernard Bresslaw as **Sir Lancelot**
Jack Douglas as **Sir Gay**
Kenneth Connor as **King Arthur**
Peter Butterworth as **Merlin**
Norman Chappell as **Sir William**
Brian Osborne as **Herald – Knight**
Desmond McNamara as **Minstrel**
Susan Valentine as **Mabel (Susan Skipper)**

Billy Cornelius as **Man-at-arms**
Brian Capron as **Trumpeter**

EPISODE 5: THE CASE OF THE COUGHING PARROT

Lord Peter Flimsey and his butler, Punter, set out to investigate the mysterious disappearance of King Ramitupum's body from his sarcophagus. Or at least they make an effort to do so.

CAST:

Jack Douglas as **Lord Peter Flimsy**
Kenneth Connor as **Punter**
Joan Sims as **Dr. Janis Crunbitt**
Peter Butterworth as **Lost Property Attendant**
David Lodge as **Inspector Bungler**
Sherrie Hewson as **Irma Klein**
Vivienne Johnson as **Freda Filey**
Norman Chappell as **Ambulance Driver**
Brian Osborne as **Harry**
Johnny Briggs as **Norman**

EPISODE 6: WHO NEEDS KITCHENER?

As the First World War looms, Sir Harry's household is busy preparing for conflict, but the new footman arrives with a rather peculiar accent!

CAST:

Kenneth Connor as **Sir Harry**
Barbara Windsor as **Lottie**
Joan Sims as **Mrs. Breeches**
Jack Douglas as **Clodson**
Bernard Bresslaw as **Klanger**
Andrew Ray as **Willie**
Sherrie Hewson as **Virginia**

Carol Hawkins as **Lilly**
Vivienne Johnson as **Teeny**
Brian Osborne as **Newsboy**

EPISODE 7: LAMP POSTS OF THE EMPIRE

A risqué parody set in the Victorian era, where newspaper reporter Mr. Stanley is tasked with locating Dr. Livingstone. The adventure is spiced up by a stunning woman on the hunt for romance, a well-spoken witch doctor who speaks flawless upper-class English, and an array of magical performances and spells.

CAST:

Barbara Windsor as **Lady Mary**
Kenneth Connor as **Stanley**
Jack Douglas as **Dick Darcy**
Bernard Bresslaw as **Dr. Pavingstone**
Peter Butterworth as **Lord Gropefinger**
Oscar James as **Witchdoctor**
Norman Chappell as **Businessman**
John Carlin as **Old Man**
Michael Nightingale as **Neighbour**
Reuben Martin as **Mabel**
Wayne Browne as **Native**

CARRY ON STAGE: THEATRE AND PLAYHOUSE ANTICS

The Carry On series expanded beyond film with three stage shows over the years, bringing its trademark humour to live theatre. These productions featured a mix of familiar faces from the film series and new talent, offering audiences a chance to enjoy the beloved characters and comedic style in a different setting.

CARRY ON LONDON! (4 OCTOBER 1973 – MARCH 1975)

Theatre: Victoria Palace Theatre, London
Written by: Talbot Rothwell, Dave Freeman, Eric Merriman
Cast: Sid James, Barbara Windsor, Kenneth Connor, Peter Butterworth, Bernard Bresslaw, Jack Douglas

Peter Rogers decided to bring the beloved franchise to the stage. Despite some regular cast members, such as Kenneth Williams and Joan Sims, declining to participate, Rogers assembled a talented group of performers, including Sid James, Barbara Windsor, Kenneth Connor, Peter Butterworth, Bernard Bresslaw, and Jack Douglas.

Initially, Sid James was hesitant about working with Jack Douglas, whose stand-up comedy background he feared might disrupt the scripted performances. However, Douglas quickly won over both the cast and audiences with his improvisational skills, ad-libbing gags and interacting effortlessly with the other performers, much to James' surprise.

The show blended comedy sketches, stand-up routines, song and dance, and speciality acts, evoking the spirit of traditional variety theatre. A key feature of the production was a series of six innuendo-filled mini sketches penned by Carry On scriptwriter Talbot Rothwell, featuring the six main performers. These sketches, inspired by some of the most popular Carry On films, including Carry On Doctor and Carry On Henry, were a highlight of the show.

One of the crowd-pleasing moments was the Emergency Ward 99 sketch, in which Bernard Bresslaw donned a Matron's outfit in a playful nod to Hattie Jacques. The Elizabethan Madrigals sketch, originally featured in the 1972 TV Christmas Special, was also a favourite, with Sid James delivering the memorable song "Balls, Balls, Banquets and Balls"—a reference to Carry On Don't Lose Your Head.

Carry On Cleo made its stage appearance as well, with Barbara Windsor as Cleo, Sid James as Caesar, and Peter Butterworth providing comic relief as Grabatiti. The show was a resounding success, with audiences delighted to see their favourite Carry On characters brought to life on stage.

CARRY ON LAUGHING: THE SLIMMING FACTORY (16 JUNE – SEPTEMBER 1976)

Theatre: Royal Opera House, Scarborough
Written by: Sam Cree
Cast: Liz Fraser, Kenneth Connor, Peter Butterworth, Jack Douglas, Anne Aston

This production was staged at the Royal Opera House in Scarborough, running throughout the summer season. It was a bold attempt at a straightforward, no-frills stage farce, basking in the Carry On legacy. Unfortunately, the show was marred by the death of Sid James just two months before its opening.

Due to Sid's passing and various other work commitments, most of the original cast members were either unable or unwilling to participate. However, three stalwart Carry On regulars decided to carry on with the production. Liz Fraser, who had recently returned to the Carry On series in Carry On Behind after having appeared in several early films as the "love interest," provided the glamour.

The plot followed a traditional farcical formula, with mistaken identities, marital troubles, and the familiar "More Tea, Vicar" humour that Ray Cooney popularised. Jack Douglas took top billing in this uninspired storyline, while Peter Butterworth stood out as the character of Willie Strokes.

WOT A CARRY ON IN BLACKPOOL (22 MAY – 25 OCTOBER 1992)

Theatre: North Pier, Blackpool
Written by: Barry Cryer, Dick Vosburgh
Cast: Bernard Bresslaw, Barbara Windsor

This production aimed to revive the spirit of Carry On London, harking back to the golden days of traditional Music Hall Vaudeville, with a mix of comic sketches, song and dance, and solo variety acts. The show's basic storyline centred around a 1940s repertory theatre company by the sea, giving writers Cryer and Vosburgh the opportunity to draw from the Carry On films and incorporate classic dialogue into the skits.

The show opens with Barbara Windsor dashing down the central aisle, exclaiming, "Cor, what a Carry On!" from which point the fun continued, with Bernard Bresslaw playing along and the two clearly enjoying themselves. While the gags may have been somewhat dated, the production was a genuine homage to the Carry On genre.

Meanwhile, back at Pinewood, Jim Dale and the cast were battling against the Spanish Inquisition and a weak Freeman script in

Carry On Columbus, but coachloads of working-class holidaymakers were having a raucous time with the real Carry On stars.

CARRY ON LEGENDS: FILMS BEYOND THE CLASSICS

The world of British comedy is vividly brought to life through four captivating biopics that delve into the personal lives, relationships, and complex legacies of beloved Carry On stars. From the fiery and tumultuous bond between Sid James and Barbara Windsor in Cor, Blimey! to the poignant exploration of Kenneth Williams' enigmatic life in Kenneth Williams: Fantabulosa!, these films reveal the human stories behind the laughter. Hattie offers an intimate glimpse into the life of Hattie Jacques, her marriage, and the challenges of love and loyalty, while Babs portrays Barbara Windsor's remarkable journey from a spirited child to an enduring icon of British television and cinema. Together, these films celebrate the triumphs and tragedies of comedic legends whose lives were as compelling off-screen as they were on.

COR, BLIMEY! (2000)

Cor, Blimey! Transports viewers to Pinewood Studios in 1963, where Sid James, portrayed as a gambling rogue and inveterate womaniser, meets Barbara Windsor while she works on Carry On Spying. James, already at odds with fellow actor Kenneth Williams, becomes smitten with Windsor. Though those around them dismiss his fascination as fleeting, the connection sparks a passionate and complex relationship.

Their entanglement weaves through iconic Carry On moments, such as Windsor's famous flying-bikini-top scene in Carry On Camping. By the time filming begins on Carry On Girls in 1973, James is deeply infatuated. Windsor, initially convinced that indulging his desires once would end his obsession, finds herself drawn into an affair that lasts years.

The narrative builds to a poignant conclusion in 1976 when their affair has ended, and James tragically dies of a heart attack during a stage performance. In the aftermath, Kenneth Williams consoles Windsor, reminding her she bears no blame for James's death, while she urges the melancholic Williams to embrace life's joys. In a touching finale, Windsor herself replaces Samantha Spiro to reflect on the bittersweet memories of their time together.

PRODUCTION

- **Challenges in Portraying Sid James**: Geoffrey Hutchings struggled to capture James, as little archive material of him off-screen existed. Hutchings relied on James's distinctive "guttural laugh" as his entry point into the character.
- **Portraying Barbara Windsor**: Samantha Spiro felt a profound responsibility while portraying Windsor, who makes a poignant appearance as herself in the film's final scene.

FACT OR FICTION?

The drama is a fictionalised account of the real-life affair between Barbara Windsor and Sid James. While the story incorporates familiar faces from the *Carry On* ensemble, including Bernard Bresslaw, Kenneth Connor, Charles Hawtrey, and Joan Sims, they remain minor characters in the narrative.

CHRONOLOGY AND CONTINUITY LIBERTIES:

The drama spans 1964 to Sid James's death in 1976 but features non-chronological storytelling and some factual inconsistencies:

- Bernard Bresslaw is seen portraying roles in *Carry On Spying* and *Carry On Henry*, which were actually played by Bernard Cribbins and Terry Scott. Bresslaw joined the *Carry On* series in 1965 with *Carry On Cowboy*.
- A reference to Jim Dale falling down hospital stairs occurs before *Carry On Cleo*, but this incident relates to *Carry On Again Doctor* in 1969.
- Barbara Windsor is shown storming off the set of *Carry On Emmannuelle* over a poor script; in reality, she never visited the set, and the film was produced two years after James's death.
- The scene where Sid James learns of Tony Hancock's death is set in 1969, though Hancock passed away in 1968.
- Kenneth Williams refers to *Carry On England*, yet this film had not been made at the time of James's death.
- James's dresser discusses moving to work on *You Only Live Twice* in a scene set in 1976, despite the Bond film's release in 1967.
- The UK government transition from Edward Heath to Harold Wilson was mentioned in 1976 but occurred in 1974.
- Williams and Windsor are depicted learning of James's death together from the news. In reality, Windsor was informed by phone after rehearsals for *Twelfth Night*, and Williams was notified by his agent.

CRITICAL RESPONSE:

- The film holds a 63% approval rating on Rotten Tomatoes, with an average score of 3.5/5.
- Mark Lawson of *The Guardian* praised the adaptation's depth and intelligence, highlighting the success of Johnson's script in transitioning the *Carry On* legacy to television.
- Lawson commended Hutchings, Spiro, and Godley for their portrayals of Sid James, Barbara Windsor, and Kenneth

Williams, respectively, describing the performances as nuanced and compelling.

CAST:

Geoffrey Hutchings as **Sid James**
Samantha Spiro as **Barbara Windsor**
David McAlister as **Gerald Thomas**
Adam Godley as **Kenneth Williams**
Hugh Walters as **Charles Hawtrey**
Steve Spiers as **Bernard Bresslaw**
Chrissie Cotterill as **Joan Sims**
Louise Delamere as **Imogen**
Derek Howard as **Kenneth Connor**
Maria Charles as **Alice Hawtrey**
Abigail McKern as **Olga Lowe**
Windsor Davies as **Sir Toby Belch**

KENNETH WILLIAMS: FANTABULOSA! (2006)

Kenneth Williams: Fantabulosa! is a 2006 BBC Four drama that casts Michael Sheen as the celebrated yet deeply complex comic actor Kenneth Williams, drawing inspiration from Williams' own revealing diaries. Cheryl Campbell portrays Lou, Kenneth's devoted mother, adding depth to the story of their relationship.

To fully embody Williams, Sheen undertook meticulous preparation, immersing himself in archival material and literary works about the actor. To capture Williams' distinctive physicality, he adhered to the cabbage soup diet, shedding 2.5 stone (35 lb; 16 kg) for the role.

Upon its premiere, the play garnered an impressive 860,000 viewers, making it BBC Four's standout programme of March 2006. A subsequent repeat brought in an additional 252,000 viewers. Praised for its authenticity and emotional weight, the production showcased Sheen's performance, which earned him the Royal Television Society Award for Best Male Actor and garnered two BAFTA nominations.

Released on DVD in October 2009 under the title **Fantabulosa! – The Kenneth Williams Story**, the play has since enjoyed numerous re-airings, cementing its place as a beloved portrayal of a comedy legend.

The drama was met with high praise, particularly for Michael Sheen's performance. Kathryn Flett of The Observer described his portrayal as "a characterisation for which the description tour-de-force is, frankly, pretty faint praise." The Times likened Sheen's performance to a brilliantly cut diamond, whose radiance is so striking that it almost overshadows the intricate craftsmanship that gives it such dazzling brilliance.

CAST:

Michael Sheen as **Kenneth Williams**
Cheryl Campbell as **Lou Williams**
Peter Wight as **Charlie Williams**
Beatie Edney as **Joan Sims**
Kenny Doughty as **Joe Orton**
Ron Cook as **Peter Eade**
Martin Trenaman as **Tony Hancock**
David Charles as **Charles Hawtrey**
Ewan Bailey as **Kenneth Halliwell**
Rachel Clarke as **Barbara Windsor**
Beatrice Comins as **St Joan/Actress**
Timothy Davies as **1st Doctor**
Stephen Critchlow as **Kenneth Horne**
Guy Henry as **Hugh Paddick**
Ged McKenna as **Sid James**
Nicholas Parsons as **Himself**
Connor Garnett Comerford as **Young Kenneth Williams**

HATTIE (2011)

Hattie is a television drama that chronicles the life of iconic British comedian Hattie Jacques, portrayed by Ruth Jones. The film delves into her marriage to John Le Mesurier and her complex relationship with their lodger, John Schofield.

Premiering in January 2011, it became a record-breaking success for BBC Four, surpassing the viewership of The Curse of Steptoe, which had held the channel's top spot since 2008. Jacques' son, Robin Le Mesurier, praised Jones' portrayal, saying she "captured my mother perfectly."

Robert Bathurst, who took on the role of John Le Mesurier in Hattie, later portrayed Sergeant Wilson in Dad's Army: The Lost Episodes (2019). This series recreated three lost episodes of the classic Dad's Army (1968), in which Le Mesurier himself had famously played the original Sergeant Wilson.

The film features scenes depicting the shooting of Carry On Cabby (1963), complete with a clapperboard displaying the final title. However, during production, the film was originally titled Call Me a Cab, with the name only being changed after filming had concluded.

CAST:

Ruth Jones as **Hattie Jacques**
Robert Bathurst as **John Le Mesurier**
Aidan Turner as **John Schofield**
Jeany Spark as **Joan Malin**
Jay Simpson as **Bruce**
Graham Fellows as **Eric Sykes**
Marcia Warren as **Esma Cannon**
Stephen Critchlow as **Gerald Thomas**
Susy Kane as **Young Actress**

Lewis MacLeod as **Eamonn Andrews**
Brian Pettifer as **Ron**
James Martin as **Reg**

BABS (2017)

Babs is a BBC biographical drama that chronicles the life of the iconic British actress Dame Barbara Windsor. Announced on 26th May 2016 by Charlotte Moore, the BBC's Acting Director of Television, the film aired just after Windsor's final appearance as Peggy Mitchell on EastEnders. Written by EastEnders scriptwriter Tony Jordan, the film takes viewers into the 1990s, where Windsor reflects on her life as she prepares for a stage performance. Through flashbacks, we witness her childhood, turbulent marriage to gangster Ronnie Knight, and her rise to stardom, particularly as a central figure in the Carry On films.

The film aired on 7th May 2017, marking Dame Barbara Windsor's 80th birthday. Upon the project's announcement, Windsor expressed her joy at Tony Jordan being selected to write the script, stating, "Tony knows the real me and what drives me, and I was especially moved by how he intends to tell my story, which will surprise many. I'm both honoured and thrilled that Tony and the BBC have brought this to life." Windsor's appearance in the film was her final on-screen performance.

In her review for The Guardian, Fiona Sturges admitted to wanting to love Babs. However, Sturges ultimately found herself puzzled by the execution, commending the performances of Jaime Winstone and Samantha Spiro, yet criticising the plot for being confusing, likening it to an EastEnders episode where Peggy apologises to the corpse of Dirty Den. She remarked that the storyline was almost as baffling as seeing Windsor in multiple versions of herself.

Conversely, Chitra Ramaswamy of The Guardian found Babs to be a "heartwarming and occasionally cliche-ridden" biopic, acknowledging that the narrative followed a familiar showbiz arc while still highlighting Winstone's strong performance.

The Telegraph awarded the film four stars, with Gerard O'Donovan calling it a "joyfully camp tribute" to Windsor, though he noted it was somewhat idealised. Meanwhile, The Times' Andrew Billen gave it a more lukewarm two-star rating.

Babs was released on DVD by IMC Vision on 15th May 2017.

CAST:

Samantha Spiro as **Babs**
Florence Keen as **Child Barbara**
Honor Kneafsey as **Teen Barbara**
Jaime Winstone as **Barbara**
Barbara Windsor as **Herself**
 Charlie Archer as **Scott Mitchell**
Nick Moran as **John Deeks**
Leanne Best as **Rose Deeks**
Nathan Harmer as **Brian Mickey**
Marty Cruikshank as **Aida Foster**
Peter Hamilton Dyer as **Producer**
Matthew Bates as **Rosie's Lawyer**
Robert East as **Divorce Judge**
Lewis Kirk as **Johnny Brandon**
Cally Lawrence as **Wardrobe Mistress**
Sue Elliott-Nichols as **Shoe Shop Manageress**
Hannah Hutch as **Woman in Shoe Shop**
Tom Machell as **Man in Shoe Shop**
Jonathan Rhodes as **Peter Noble**
Laurent Maurel as **Monsieur Vincent**
Alex Macqueen as **Peter Charlesworth**
Ross Green as **Ronnie Scott**

Jacob Krichefski as **Slim Cattan**
James Atherton as **Cliff (Saxophonist)**
Luke Allen-Gale as **Ronnie Knight**
Todd Von Joel as **Neil**
Dean Roberts as **Stan**
Jerry-Jane Pears as **Jayne Mansfield**
Rebecca Lee as **Jayne's Assistant**
Nicola Munns as **Young Actress**
Zoë Wanamaker as **Joan Littlewood**
Daniel Ben Zenou as **Lionel Bart**
Lewis Maiella as **Chuck**
Toby Wharton as **Charlie Kray**
Rob Compton as **Ronnie Kray / Reggie Kray**
Nicholas Asbury as **Gerald Thomas**
Robin Sebastian as **Kenneth Williams**
Rob Hughes as **Bernard Cribbins**
Rose Robinson as **Hat Girl**
Tom Forbes as **Warren Beatty**
Joe Stilgoe as **Shepard Coleman**
Julia Ford as **Julie Deeks**

THE LOST STORIES: UNFILMED CARRY ON SCRIPTS

While the Carry On series is renowned for its hilarious and sometimes absurd adventures, there are several films that, despite being scripted, never made it to the screen. These "lost stories" offer a fascinating glimpse into the projects that never quite came to fruition.

Carry On Smoking (1961) was a proposed comedy centred around a fire station, following the antics of a group of inept new recruits trying to become firefighters. The film was expected to feature Williams, Connor, and Phillips, likely portraying the hapless trainees. It seemed the team intended to lampoon all three emergency services, having already satirised the police force and hospitals. However, concerns arose that the film could face backlash if a major fire occurred near its release, potentially being viewed as insensitive.

Carry On Spaceman (1961) written by Norman Hudis, was envisioned as a satirical comedy inspired by the Space Race. The film, intended to be shot in black and white, would have followed the misadventures of three bungling astronauts during their training and eventual space mission. Kenneth Williams, Kenneth Connor, and Leslie Phillips were slated to star. Initially planned to follow Carry On Cruising (1962), the project sought to present a European perspective on the Space Race. However, due to its high estimated costs and the producers' desire for a simpler venture after their first colour film, the idea was ultimately shelved.

Carry On Flying (1962) was another script by Norman Hudis, this time centred on a group of hapless RAF recruits. The film progressed to pre-production, with newcomer Jim Dale set to star, but it was ultimately shelved. Planned for late 1962, the project was intended as a light-hearted parody of the RAF. When the idea failed to materialise, producer Peter Rogers turned his attention to a script Gerald Thomas had received, titled Call Me a Cab (Which later became Carry On Cabby).

Carry On Robin (1965) was the planned Carry On spoof of the Robin Hood legend, with the title even registered by Peter Rogers with the British Film Producers Association. However, the project never came to pass. While the Robin Hood story offered plenty of room for comedic interpretation, the team would likely have approached it with their usual irreverence, prioritising laughs over historical accuracy.

Rumours suggested that Jim Dale was in line to play Robin Hood, which would have relegated Sid James to a secondary role. However, Sid favoured the idea of a western parody, particularly one that allowed him to work with horses. This led to Carry On Cowboy becoming the more practical and appealing choice, leaving Carry On Robin forgotten.

Carry On Escaping (1973) was proposed by Talbot Rothwell, inspired by the enduring popularity of World War II films and the success of the BBC series Colditz, which had attracted high ratings with its international cast. The idea stemmed from a suggestion by Peter Butterworth, Rothwell's close friend, whom he had met while they were both detained in a prisoner-of-war camp. Butterworth had been part of a concert party that masked the sounds of escaping prisoners—a real-life experience that could have lent authenticity to the script.

The film would have likely parodied classics like The Great Escape (1963), but there were concerns it might be seen as disrespectful to the bravery of those involved in such events. Despite the interest in the concept, the idea was shelved, and the team pivoted to other projects. Though the war theme resurfaced in 1976's Carry On England, the next film to hit screens after the proposal was Carry On Girls.

Carry On Again Nurse was originally planned for production in 1968 as a direct sequel to Carry On Nurse, but the project failed to come together. Over a decade later, in 1979, it was announced as the follow-up to Carry On Emmanuelle. However, following the poor performance of Emmanuelle, the idea was shelved once more. A fresh attempt to revive the project came in early 1988, by which time it had been renamed Carry On Nursing and was scripted by George Layton and Jonathan Lynn.

Sadly, the deaths of Kenneth Williams and Charles Hawtrey, combined with a prohibitive £1.5 million budget, ultimately ended any hope of the film being made.

Carry On Dallas (1980) would have featured Kenneth Williams in the role of a JR Ewing-type character. The concept envisioned Williams playing the complete opposite of Larry Hagman's tough, savvy businessman, instead portraying a weak, ineffectual fool lacking any business acumen. The idea had strong potential. However, the project came to a halt when Lorimar, the US production company behind Dallas, demanded a substantial fee to use the basic concept. The fee they requested was twenty times the total budget of the Carry On film, effectively bringing the project to an end.

Carry On Down Under (1981) was a film that Gerald Thomas explored locations for in Australia; while the idea gained renewed interest in the late 1980s, spurred by the success of the Australian soap Neighbours, the original plot had no connection to the show. The project progressed to the scripting stage, with a treatment by Vince Powell. The film even had potential backing from the Australian Film Commission. Unfortunately, the funding fell through, and the project was ultimately abandoned.

Carry On London (2008) was a modern attempt to revive the iconic series, set around a limousine company transporting celebrities to an awards show. Despite several cast changes and numerous false starts, the film never came to fruition after the death of producer Peter Rogers in 2009.

Previously, in 2003, Carry On London (not to be confused with the 1975 stage play) was announced, with Shaun Williamson—known for his role as Barry in EastEnders—set to star. The cast was expected to include Paul O'Grady, Daniella Westbrook, and Frank Skinner, but the project struggled to come together, eventually entering a prolonged period of development hell, during which it was even referred to, rather unexpectedly, as Carry On Bananas.

ITV issued a statement, saying: "We know the British public love Carry On, and we welcome working with anyone interested in keeping this much-loved brand alive."

This wasn't the first attempt to resurrect the Carry On franchise. In 2016, Jonathan Sothcott of Hereford Films announced plans for a new series of Carry On films, starting with Carry On Doctors, followed by Carry On Campus. Tim Dawson and Susan Nickson, the writers behind the BBC sitcom Two Pints of Lager and a Packet of Crisps, were lined up to write the scripts.

FILMOGRAPHY: A SCREEN LEGACY

Below is a curated filmography of some of our Carry On stars, featuring their most notable roles. Please note that this is not an exhaustive list of their credits but rather a selection of key productions that highlight their impressive careers beyond the Carry On series.

KENNETH WILLIAMS

FILM:

Trent's Last Case (1952), **Valley of Song** (1953), **The Beggar's Opera** (1953), **Innocents in Paris** (1953), **The Seekers** (1954), **Three Men in a Boat** (1956), **Tommy the Toreador** (1959), **Make Mine Mink** (1960), **His and Hers** (1961), **Raising the Wind** (1961), **Twice Round the Daffodils** (1962), **The Hound of the Baskervilles** (1978), **The Thief and the Cobbler** (1993).

TELEVISION:

Wogan's Radio Fun (1987), **International Cabaret** (1966–1974), **The Kenneth Williams Show** (1970–1976), **Jackanory** (1968–1986), **Willo the Wisp** (1981), **Galloping Galaxies** (1985–1986), **An Audience with Kenneth Williams** (1983), **Bilko on Parade** (1984), **Parkinson in Australia** (1981), **What's My Line?**, **Some You Win**, **Whizzkids Guide** (1981), **Tomorrow's World** (1981), **Let's Make a Musical** (1977), **Going Places** (1975), **Meanwhile, on BBC2** (1971), **Join Jim Dale** (1969), **The Wednesday Play** (1964), **BBC Sunday Night Theatre** (1952–1958), **Saint Joan** (1958), **Sword of Freedom**, **The School**, **Dick and the Duchess** (1957), **The Armoured Car**, **Misalliance** (1954), **Countdown**.

JOAN SIMS

FILM:

The Square Ring (1953), Will Any Gentleman...? (1953), Trouble in Store (1953), Meet Mr. Lucifer (1953), Doctor in the House (1954), What Every Woman Wants (1954), The Young Lovers (1954), The Belles of St. Trinian's (1954), To Dorothy a Son (1954), The Sea Shall Not Have Them (1954), As Long as They're Happy (1955), Colonel March Investigates (1955), Doctor at Sea (1955), Stars in Your Eyes (1956), Lost (1956), The Silken Affair (1956), Keep It Clean (1956), Dry Rot (1956), Carry On Admiral (1957), Just My Luck (1957), The Naked Truth (1957), No Time for Tears (1957), Davy (1958), Passport to Shame (1958), Please Turn Over (1959), The Captain's Table (1959), Life in Emergency Ward 10 (1959), Upstairs and Downstairs (1959), Watch Your Stern (1960), Doctor in Love (1960), His and Hers (1961), Mr. Topaze (1961), No My Darling Daughter (1961), The Iron Maiden (1962), A Pair of Briefs (1962), Twice Round the Daffodils (1962), Nurse on Wheels (1963), Strictly for the Birds (1963), San Ferry Ann (1965), The Big Job (1965), Doctor in Clover (1966), Don't Just Lie There, Say Something! (1973), Not Now, Darling (1974), The Alf Garnett Saga (1972), One of Our Dinosaurs Is Missing (1975), The Magnificent Seven Deadly Sins (1971), The Fool (1990), The Princess and the Cobbler (1993).

TELEVISION:

The Adventures of Robin Hood (1955), The Buccaneers (1956), A Journey to London (1975, TV film), Love Among the Ruins (1975, TV film), Hay Fever (1984, TV film), A Murder Is Announced (1985, TV film), Doctor Who – The Trial of a Time Lord (1986), Only Fools and Horses – "The Frog's Legacy" (1987), Victoria Wood – Episode 5 (1989), On the Up (1990–1992), One Foot in the Algarve (1993), As Time Goes By (1994–1998), The Canterville Ghost (1996, TV film), **Hetty Wainthropp Investigates** (1997), **The Last of the Blonde Bombshells** (2000, TV film).

CHARLES HAWTREY

FILM:

Tell Your Children (1922), **This Freedom** (1923), **Marry Me** (1932), **The Melody-Maker** (1933), **Mayfair Girl** (1933), **Smithy** (1933), **High Finance** (1933), **As Good as New** (1933), **Trouble in Store** (1934), **Hyde Park** (1934), **Little Stranger** (1934), **Murder at Monte Carlo** (1935), **Boys Will Be Boys** (1935), **Windfall** (1935), **Man of the Moment** (1935), **Get Off My Foot** (1935), **Well Done, Henry** (1936), **Cheer Up** (1936), **The Brown Wallet** (1936), **Sabotage** (1936), **Good Morning, Boys** (1937), **Melody and Romance** (1937), **Where's That Fire?** (1940), **Jailbirds** (1940), **The Ghost of St. Michael's** (1941), **The Goose Steps Out** (1942), **Let the People Sing** (1942), **Much Too Shy** (1942), **Bell-Bottom George** (1943), **A Canterbury Tale** (1944), **Meet Me at Dawn** (1947), **The End of the River** (1947), **The Story of Shirley Yorke** (1948), **Passport to Pimlico** (1949), **The Lost People** (1949), **Dark Secret** (1949), **Room to Let** (1950), **Smart Alec** (1951), **The Galloping Major** (1951), **Hammer the Toff** (1952), **Brandy for the Parson** (1952), **You're Only Young Twice** (1952), **Five Days** (1954), **To Dorothy a Son** (1954), **As Long as They're Happy** (1955), **Timeslip** (1955), **Simon and Laura** (1955), **Man of the Moment** (1955), **Jumping for Joy** (1956), **Who Done It?** (1956), **The March Hare** (1956), **I Only Arsked!** (1958), **Please Turn Over** (1959), **Inn for Trouble** (1960), **Dentist on the Job** (1961), **What a Whopper** (1961), **Zeta One** (1969), **Stop Exchange** (1970), **The Terrornauts** (1967).

TELEVISION:

Tess and Tim (1956), **Wolfe at the Door** (1956), **Laughter in Store** (1957), **The Army Game** (1957–1958), **Our House** (1960), **Best of Friends** (1963), **Grasshopper Island** (1970), **The Princess and the**

Pea (1979), The Plank (1979), Movie Memories (1981), Runaround (1981), Super Gran (1987).

SID JAMES

FILM:

Black Memory (1947), The October Man (1947), Night Beat (1947), No Orchids for Miss Blandish (1948), The Small Back Room (1949), Once a Jolly Swagman (1949), Paper Orchid (1949), Give Us This Day (1949), Man in Black (1949), Last Holiday (1950), The Lady Craved Excitement (1950), Talk of a Million (1951), The Galloping Major (1951), The Lavender Hill Mob (1951), Lady Godiva Rides Again (1951), The Magic Box (1951), I Believe in You (1952), The Tall Headlines (1952), Emergency Call (1952), Time Gentlemen, Please! (1952), Gift Horse (1952), Father's Doing Fine (1952), Venetian Bird (1952), Miss Robin Hood (1952), Cosh Boy (1953), The Yellow Balloon (1953), The Titfield Thunderbolt (1953), The Flanagan Boy (1953), The Square Ring (1953), Will Any Gentleman...? (1953), Park Plaza 605 (1953), Is Your Honeymoon Really Necessary? (1953), Escape by Night (1953), The Wedding of Lilli Marlene (1953), The Weak and the Wicked (1954), The House Across the Lake (1954), The Rainbow Jacket (1954), Father Brown (1954), Seagulls Over Sorrento (1954), For Better, for Worse (1954), The Belles of St. Trinian's (1954), The Crowded Day (1954), Orders Are Orders (1954), Aunt Clara (1954), Out of the Clouds (1955), The Glass Cage (1955), A Kid for Two Farthings (1955), John and Julie (1955), The Deep Blue Sea (1955), Joe MacBeth (1955), It's a Great Day (1955), A Yank in Ermine (1955), Ramsbottom Rides Again (1956), Wicked as They Come (1956), Trapeze (1956), The Iron Petticoat (1956), Dry Rot (1956), The Extra Day (1956), Interpol (1957), The Smallest Show on Earth (1957), Quatermass 2 (1957), The Shiralee (1957), Hell Drivers (1957), The Story of Esther Costello (1957), Campbell's Kingdom (1957), A King in New York (1957), The Silent Enemy (1958), Another Time, Another Place

(1958), **Next to No Time** (1958), **The Man Inside** (1958), **I Was Monty's Double** (1958), **The Sheriff of Fractured Jaw** (1958), **Make Mine a Million** (1959), **Too Many Crooks** (1959), **I'm All Right Jack** (1959), **The 39 Steps** (1959), **Idol on Parade** (1959), **Upstairs and Downstairs** (1959), **Desert Mice** (1959), **Tommy the Toreador** (1959), **Look at Life** (1959), **And the Same to You** (1960), **Watch Your Stern** (1960), **The Pure Hell of St. Trinian's** (1960), **Look at Life** (1961), **A Weekend with Lulu** (1961), **The Green Helmet** (1961), **Double Bunk** (1961), **Raising the Wind** (1961), **What a Carve Up!** (1961), **What a Whopper** (1961), **We Joined the Navy** (1962), **The Beauty Jungle** (1964), **Tokoloshe** (1965), **The Big Job** (1965), **Three Hats for Lisa** (1966), **Where the Bullets Fly** (1966), **Stop Exchange** (1970),

TELEVISION:

The Adventures of Robin Hood (1955–1959), **Hancock's Half Hour** (1956–1961), **The Crime of the Century** (1956–1957), **East End, West End** (1958), **Citizen James** (1960–1962), **"Taxi!"** (1963–1964), **Sid and Dora** (1965), **George and the Dragon** (1966–1968), **Two in Clover** (1969–1970), **Bless This House** (1971–1976).

KENNETH CONNOR

FILM:

Poison Pen (1939), **The Passionate Pilgrim** (1949), **Over The Odds** (1950), **Don't Say Die** (1950), **Rush Job** (1951), **Elstree Story** (1952), **Miss Robin Hood** (1952), **There Was a Young Lady** (1953), **Marilyn** (1953), **The Black Rider** (1954), **The Ladykillers** (1955), **Davy** (1957), **Make Mine a Million** (1959), **Dentist in the Chair** (1960), **Watch Your Stern** (1960), **His and Hers** (1961), **A Weekend with Lulu** (1961), **Nearly a Nasty Accident** (1961), **Dentist on the Job** (1961), **What a Carve Up!** (1961), **Gonks Go Beat** (1965), **Cuckoo Patrol** (1967), **Danny the Dragon** (1967), **Captain Nemo and the Underwater City** (1969), **Rhubarb** (1969).

TELEVISION:

The Passionate Pilgrim (1949), Oranges and Lemons (1949), Over the Odds (1950), Rush Job (1951), The Boy with a Cart (1951), Winnie-the-Pooh (1952), It's a Small World (1952), The Sand Castle (1952), Shadow Pictures (1952), Huckleberry Finn (1952), BBC Sunday-Night Theatre (1953), Tom's Goblin (1953), The Rose and the Ring (1953), The Grove Family (1954–1955), Stage by Stage (1954), The Three Princes (1954), This Is Show Business, with Vic Oliver (1954), Will O' the Gris (1955), The Farmer's Wife (1955), The Idiot Weekly, Price 2d (1956), A Show Called Fred (1956), Son of Fred (1956), The Charlie Farnsbarns Show (1956), Alfred Marks Time (1956), Emney Enterprises (1955–1956), Pantomania: Babes in the Wood (1957), The Black and White Minstrel Show (1958–1966), Hi, Summer! (1957–1960), Torchy the Battery Boy (1960), Four Feather Falls (1960), The Sid James Show (1961), Don't Say a Word (1963–1964), Room at the Bottom (1966), Danny the Dragon (1967), On the House (1970–1971), Jokers Wild (1970), The Kenneth Connor Show (1972), 'Allo 'Allo! (1984–1992), Hi-de-Hi! (1986–1988), Blackadder the Third (1987), Rentaghost (1982–1984), You Rang, M'Lord? (1990), The Memoirs of Sherlock Holmes (1994).

PETER BUTTERWORTH

FILM:

William Comes to Town (1948), Murder at the Windmill a.k.a. Mystery at the Burlesque (1949), Miss Pilgrim's Progress (1949), The Adventures of Jane (1949), The Body Said No! (1950), Night and the City (1950), Double Confession (1950), Paul Temple's Triumph (1950), Mister Drake's Duck (1951), Circle of Danger (1951), Appointment with Venus (1951), The Case of the Missing Scene (1951), Island Rescue (1951), Old Mother Riley's Jungle Treasure (1951), Saturday Island a.k.a. Island of Desire (1952), Penny Princess (1952), Will Any Gentleman...? (1953), Colonel

March Investigates (1953), **Is Your Honeymoon Really Necessary?** (1953), **Watch Out** (1953, short), **A Good Pull-up** (1953, short), **The Gay Dog** (1954), **Fun at St. Fanny's** (1956), **Blow Your Own Trumpet** (1958), **Tom Thumb** (1958), **The Spider's Web** (1960), **Escort for Hire** (1960), **Murder, She Said** (1961), **Fate Takes a Hand** (1961), **The Day the Earth Caught Fire** (1961), **She'll Have to Go** a.k.a. **Maid for Murder** (1962), **Kill or Cure** (1962), **Live Now, Pay Later** (1962), **The Prince and the Pauper** (1962), **The Rescue Squad** (1963), **The Switch** (1963), **The Odd Man, "Prince on a White Horse"** (1963), **Doctor in Distress** (1963), **The Edgar Wallace Mystery Theatre, "Never Mention Murder"** (1964), **A Home of Your Own** (1965), **The Amorous Adventures of Moll Flanders** (1965), **Funny Thing Happened on the Way to the Forum** (1966), **Ouch!** (1967, short), **Danny the Dragon** (1967), **Prudence and the Pill** (1968), **The Magnificent Seven Deadly Sins** (1971), **A Class by Himself** (1972), **Bless This House** (1972), **Not Now Darling** (1973), **Robin and Marian** (1976), **The Ritz** (1976), **What's Up Nurse!** (1978), **The First Great Train Robbery** a.k.a. **The Great Train Robbery** (1979).

TELEVISION:

By Candlelight (1949), **How Do You View?** (1950–1951), **BBC Sunday Night Theatre, "The Happy Sunday Afternoon"** (1951), **Saturday Special** (1951–1953), **Whirlygig** (1951), **The Passing Show** (1951), **Aladdin** (1951), **Trial Gallop** (1952), **Friends and Neighbours** (1954), **Theatre Royal, "The Stocking"** (1955), **Those Kids** (1956), **ITV Play of the Week, "I Killed the Count"** (1956), **Armchair Theatre, "The Common Man"** (1956), **Armchair Theatre, "Start from Scratch"** (1957), **Armchair Theatre, "Off the Deep End"** (1957), **Any Old Iron?** (1957), **The Anne Shelton Show** (1959), **No Hiding Place, "Everybody Loves Jerry"** (1959), **Inside Story, "A Present for Penny"** (1960), **Meet the Champ** (1960), **The Cheaters** (1961–1962), **Armchair Theatre, "His Polyvinyl Girl"** (1961), **Alfred Marks Time** (1961), **ITV Television Playhouse, "Mr. Cole and the Middle Kingdom"** (1961), **Armchair Theatre, "The Fishing Match"**

(1962), Bulldog Breed, "The New Garage" and "The New Digs" (1962), Dixon of Dock Green, "Dead Jammy" (1962), The Danny Thomas Show, "A Hunting We Will Go" (1962), The Magical World of Disney (1962–1963), ITV Play of the Week, "The Kidnapping of Mary Smith" (1963), ITV Play of the Week, "Cunningham 5101" (1963), BBC Sunday-Night Play, "The Holly Road Rig" (1963), Emergency Ward 10 (1964), Festival, "Police" (1964), The Roy Castle Show (1964), Drama 61-67, "Drama '64: A Menace to Decent People" (1964), Armchair Mystery Theatre, "The Blackmailing of Mr S" (1964), Love Story, "The Apprentices" (1964), Just Jimmy, "Chips with Nothing" (1964), Danger Man a.k.a. Secret Agent, "The Ubiquitous Mr. Lovegrove" (1965), ITV Play of the Week, "We Thought You'd Like to Be Caesar" (1965), Public Eye, "A Harsh World for Zealots" (1965), Six of the Best, "Porterhouse: Private Eye" (1965), Doctor Who: The Time Meddler (1965) Doctor Who: The Daleks' Master Plan (1966), Hugh and I, "It Never Rains" (1966), The Frankie Howerd Show (1966), The Informer, "Keep off the Grass" (1967), Danny the Dragon (1967), Scott on... (1968–1972), The Sooty Show (1968–1974), Inside George Webley, "Get Well Soon" (1968), The Wednesday Play, "The Fabulous Frump" (1969), Wink to Me Only, "The Lost Chord" (1969), Nearest and Dearest, "Now Is the Hour" (1969), Catweazle, (1970–1971), Ours Is a Nice House, "Judge for Yourself" (1970), Kindly Leave the Kerb (1971), A Class by Himself (1972), Odd Man Out (1977), Dad's Army, "The Face on the Poster" (1975), A Bunch of Fives, "A Cry for Help" (1977), Odd Man Out (1977), The Dancing Princesses (1978), Afternoon Off (1979).

HATTIE JACQUES

FILM:

Green for Danger (1946), Nicholas Nickleby (1947), Oliver Twist (1948), Trottie True (1949), The Spider and the Fly (1949), Waterfront (1950), Chance of a Lifetime (1950), Scrooge (1951), No

Haunt for a Gentleman (1952), Mother Riley Meets the Vampire (1952), The Pickwick Papers (1952), All Hallowe'en (1952), The Pleasure Garden (1953), Our Girl Friday (1953), Up to His Neck (1954), The Love Lottery (1954), As Long as They're Happy (1955), Now and Forever (1956), The Square Peg (1958), Left Right and Centre (1959), The Night We Dropped a Clanger (1959), Follow a Star (1959), The Navy Lark (1959), Make Mine Mink (1960), School for Scoundrels (1960), Watch Your Stern (1960), In the Doghouse (1961), She'll Have to Go (1962), The Punch and Judy Man (1963), The Plank (1967), The Bobo (1967), Rhubarb (1969), Monte Carlo or Bust! (1969), Crooks and Coronets (1969), The Magic Christian (1969), Danger Point (1971), You'd Better Go in Disguise, Three for All (1975).

TELEVISION:

Late Joys Revue (1946), No, No, Nanette (1948), Out of This World (1950), Panorama (1954), Happy Holidays (1954), Plunder (1955), The Granville Melodramas (1955), Tribute to Henry Hall (1956), The Tony Hancock Show (1956), Pantomania (1956), Hancock's Half Hour (1957), A Cup of Kindness (1959), Gala Opening (1959), Hancock's Half Hour, "The Cruise" (1959), Sykes and a... (1960), Royal Variety Performance (1960), Twentieth Century Theatre, "The Insect Play" (1960), Sykes and a... (1960), Our House (1960), Sally Ann Howes Variety Show (1961), Juke Box Jury (1960), Our House (1961), Billy Cotton Band Show (1961), Compact (1962), That Was the Week That Was (1962), Christmas Night with the Stars (1962), This Is Your Life (1963), Miss Adventure (1964), A Choice of Coward: Blithe Spirit (1964), Cribbins (1965), Jackanory (1966), Titi-Pu (1967), Theatre 625, "The Memorandum" (1967), Sykes Versus ITV (1967), Knock Three Times (1968), Inside George Webley (1968), The World of Beachcomber (1968), Howerd's Hour (1968), Join Jim Dale (1969), Pickwick (1969), Catweazle (1970), Charley's Grants (1970), Dangerpoint (1971), Ask Aspel (1971), Sykes and a Big, Big Show (1971), Frankie Howerd: The Laughing

Stock of Television (1971), Doctor at Large: "Cynthia Darling" (1971), Sykes – With the Lid Off (1971), Christmas Night with the Stars (1971), Max Bygraves at the Royalty (1972), Max Bygraves at the Royalty (1972), Pebble Mill at One (1973), Call My Bluff (1973), Celebrity Squares (1975), Wogan's World (1975), Looks Familiar (1975), 2nd House: The Sound of Laughter (1975), Sykes: "Christmas Party" (1975), Multi-Coloured Swap Shop (1978), Play It Again, Hattie Jacques (1980), Rhubarb Rhubarb (1980).

BERNARD BRESSLAW

FILM:

The Men of Sherwood Forest (1954), The Glass Cage (1955), Satellite in the Sky (1956), Up in the World (1956), High Tide at Noon (1957), Blood of the Vampire (1958), I Only Arsked! (1958), Too Many Crooks (1959), The Ugly Duckling (1959), It's All Happening (1962), Morgan: A Suitable Case for Treatment (1966), Moon Zero Two (1969), Spring and Port Wine (1970), Up Pompeii (1971), The Magnificent Seven Deadly Sins (1971), Blinker's Spy-Spotter (1972), Vampira (1974), One of Our Dinosaurs Is Missing (1975), In the Movies it Doesn't Hurt (1975), Joseph Andrews (1977), Jabberwocky (1977), The Fifth Musketeer (1979), Hawk the Slayer (1980), Krull (1983), Asterix and the Big Fight (1989), Leon the Pig Farmer (1992), Bernard Bresslaw: A Story About Bernard Bresslaw (2009).

TELEVISION:

The Adventures of Robin Hood: The Black Patch, The Army Game, Our House (1961–1962), Danger Man: The Outcast (1964), Doctor Who: The Ice Warriors (1967), The Goodies (1971), The Book Tower (1987), T-Bag (1987), Terry and June (1982), Sykes (1974), Doctor in the House (1969), Mann's Best Friends (1984), The Book Tower (1987–1988).

JIM DALE

FILM:

Break-In (1956), Six Five Special (1958), Raising the Wind (1961), The Iron Maiden (1962), Nurse on Wheels (1963), The Big Job (1965), The Plank (1967), Lock Up Your Daughters (1969), Digby, the Biggest Dog in the World (1973), The National Health (1973), Adolf Hitler: My Part in His Downfall (1973), Pete's Dragon (1977), Joseph Andrews (1977), Hot Lead and Cold Feet (1978), Unidentified Flying Oddball (1979), Scandalous (1984), The Hunchback (1997), Pushing Daisies (2007).

TELEVISION:

Six-Five Special (1957), Thank Your Lucky Stars (1965–1966), Join Jim Dale (1969), Sunday Night at the London Palladium (1973), Cinderella Ballet (1981), Adventures of Huckleberry Finn (1986), The American Clock (1993), The Bill Cosby Show (1998), The Ellen Burstyn Show, The Dinah Shore Show, Meet Jim Dale, The Jim Dale Show, The Equalizer: Mama's Boy.

BARBARA WINDSOR

FILM:

The Belles of St Trinian's (1954), Lost (1956), Make Mine a Million (1959), Too Hot to Handle (1960), Flame in the Streets (1961), On the Fiddle (1961), Hair of the Dog (1962), Death Trap (1962), Sparrows Can't Sing (1963), Crooks in Cloisters (1964), San Ferry Ann (1965), A Study in Terror (1965), Chitty Chitty Bang Bang (1968), The Boy Friend (1971) Not Now, Darling (1973), Comrades (1986), It Couldn't Happen Here (1987), Pussy in Boots (1994), Second Star to the Left (2001), Alice in Wonderland (2010), Alice Through the Looking Glass (2016).

TELEVISION:

Dreamer's Highway (1954–1955), The Rag Trade (1961–1963), The Edgar Wallace Mystery Theatre (1962), A Christmas Night with the Stars (1962), The Plane Makers (1963), The Rag Trade (1963), Comedy Playhouse (1964), Two Plus Two (1964), The Des O'Connor Show (1965), Before the Fringe (1967), Dad's Army (1968), Ooh La La! (1968), Wild, Wild Women (1968–1969), The Rolf Harris Show (1969), Comedy Playhouse (1970), Up Pompeii! (1970), Ooh La La! (1973), The Bob Monkhouse Offensive (1973), The Punch Review (1973), Whodunnit? (1973), The Mike Reid Show (1976), Both Ends Meet (1980), Worzel Gummidge (1980), Filthy Rich & Catflap (1987), Super Gran (1987), The Grand Knockout Tournament (1987), The Nephew (1988), Terry in Pantoland (1988), Norbert Smith: A Life (1989), Bluebirds (1989), Family Fortunes (1990), You Rang, M'Lord? (1991), Double Vision (1992), Frank Stubbs (1993), The Great Bong (1993), EastEnders (1994–2010, 2013–2016), One Foot in the Grave (1995), The Nearly Complete and Utter History of Everything (1999), Cor, Blimey! (2000), Second Star to the Left (2001), Walk on the Wild Side (2009), Little Crackers (2011), Come Fly With Me (2011), Children in Need (2015), The Tube: Going Underground (2016), Babs (2017).

Explore More: A Handpicked Selection of Similar Productions for Your Next Watch

Gerald Thomas also directed several other films that were produced by Peter Rogers, including **Please Turn Over** (1959), **Watch Your Stern** (1960), **No Kidding** (1960), **Raising the Wind** (1961), **Twice Round the Daffodils** (1962), **Nurse on Wheels** (1963), **The Big Job** (1965), and the television spin-off **Bless This House** (1972). While these films shared the same writers and occasionally the same cast and crew as the Carry On series, they are not considered part of the franchise.

Additionally, **Carry On Admiral** (1957), which also features Joan Sims, is often mistaken as part of the Carry On Collection.

CARRY ON QUOTING

Come come, Matron. Surely you've seen a temperature taken like this before?

Look at you. Standing as if you're pregnant!

It wouldn't surprise me, the way I'm mucked about.

Do you provide substitutes?

No! This is a respectable firm.

Are you satisfied with your quipment, Miss Allcock?

As a connoisseur of police personalities, let me state that I have never before been arrested with such charm. Never. I salute her.

If you've got a heart of oak, it's got a worm in it.

I'm going to be blunt, and make some very cutting remarks.

When you get to be a cab driver you cut yourself right off from the rest of the human race. Everybody's got it in for you and nobody loves you. In no time at all you find that you're about as popular as a wickerwork seat in a nudist camp, and you know what sort of impression that makes on people.

Oh, Mr. Simpkins, that was wonderful. I'm sure I'll never get my drawers off as slickly as that.

Oh, Vienna! Lovely! I've always wanted to see Vienna before I die

But you're my personal bodyguard and champion gladiator! I don't want to die! I may not be a very good live emperor but I'd be a worse one dead!

Infamy! Infamy! They've all got it in for me

- I once talked peace with a Sioux, but you can't trust them. One moment it was peace on, the next it was peace off.

- FRYING TONIGHT!

- Slobotham, I'm beginning to think he's right. There is something funny going on in this house.

- Salt Tablets, The Pill... The Pill? What do you suppose they use that for?

- Oh, drop it in the basket, I'll read it later.

- You may not realise it but I was once a weak man

  Once a week is enough for any man.

- They don't want rubber sheets, they want straightjackets.

- Oh dear! I seem to have got a little plastered!

- Sir, I do not object to jiggery but I take exception to pokery!

- Joan may think you're a gentleman but personally I've got sore misgivings

- I'm flabbergasted! My gast has never been so flabbered!

- "Wouldn't eat the mu-". Thank you, "Dr. Crippen". Don't call us, we'll call you.

- Oh, Fawkes!

Carry On Revisited | 219

> Well I could make you some beans on toast or something?
>
> No, nothing too elaborate, thank

> By the way; your mail.
>
> Yes, I am. And I can prove it, d'you hear. Prove it.

> Your blade, ma'am. You handle it far too well for my liking!
>
> I shouldn't worry. You don't look as if you've got much to

> I tried it once and didn't like it.

> You and a bunch of beauty queens? It's like asking Dracula to be in charge of a blood bank!

> Don't worry me and Professor Crump will soon be having it off.

> Now, grit your teeth and we will have it off in a minute

> Why me? You could have Tom, Dick or Harry
>
> I don't want Tom or Harry!

> You mean, the sharks won't eat me whole?
>
> Oh, no! I'm told they spit that bit out first!

CARRY ON GUESSING: THE ULTIMATE CARRY ON QUIZ

	Questions
1	What was the first Carry On film to be shot in colour?
2	Name all four medical films, in order of their release?
3	(Sergeant) What was the first line of dialogue ever spoken?
4	(Constable) Which character was superstitious?
5	(Regardless) What disaster befalls Helping Hand's new filing system?
6	(Emmannuelle) Who is the character Lyons, and which actor portrayed him?
7	Which two films were originally released without the Carry On prefix?
8	(Dick) What is the name of the new police force established by King George II to combat crime?
9	(Spying) What is the name of Barbara Windsor's character and codename?
10	(Cleo) What was the name of the Roman bodyguard who was killed by Horsa?
11	(Cowboy) Which character does Kenneth Williams play?
12	(England) What comedic incident occurs with Captain Melly's uniform during training?
13	(Head) Which revolutionary leader is trying to capture The Black Fingernail?
14	(Camel) What is the name of the café where Sergeant Nocker enjoys himself during "patrol"?
15	What Carry On Film was the last to be shot in black and white?
16	(Doctor) What plan do the hospital patients hatch to get revenge on Dr. Tinkle and Matron?
17	(Khyber) What character does Terry Scott portray?
18	(Camping) Joan Sims plays which character?
19	(Again Doctor) Which actor made a cameo appearance as Mr. Pullen?
20	(Girls) What was unique about Valerie Leon's performance?
21	(Loving) Which actor is introduced as a sinister client referred to as Dr. Crippen?
22	Name the actress who played Jenny Grubb and in which Carry On Film?
23	(Henry) What was the original alternative title planned for the production and what film inspired this pun?
24	(Convenience) Which horse did Sid bet on after Joey's prediction?
25	(Matron) Which character becomes suspicious of Cyril's true identity?
26	(Abroad) What incident lands the holidaymakers in jail during their trip?
27	(Girls) Which character is outraged by the idea of the beauty contest and storms out of the council meeting?
28	What year was Carry On Emmannuelle released?
29	(Behind) Who were the two friends who went on a caravanning holiday together?

Carry On Revisited | 221

30	(England) Which actor reprises a similar character from the sitcom It Ain't Half Hot Mum?
31	(Screaming) Which character is transformed into a hairy monster man by Valeria & Dr. Orlando Watt?
32	(Columbus) Which character is portrayed by Julian Clary?
33	(England) Who played Gunner Shorthouse?
34	Which Carry On film had Marianne Stone's character cut from the final version, despite being credited?
35	(Nurse) What is the name of the hospital?
36	What is the title of the fifth film in the Carry On series?
37	(Cruising) What is the name of the cruise ship?
38	(Screaming) Who played the role of Detective Sergeant Sidney Bung?
39	(Teacher) Which young actor, later famous, played a pupil?
40	(Emmannuelle) What is the name of the chat show host who Emmannuelle has an affair with?
41	(Spying) Who plays Harold Crump and what is his codename?
42	What is the title of the eighth film in the Carry On series?
43	(Sergeant) Which actor played Sergeant Grimshaw?
44	(Jack) Who wrote the screenplay?
45	(Jack) What role does Jim Dale play?
46	(Cleo) Who is Sosages?
47	(Behind) Which three actors made their final Carry On appearances?
48	(Screaming) What is the name of the monster that abducts Doris Mann in the woods?
49	(Khyber) What is the name of the Khasi's warlord ally?
50	(Screaming) Why are Sidney and Valeria unable to transform Emily back into her human form?
51	(Camping) What was the finishing school called?
52	(Cleo) What was the name of the caveman character played by Jim Dale?
53	(Camel) What is the name of the main character who joins the French Foreign Legion?
54	(Cowboy) What is the name of the character played by Angela Douglas?
55	(England) Why were Kenneth Williams and Barbara Windsor unavailable for filming?
56	(Doctor) What is the name of Frankie Howerd's character?
57	(Camping) What do Sid and Bernie discover upon arriving at the Paradise campsite?
58	(Screaming) Which character is turned into a mannequin after being captured by Oddbod Junior?
59	Which actor made their Carry On debut due to Joan Sims falling ill?
60	(Regardless) What pet does Francis have to walk?
61	What was the first film in the Carry On series to feature both Peter Butterworth and Bernard Bresslaw?
62	(Spying) Which Carry On regular makes their first appearance in the series?
63	(Constable) Why was the police station understaffed?

64	(Khyber) What scandal triggers the Khasi's plans to incite rebellion?
65	(Again Doctor) What incident at the hospital leads to Nookey causing a massive short circuit?
66	(Jungle) Who is the jungle boy that rescues June?
67	(Convenience) What alternate title was used for this film outside the UK?
68	(Screaming) Who provided the voice of Oddbod Junior?
69	Which actor's mother accidentally set her handbag on fire during filming?
70	(Cleo) Which actress played the title role of Cleopatra (and what was her first Carry On Appearance?
71	(Loving) What is the name of the dating agency run by Sid Bliss and Sophie Plummett?
72	(Matron) Which character is a hypochondriac convinced he is undergoing a sex change?
73	(Nurse) Which patient falls in love with Nurse Denton?
74	(Abroad) What is the name of the Mediterranean island where the characters go on holiday?
75	(Jack) What was the original title of the film before it became part of the Carry On series?
76	(Girls) Which character transforms from a prim persona into a glamorous contestant, stepping in to save the contest?
77	(Cabby) What happens to Peggy and Sally towards the end of the film?
78	(Girls) Why did Kenneth Williams and Charles Hawtrey not appear?
79	(Behind) What type of expert was Anna Vrooshka?
80	(Jungle) Name the character played by Joan Sims?
81	(Sergeant) Who are the two main characters introduced as a married couple?
82	(Cruising) What song does Dr Binn serenade Flo with?
83	(Spying) Identify the actor and their character associated with the codename "Yellow Peril."
84	(Henry) Who was originally considered for the role of Henry VIII?
85	(Loving) Which character undergoes a makeover to become a model?
86	Which films were named among the five worst in the Carry On series by the British Film Institute in a 2018 retrospective?
87	(Dick) How does the Bow Street Runners learn about Turpin's distinguishing feature?
88	(Behind) Who wrote the script, making it the first in 13 years not written by Talbot Rothwell?
89	(Girls) Who played Larry?
90	(England) What humorous name is given to the private bunker used by the 1313 Battery?
91	(Spying) What happens to the chemical formula?
92	(Loving) What is the profession of Percival Snooper, played by Kenneth Williams?
93	(Loving) Who plays the volatile wrestler Gripper Burke?
94	In which Carry On films did Margaret Nolan make her first and final appearances?
95	(Emmannuelle) How does Theodore Valentine retaliate against Emmannuelle?

Carry On Revisited | 223

96	(Columbus) Who plays King Ferdinand and Queen Isabella of Spain?
97	Who appeared in all four of the Carry On Christmas TV specials?
98	(Constable) Which series regular made his first appearance?
99	(Regardless) Who composed the music?
100	(Sergeant) Which character is a chronic hypochondriac?
101	What year was Carry On Cabby released?
102	(Cruising) Name the characters played by Sid James and Esma Cannon?
103	(Nurse) Which nurse is known for being clumsy and accidentally calls the fire brigade?
104	(Jack) Which actress plays Sally?
105	(Regardless) What is the name of the job agency?
106	(Spying) Who is revealed to be a double agent working for SNOG?
107	(Teacher) Which actor played Mr William Wakefield?
108	(Cowboy) What is the name of the town where the majority of the film takes place?
109	(Screaming) What happens to Dr. Orlando Watt and Rubbatiti in their final moments?
110	(Head) What is the nickname given to the mysterious hero who rescues French nobles from execution?
111	(Camel) Which character is portrayed as the leader of the attacking forces against the fort?
112	(Constable) Which female character does PC Charles Constable fall in love?
113	(Jack) How does the crew of the Venus manage to defeat five Spanish ships towards the end of the film?
114	(Cleo) Which actor plays the soothsayer that warns Caesar of the plot to kill him and what connection does the actor have with Carry On Sergeant?
115	(Camel) How much was Phil Silvers paid for his role, causing animosity among the regular cast?
116	(Cabby) What is the name of Charlie's original taxi company?
117	(Screaming) Which actor was initially offered the role of Valeria, but declined it?
118	(Head) What is the name of Sir Rodney Ffing's true love?
119	Frankie Howerd appeared in two Carry On Films, which were they?
120	(Khyber) What is the name of the fictional Highland regiment?
121	(Spying) What special ability does Daphne Honeybutt have?
122	(Cruising) What is the name of the character played by Kenneth Connor?
123	(Camping) Which character (played by which actor?) vows never to go camping again?
124	(Again Doctor) What is the full name of the character Hattie Jacques plays?
125	(Cleo) What happens to Agrippa and his fellow assassins?
126	(Khyber) What is Brother Belcher's reaction to the events at the Residency?
127	(Jungle) Name the two tribes?
128	(Henry) Name the characters played by Charles Hawtrey and Barbara Windsor?

129	(Again Doctor) What causes trouble for Dr. Jimmy Nookey at the beginning of the film?
130	(Convenience) What is the name of the ceramics factory?
131	(Matron) What is the main objective of Sid Carter's gang?
132	(Teacher) What school served as the exterior location?
133	(Doctor) Name the character who fakes their symptoms to stay in the hospital?
134	(Regardless) How many languages can Kenneth Williams' character speak and what is his name?
135	(Camel) Which actress makes her first Carry On appearance as Corktip?
136	(Nurse) What prank do Nurse Dawson and Nurse Axwell play on the Colonel?
137	(Camping) Which actress famously starred as Miss Dobbin, the camping store assistant?
138	(Constable) What mistake does PC Stanley Benson make while on duty?
139	(Cruising) Why did Charles Hawtrey not appear?
140	(Sergeant) What gift do the platoon members give Sergeant Grimshaw on his last day?
141	(Spying) Which actor had previously appeared in The Third Man?
142	(Head) Which French noble is rescued by The Black Fingernail disguised as an insurance salesman?
143	How did Carry On Doctor perform at the British box office in 1968?
144	In what year was Carry On Up the Khyber included in the BFI's list of greatest British films, and at what position?
145	(Jungle) Name Bernard Bresslaw's character?
146	(Loving) Who plays the seamstress Esme Crowfoot?
147	(Henry) What comedic twist prevents Henry VIII from consummating his marriage with Marie of Normandy?
148	(Convenience) Which character is responsible for designing the controversial bidet?
149	(Abroad) Who played the brothel keeper and what is her connection to Sid James?
150	(Girls) Which character (and actor) was upgraded to a main role, marking their third appearance in the series?
151	(Dick) Which character leads the Bow Street Runners and is determined to catch Dick Turpin?
152	(Dick) Which three main actors made their final appearances?
153	(Behind) What was unique about the casting of Joan Sims and Patsy Rowlands as mother and daughter?
154	(England) Which Carry On regular plays the role of Captain S Melly?
155	(Columbus) Who portrayed Fatima?
156	(Columbus) Who was originally cast to play the King of Spain before his death?
157	(Spying) What issue did the film's poster face in relation to its artwork?
158	(Cleo) What happens to Horsa and Hengist at the end?
159	(Teacher) What is the name of the senior pupil who overhears Mr Wakefield's plans?
160	(Emmannuelle) What is Émile Prévert's main hobby?

161	(Sergeant) What was the original title of the screenplay?
162	(Cruising) Which actor made their only Carry On appearance and what was their character name and profession?
163	(Jack) Why is Albert Poop-Decker considered an incompetent seaman?
164	(Spying) Who plays Desmond Simkins, what was his codename and where has he always wanted to visit?
165	(Camel) Where were the Sahara scenes filmed?
166	(Cabby) Which actor made their first appearance?
167	What film followed Carry On Cleo in the Carry On series?
168	(Henry) What inspired the film's promotional tagline, A Great Guy With His Chopper?
169	(Again Doctor) Who is responsible for spiking Dr. Nookey's drink at the staff party?
170	What play was Carry On Nurse adapted from?
171	(Camping) What motivates Sid Boggle and Bernie Lugg to take their girlfriends on a camping holiday?
172	(Camping) What noisy group disrupts the campsite with a rave?
173	Which actor made their debut in Carry On Loving, and what was the title of their second (and final) appearance?
174	(Again Doctor) What role does Patsy Rowlands play?
175	(Girls) What comedic mishap occurs involving the Mayor during a photoshoot?
176	(Cowboy) Which actress played the sharp-shooting Belle Armitage?
177	Bill Owen and Esma Cannon made their final appearances in which Carry On?
178	(Teacher) Name the characters that visit the school to conduct an inspection? Name the actors who portray them.
179	(Henry) Which series regular played Lord Hampton of Wick?
180	(Regardless) What is the final outcome for the landlord's property?
181	(Girls) What is the real name of Hope Springs, played by Barbara Windsor?
182	What Brighton-based hotel, owned by an actress from Carry On Sergeant, served as an exterior filming location for Carry On Girls?
183	(Dick) Where do Fancey and Strapp go undercover to gather information about Turpin?
184	Which Carry On film was the longest, with a runtime of one hour and thirty-seven minutes?
185	(Behind) What surprising discovery does Daphne make about her estranged husband Henry Barnes?
186	(England) What was the reason for Sid James's absence from the film?
187	(Emmannuelle) Who played the character of Emmannuelle Prévert?
188	In which Carry On film did Joan Sims first appear?
189	What is the connection between Carry On Columbus and Carry On Jack in terms of filming locations?
190	Who made his debut in Carry On Matron with a cameo appearance, and then appeared in all subsequent films?
191	Patsy Rowlands often played characters that started off as meek and transformed into more assertive women. How many Carry On films did she appear in?

192	In which Carry On film did Dora Bryan play the character Nora?
193	(Cabby) Why does Peggy Hawkins start her own rival taxi company and what is it called?
194	(Head) Who accompanies Citizen Camembert and his lover, Desirée, to England disguised as the Comte and Comtesse de la Plume de ma Tante?
195	Which was the first Carry On film to reach a budget of £100,000?
196	(Camel) What is Bo's humorous response after being blown up during a cricket game?
197	(Khyber) Which actor portrayed Captain Keene?
198	(Sergeant) Which barracks were used for filming?
199	(Nurse) What causes the patients to become intoxicated?
200	In which three Carry On films did Bernard Cribbins appear, and what were the names of his characters?
201	Which Carry On film was the first not to feature Kenneth Williams?
202	(Behind) Why was Sid James absent?
203	(Emmannuelle) Name the characters played by Joan Sims and Peter Butterworth?
204	(Abroad) What unusual joke is included in the opening credits?
205	Name the five best Carry On films as voted for by the British Film Institute in 2018
206	(Convenience) What significant outdoor location is featured during the annual works outing?
207	(Girls) What role does the character Peter Potter reluctantly take on during the Women's Things publicity stunt?
208	(Henry) Which two actors reunited for the first time in seven years?
209	(Khyber) What comedic element gives the film its title's risqué humour?
210	Which Carry On film was the highest-grossing movie at the UK box office in 1969?
211	(Henry) How does King Francis of France contribute to the plot?
212	(Spying) What does the antagonist organisation STENCH stand for?
213	(Cruising) Where were the exterior scenes filmed?
214	(Again Doctor) How does Dr. Nookey profit from the weight-loss serum?
215	(Emmannuelle) What is the primary setting for the film's opening scene?
216	(Abroad) marked Charles Hawtrey's last appearance. How many films did he appear in?
217	(Khyber) Which classic war film's props were used to dress the soldiers?
218	What was the final Carry On film for actors Julian Holloway and Patricia Franklin?
219	(Convenience) What role does Sid James play and how does it differ from his usual Carry On persona?
220	(Jungle) Name the character (and actor) who plays Professor Tinkle's assistant?
221	(Jungle) Which character (and actor) is the leader of the all-female Lubby-Dubby tribe?
222	(Teacher) What class does Mr Gregory Adams teach?
223	Which writer worked on the early Carry On films (1958–1962)?
224	(Matron) Name the character played by Charles Hawtrey?
225	(Nurse) What is the Colonel's favourite activity?

226	(Head) Name the roles played by Sid James, Peter Butterworth and Jim Dale?
227	(Teacher) Why do the pupils try to sabotage the inspection?
228	(Jack) Who composed the music?
229	(Abroad) Which notable actress returned to the series after a 13-year absence?
230	(Cleo) What was Kenneth Williams' famous line?
231	(Constable) What location was used for the exterior of the police station?
232	(Cleo) What was the name of the firm that sold Horsa as a slave?
233	(Spying) What is the connection between STENCH and the chief of the Secret Service?
234	(Doctor) What is the name of Jim Dales character?
235	(Regardless) What job does Bert Handy mistakenly end up doing at a hospital?
236	What accolade did Carry On Camping receive in a 2008 Daily Mirror survey?
237	(Henry) What happened to the unused madrigals written for the original version of this film?
238	(Cowboy) Which character is the leader of the Indians and which actor portrays him?
239	(Cowboy) What is the occupation of Marshal P. Knutt, played by Jim Dale?
240	(Jack) What happens to Captain Fearless towards the end of the film?
241	(Khyber) What role does Angela Douglas play?
242	(Camping) What happens to disrupt the happiness of Sid and Bernie when their girlfriends agree to share a tent?
243	(Screaming) What is the name of the creepy mansion where much of the action takes place?
244	(Screaming) Who creates the second Oddbod creature, Oddbod Junior?
245	(Head) What object does Sir Rodney leave with Jacqueline as a symbol of his love?
246	(Camel) Why did filming have to be halted at Camber Sands?
247	(Convenience) Name the union representative and how does his behaviour disrupt the factory?
248	(Matron) What comedic role does Joan Sims play?
249	(Cabby) What was the original planned title, before it became part of the Carry On series?
250	What was the first Carry On film to be produced by the Rank Organisation?
251	Which other Carry On film reused some of the sets from Carry On Follow That Camel?
252	(Jack) What characters do Kenneth Williams and Charles Hawtrey play?
253	(England) Why do the battery members sabotage an inspection by the Brigadier?
254	(Dick) Name the character portrayed by Jack Douglas?
255	(Screaming) What was the original relationship between Valeria and Orlando Watt, which was later changed at the request of Kenneth Williams?
256	(Screaming) Which actor, known for his popularity with American audiences, was added to the cast at the last minute and what was his character's name?
257	Which Carry On film was the last for Terry Scott and what was his character name?
258	(Cowboy) What theme song was featured and who sung it?
259	(Doctor) Name the actress (and her character) who causes trouble for Dr. Tinkle?

260	(Doctor) What real-life building doubled as the hospital?
261	(Khyber) What comical tactic is used at the end to scare off the invading Afghan army?
262	(Khyber) Where were the scenes for the Khyber Pass filmed?
263	(Camping) Name the character (and actor) who plays the farmer and owner of the campsite?
264	(Camel) Phil Silvers plays which role?
265	(Camel) What is the alternative title for screenings outside the UK?
266	(Matron) What disguise does Sid Carter use during the gang's attempted robbery?
267	(Abroad) What mishap occurs with the hotel?
268	(Behind) What mistake did Major Leap make when arranging entertainment for the caravanners?
269	(Dick) What incriminating evidence leads to Harriett's temporary capture?
270	(Girls) How does the character Hope Springs respond when she believes Dawn Brakes has stolen her bikini?
271	(Again Doctor) What unexpected side effect does the weight-loss serum cause?
272	(Head) What happens to Citizen Camembert and Bidet at the end?
273	(Screaming) Which actor was set to play Detective Sergeant Sidney Bung and why did they decline the role?
274	(Cowboy) Which character is killed in the opening scenes, prompting the arrival of Marshal Knutt?
275	(Jack) What is the filming location for the HMS Venus scene?
276	(Abroad) Which character develops a romance with Brother Bernard?
277	(Matron) Which two Carry On regulars were absent?
278	(Camel) Which famous book does this Carry On parody?
279	(Camping) Which real-life cinema featured in the opening scene?
280	How did Carry On Up the Khyber perform at the UK box office in 1969?
281	(Doctor) What event restores Dr. Kilmore's reputation at the end of the film?
282	(England) Name the characters played by Joan Sims, Judy Geeson and Jack Douglas?
283	(Dick) Which actor played Sir Roger Daley, a key figure leading the effort to capture Dick Turpin?
284	(Girls) What is the name of the publicist who helps Sidney organise the beauty contest?
285	(Convenience) Why was the film considered the first box office failure of the series?
286	(Henry) Which musical piece is referenced in the opening theme, and who arranged it?
287	(Jungle) Name the character and the actor who plays the ornithologist leading the expedition?
288	(Again Doctor) Charles Hawtrey dresses as a female patient to try to steal the serum, name their male and female character name?
289	(Head) How does Desirée manipulate Sir Rodney Ffing?
290	(Screaming) Who was the original actor planned to play the role of Dan Dann before Charles Hawtrey replaced him?

291	(Cowboy) Where does Marshal Knutt conceal himself while fighting the Rumpo Kid's gang?
292	(Cleo) What was the original intended use of the costumes and sets?
293	(Spying) What was the original codename for Charles Hawtrey's character and why was it changed?
294	(Jack) What motivates Sally to go to sea?
295	(Behind) What natural event caused the tunnels of the archaeological dig to collapse?
296	(Abroad) What is the final scene and where does it take place?
297	(Matron) What filming location served as the exterior for Finisham Maternity Hospital?
298	(Khyber) Which costumes from an earlier film were rented for the Highland regiment?
299	(Doctor) What embarrassing situation does Dr. Kilmore face on the hospital roof?
300	(Columbus) Who plays the role of the Sultan?
301	(Head) Which actress made her only Carry On appearance?
302	(Dick) What role does Joan Sims play and what is the nature of her character?
303	(Camping) Who had a heavily cut lead role?

QUIZ ANSWERS

	Answers
1	Carry On Cruising
2	Nurse (1959), Doctor (1967), Again Doctor (1969) and Matron (1972)
3	"Congratulations. May all your troubles be little ones and remember, the first 10 years are the worst. With love from Granny."
4	PC Charles Constable
5	The cleaner accidentally mixes up the job cards, leading to chaos
6	Lyons is the butler, portrayed by Jack Douglas
7	Don't Lose Your Head and Follow That Camel
8	The Bow Street Runners
9	Daphne Honeybutt (codename Brown Cow)
10	Bilius
11	Judge Burke
12	His uniform is sabotaged, leaving him red-faced and bare-cheeked
13	Citizen Camembert
14	Café Zig-Zig
15	Carry On Spying
16	They stage a nocturnal mutiny and force them to confess their wrongdoings
17	Sergeant Major MacNutt
18	Joan Fussey (Sid Boggle's prudish girlfriend)
19	Wilfrid Brambell
20	Her voice was dubbed by co-star June Whitfield
21	Peter Butterworth
22	Imogen Hassall (Carry On Loving)
23	Anne of a Thousand Lays, inspired by the Richard Burton film Anne of the Thousand Days
24	Peewit The Third
25	Nurse Susan Ball
26	They are arrested after causing a riot at Madame Fifi's brothel
27	Councillor Augusta Prodworthy
28	1978
29	Fred Ramsden and Ernie Bragg
30	Windsor Davies as Sergeant Major "Tiger" Bloomer
31	Detective Sergeant Sidney Bung
32	Don Juan Diego

33	Melvyn Hayes
34	Marianne Stone's character was cut from Matron, though she remained credited
35	Haven Hospital
36	Carry On Regardless
37	SS Happy Wanderer
38	Harry H. Corbett
39	Richard O'Sullivan
40	Harold Hump (portrayed by Henry McGee)
41	Bernard Cribbins (codename Bluebottle)
42	Carry On Jack
43	William Hartnell
44	Talbot Rothwell
45	He appears in a cameo as a sedan chair carrier
46	Cleopatra's bodyguard, whom Hengist defeats in combat
47	Bernard Bresslaw, Patsy Rowlands, and Liz Fraser
48	Oddbod
49	Bungdit Din
50	They only have gas!
51	Chayste Place
52	Horsa
53	Bertram Oliphant "Bo" West
54	Annie Oakley
55	Kenneth Williams was performing in Signed and Sealed, and Barbara Windsor was appearing in Twelfth Night at the Chichester Festival Theatre
56	Francis Kitchener Bigger
57	It is a regular family campsite, not the nudist camp they expected
58	Emily Bung (Joan Sims)
59	Dilys Laye
60	A chimpanzee
61	Carry On Cowboy
62	Barbara Windsor
63	Due to a flu epidemic
64	A soldier from the 3rd Foot and Mouth Regiment is found wearing underpants under his kilt
65	A mishap with the X-ray machine
66	Ug, played by Terry Scott
67	The alternate title was Carry On Round the Bend
68	Gerald Thomas (uncredited)
69	Charles Hawtrey
70	Amanda Barrie (Carry On Cabby was her first appearance)

71	Wedded Bliss
72	Sir Bernard Cutting, the hospital registrar
73	Ted York
74	The island is called Elsbels, located on the Costa Bomm
75	Up the Armada
76	Paula Perkins
77	They are hijacked by gangsters but use the taxi radio to subtly reveal their location, leading to their rescue by Charlie and the other Speedee drivers
78	Kenneth Williams had stage commitments, and Charles Hawtrey was dropped due to unreliability
79	She was a Roman archaeology expert
80	Lady Evelyn Bagley
81	Mary Sage and Charlie Sage
82	Bella Marie
83	Charles Hawtrey (Charlie Bind)
84	Harry Secombe
85	Jenny Grubb
86	Carry On Girls (1973), Carry On England (1976), That's Carry On! (1977), Carry On Emmannuelle (1978), and Carry On Columbus (1992)
87	From Maggie, a midwife, who reveals he has a curious birthmark
88	Dave Freeman
89	Robin Askwith
90	The private bunker is referred to as the "Snoggery."
91	The agents destroy it by eating the formula papers with soup and bread
92	Marriage counsellor
93	Bernard Bresslaw
94	Carry On Cowboy and Carry On Dick
95	Theodore reveals Emmannuelle's sexual escapades to the press
96	Leslie Phillips and June Whitfield
97	Barbara Windsor
98	Sid James
99	Bruce Montgomery
100	Horace Strong
101	1963
102	Captain Wellington Crowther & Bridget Madderley
103	Nurse Dawson
104	Juliet Mills
105	Helping Hand
106	Lila, who has a crush on Desmond Simpkins
107	Ted Ray

108	Stodge City
109	They fall into a boiling vat and die
110	The Black Fingernail
111	Sheikh Abdul Abulbul
112	WPC Gloria Passworthy
113	A fire ignites the ship's cannons, which accidentally hit all five Spanish ships
114	Jon Pertwee - who played the title role of Doctor Who, as did William Hartnell who portrayed Grimshaw in Sergeant.
115	£30,000
116	Speedee Taxis
117	Deborah Kerr
118	Jacqueline
119	Carry On Doctor and Carry On Up The Jungle
120	The 3rd Foot and Mouth Regiment
121	A photographic memory
122	Dr Arthur Binn
123	Peter Potter, played by Terry Scott
124	Matron Miss Soaper
125	They are killed by Horsa and the galley slaves
126	He calls the group "raving mad" after observing their stiff-upper-lip behaviour during the attack
127	The Nosha tribe and The Lubby-Dubby tribe
128	Charles Hawtrey as Sir Roger de Lodgerley and Barbara Windsor as Bettina
129	He enters the women's washroom by mistake, causing Miss Armitage to panic
130	The factory is called W.C. Boggs & Son
131	The gang plans to steal contraceptive pills from Finisham Maternity Hospital to sell abroad
132	Drayton Green Primary School, Ealing
133	Charlie Roper, played by Sid James
134	He can speak 16 languages - Francis Courtenay
135	Anita Harris
136	They replace a rectal thermometer with a daffodil
137	Valerie Leon
138	He nearly arrests a plainclothes detective
139	He was dropped for demanding star billing
140	A cigarette lighter
141	Eric Pohlmann, who played The Fat Man, had a minor role in The Third Man and voiced SPECTRE No. 1 in From Russia with Love.
142	The Duc de Pommfrit
143	It was the third biggest general release hit of the year

144	In 1999, it was placed 99th on the list
145	Upsidasi
146	Joan Sims
147	Marie eats garlic, claiming it is a Normandy tradition before coitus, which repulses Henry
148	Charles Coote
149	Olga Lowe played Madame Fifi and was one of the first actresses to work with Sid James in the UK
150	Jack Douglas, playing the character William
151	Captain Desmond Fancey
152	Sid James, Hattie Jacques, and Barbara Windsor
153	Joan Sims was only eight months older than Patsy Rowlands
154	Kenneth Connor
155	Sara Crowe
156	Frankie Howerd
157	The artwork was deemed too similar to the From Russia with Love poster, leading to changes being made
158	They return to Britain after Caesar is assassinated
159	Robin Stevens
160	Émile Prévert is dedicated to bodybuilding
161	The Bull Boys
162	Lance Percival (Wilfred Haines, Ship's Cook)
163	He has taken eight and a half years to qualify as a midshipman and repeatedly makes errors on the ship
164	Kenneth Williams (codename Red Admiral) – Vienna
165	Camber Sands near Rye, East Sussex
166	Jim Dale
167	Carry On Cowboy
168	The tagline was inspired by the rising popularity of modified motorcycles, nicknamed "choppers."
169	Dr. Stoppidge
170	Ring for Catty by Patrick Cargill and Jack Beale
171	They hope the nudist environment at "Paradise" will relax their girlfriends' strict moral standards
172	A group of hippies led by the band "The Flowerbuds"
173	Richard O'Callaghan (Carry On at Your Convenience)
174	Miss Fosdick
175	The Mayor loses his trousers during a catfight scene
176	Joan Sims
177	Carry On Cabby
178	Miss Felicity Wheeler (Rosalind Knight) and Mr Alistair Grigg (Leslie Phillips)

179	Kenneth Connor
180	The house is demolished to make way for a luxury block of flats
181	Muriel Bloggs
182	The Clarges Hotel, owned by Dora Bryan
183	The Old Cock Inn
184	Carry On Screaming!
185	She finds out he is living as a downtrodden odd-job man at the caravan site, despite having won the pools
186	He was performing in The Mating Season and passed away after suffering a heart attack on stage during the play's opening night
187	Suzanne Danielle
188	Carry On Nurse
189	Carry On Columbus was shot at Frensham Common, a location previously used for Carry On Jack nearly 30 years earlier.
190	Jack Douglas
191	9
192	Carry On Sergeant
193	She feels neglected by her husband, Charlie, and wants to teach him a lesson after he misses their fifteenth wedding anniversary. (GlamCabs)
194	Citizen Bidet
195	Carry On Regardless
196	"Not out!"
197	Roy Castle
198	Stoughton Barracks
199	Champagne and laughing gas
200	Carry On Jack (Midshipman Albert Poop-Decker) Carry On Spying (Harold Crump) Carry On Columbus (Mordecai Mendoza)
201	Carry On Cabby
202	He was busy touring in a play
203	Mrs. Dangle and Richmond
204	A fictional "Sun Tan Lo Tion" is listed as the "Technical Director."
205	Carry On Cleo, Carry On Screaming! Carry On Up the Khyber, Carry On Camping and Carry On Matron
206	Brighton
207	He dresses as a man in a frock
208	Kenneth Williams and Kenneth Connor (Carry On Cleo was their previous appearance together)
209	"Khyber" is rhyming slang for "arse" in Cockney rhyming slang.
210	Carry On Camping
211	King Francis offers ten thousand gold pieces for Henry's marriage to Marie, complicating Henry's plans to divorce her
212	The Society for the Total Extinction of Non-Conforming Humans

213	Tilbury Docks
214	He opens a new surgery and makes a fortune from the serum
215	The film opens with Emmannuelle Prévert on a flight aboard Concorde
216	23
217	The pith helmets and webbing were borrowed from the film Zulu
218	Carry On England marked their last appearances in the series
219	Sid James plays Sid Plummer, a put-upon family man and factory foreman, which is a departure from his usual girl-chasing roles
220	Claude Chumley (Kenneth Connor)
221	Leda, played by Valerie Leon.
222	Science
223	Norman Hudis
224	Doctor Francis A Goode
225	Gambling
226	Sir Rodney Ffing, Citizen Bidet and Lord Darcy Pue
227	To prevent Mr Wakefield from leaving the school
228	Eric Rogers
229	June Whitfield returned to the series, having last appeared in Carry On Nurse
230	"Infamy, infamy, they've all got it in for me!"
231	Hanwell Library, Cherrington Road, W7
232	Marcus et Spencius
233	STENCH's underground base is located directly below the office of the chief of the Secret Service
234	Dr. Jim Kilmore
235	He is mistaken for an eminent diagnostician and taken on a tour of the hospital
236	It was voted the nation's favourite Carry On film
237	They were later performed in the 1972 Carry On Christmas special and the 1973 stage show Carry On London
238	Chief Big Heap (Charles Hawtrey)
239	Sanitation engineer
240	He develops gangrene in his foot, loses his leg, and is later promoted to Admiral with a desk job.
241	Princess Jelhi, the Khasi's daughter. (her final Carry On appearance)
242	Joan's mother, Mrs Fussey, turns up unexpectedly
243	Bide-A-Wee Rest Home
244	The police scientist (Jon Pertwee)
245	A silver locket containing his mother's false teeth
246	Snow was present on the sands
247	Vic Spanner - whose constant strikes and laziness disrupt the factory's operations
248	She plays Mrs Tidey, a gluttonous patient more interested in food than her impending childbirth

249	Call Me A Cab
250	Carry On Don't Lose Your Head.
251	Carry On Up the Khyber
252	Captain Fearless and Walter Sweetley
253	They hope it will lead to Captain Melly being reassigned elsewhere
254	Sergeant Jock Strapp
255	Originally father and daughter, but changed to brother and sister
256	Charles Hawtrey (Dan Dann)
257	Carry On Matron - Dr Prodd
258	"This is the Night for Love," sung by Angela Douglas
259	Barbara Windsor - Nurse Sandra May
260	Maidenhead Town Hall
261	The soldiers lift their kilts to reveal they are not wearing underwear
262	The scenes were filmed beneath the summit of Snowdon in North Wales
263	Joshua Fiddler (Peter Butterworth)
264	Sergeant Ernie Nocker
265	Carry On In The Legion
266	Sid disguises himself as a foreign doctor named "Dr Zhivago"
267	The hotel is only half-finished, with numerous faults and ongoing construction
268	He accidentally booked a stripper, Veronica, instead of a singer
269	Lady Daley recognises a bracelet Harriett is wearing as stolen property
270	She starts a catfight
271	It causes sex changes
272	They are executed by a double guillotine, with The Black Fingernail revealed as the executioner
273	Sid James, who had commitment to a pantomime at the London Palladium
274	Sheriff Albert Earp (Jon Pertwee)
275	Kimmeridge Bay, Dorset
276	Marge Dawes
277	Jim Dale and Peter Butterworth
278	Beau Geste by PC Wren
279	The Everyman Cinema in Gerrards Cross, Buckinghamshire
280	It was the second most popular film of the year
281	The patients' mutiny exposes the lies of Dr. Tinkle and Matron
282	Private Ffoukes-Sharpe, Sergeant Tilly Willing and Bombardier
283	Bernard Bresslaw
284	Peter Potter
285	The film's portrayal of trade union activists as buffoons alienated its traditional working-class audience
286	A version of Greensleeves, arranged by Eric Rogers, serves as the opening theme.

287	Professor Inigo Tinkle, played by Frankie Howerd
288	Doctor Ernest Stoppidge and Lady Puddleton
289	She pretends to be Camembert's flamboyant sister to get close to him, later falling in love with him
290	Sydney Bromley
291	In the drainage tunnels beneath the main street
292	They were originally intended for the 1963 film Cleopatra
293	His original code name was "James Bind agent 006½," but it was changed to Charlie Bind after Albert R. Broccoli, producer of the James Bond series, threatened legal action
294	She is searching for her childhood sweetheart, Roger
295	Heavy rain
296	The characters gather for an Elsbels reunion at Vic and Cora's pub
297	Heatherwood Hospital in Ascot, Berkshire
298	The regimental tartans and bonnet badges from Tunes of Glory (1960)
299	He is accused of inappropriate behaviour while trying to rescue Nurse May
300	Rik Mayall
301	Dany Robin
302	She plays Madame Desiree, a faux-French show-woman with a risqué act
303	Julian Holloway had a heavily cut lead role

Printed in Dunstable, United Kingdom